KRAZY KAT

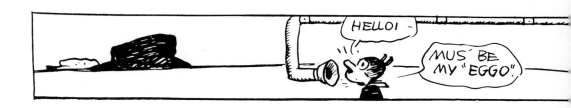

KRAZY KAT

THE COMIC ART OF GEORGE HERRIMAN

By Patrick McDonnell

Karen O'Connell

Georgia Riley de Havenon

Harry N. Abrams, Inc.,

Publishers, New York

Project Director: Darlene Geis

Designer: Samuel N. Antupit

Printed and bound in Japan

Library of Congress Cataloging-in-Publication Data
Herriman, George, 1880–1944.
    Krazy Kat: the comic art of George Herriman.
    Bibliography: p.
    I. McDonnell, Patrick. II. O'Connell, Karen.
III. De Havenon, Georgia Riley. IV. Title
PN6728.K7H4   1986   741.5′092′4   85–20000
ISBN 0–8109–1211–2
ISBN 0–8109–2313–0 (pbk.)

CONTENTS

A Note About the Illustrations   9

Introduction: The Krazy Kat
That Walks by Himself
by Gilbert Seldes   13

Krazy Kat: The Art of George Herriman   25

Acknowledgments   213

Chronology   215

Selected Bibliography   221

Picture Credits   223

Original watercolor of Ignatz Mouse, Officer Pupp, and *Krazy Kat* sent to a fan, c. 1925

Krazy Kat, original for a Sunday page, November 11, 1917, hand colored as a gift for fellow cartoonist, P. C. Springer

Krazy Kat, original for a Sunday page, June 22, 1919

A NOTE ABOUT THE ILLUS- TRATIONS

The illustrations in this book have been gathered from several different sources. A brief explanation should help the reader to better understand and enjoy them. First, the nomenclature. In comic-strip terminology there are "Sunday pages" and "dailies." The former are the large-format rectangular comics which are customarily published on Sundays. The dailies, which not surprisingly appear daily, are long, thin, horizontal strips made up of a row of four or five panels. On occasion *Krazy Kat*, which followed no set rules, had its panels arranged vertically. A panel is usually one section of a comic strip, but it can also be a cartoon consisting of a single drawing.

The earliest Herriman comic strips that are reproduced here in color are reprinted from old newspaper pages. Few pieces of Herriman's original art from the years 1900 to 1910 still exist, and they are most often sports or political panel cartoons. The *Krazy Kat* Sunday pages in black and white, consisting of pen and ink drawings, each measuring approximately 20 by 17 inches, have almost all been reproduced from the original artwork. The dailies reprinted here were shot for the most part from King Features Syndicate photostats and from the originals when they were available.

Relatively large, Herriman's drawings are skillfully rendered with a strength and clarity which give them an energetic presence. He sketched minimally, using light lead pencil, loosely indicating the placement of panels and characters directly on the bristol board. These pencil notes he then inked over in pen and brush. At times, Herriman would not follow his pencil guidelines at all, improvising instead with pen and ink.

Herriman was a master technician; there are no whiteouts or paste-ups to hide mistakes. The white lines are actually scratched into the black, inked areas. The cartoonist used this technique more and more frequently over the years and his last drawings have as much scratched work as pen-line work.

The *Krazy Kat* Sunday pages from 1934 to 1944 which appear here in color are taken from actual newspaper pages. The printers added the color right at the press, following color guides indicated by the artist. The original art of this period was, as in the earlier strips, drawn in black and white.

The original watercolors in this book include a few Sunday pages of *Krazy Kat* which were hand colored by Herriman himself. "I want to color it—it adds a bit to it—" he wrote to Gilbert Seldes about one he gave to him. Made as gifts, they usually have an inscription across the bottom. Although these hand-colored comics are extremely rare, a number of previously unknown pieces turned up during the research undertaken in the course of writing this book. Herriman's handling of the medium was very accomplished, as can be seen in the delicate translucent washes of layered color on page 110. The sensitive tonalities of these watercolors are in sharp contrast with the strong, vibrant colors of the later strips and reflect the difference between art which was designed to have an impact on the printed page and that which was a more intimate expression of the artist's feelings.

Dates indicated on the original artwork by the artist and the copyright insignia, when available, were used in dating the pieces. Early comic pages do not have such notations, and in these cases we relied on the date of publication printed on the newspaper. Since different papers ran syndicated material on different days, the date given for a piece may vary by a day or so.

Even though it has stopped appearing in newspapers, *Krazy Kat* has kept its high repute. In recent years it has been recognized as a work of art, perhaps due to the perspective of intervening time and our ability to judge a cartoon strip in a different light. There have been numerous exhibitions of original *Krazy Kat* drawings. The first such show took place in 1972 at the University of Arizona, and subsequently there were three exhibitions at the Graham Gallery on Madison Avenue in New York, as well as several museum shows. In a 1982 review of a Graham Gallery exhibition, the art critic Hilton Kramer wrote in the *New York Times*, ". . . the boundaries as well as the governing tastes of both popular culture and the fine arts have shifted so radically in the interim that the *Krazy Kat* drawings are likely to look more like classics than a good many paintings and sculptures that are nowadays on view." The occasional reprint of a *Krazy Kat* comic strip has produced many enthusiastic devotees, a new generation of admirers as fervent as the first.

P. McD.
K. O'C.
G. R. de H.

Krazy Kat, Sunday page, December 21, 1941

Krazy Kat, Sunday page, June 11, 1939

INTRO-
DUCTION

n 1924 Gilbert Seldes, a noted art critic of the time, sang the praises of a comic strip called *Krazy Kat* in a chapter of his book on art and popular culture, *The Seven Lively Arts*. Since this chapter was written at the midpoint of Herriman's career, Seldes could not yet have known the full scope of *Krazy Kat*. Furthermore, there are some inaccuracies in dates and spellings, explained by Seldes's note in the first edition: "This book was written while on holiday some three thousand miles away from data, documents, and means of verification. It is written from memory, and although I have had time and have tried to check up, I feel sure that the safest thing to do is to let it go...with [this] caveat...." His critique, nonetheless, still stands as a perceptive and often quoted evaluation of what Seldes called "the most amusing and fantastic and satisfactory work of art produced in America today."

In a letter to Seldes, Herriman expressed his appreciation:

...now I've got an inflated "mouse"—a "kop" busting with Ego—and a "kat" gone clean Kookoo—on my hands.... Gilbert being just weaklings guess they can't hold their good fortune—and I don't blame them—you said some nice things—werra—werra nice things—

The "werra—werra nice things" are reprinted here, with the kind permission of Timothy Seldes.

Krazy Kat, original for a Sunday page, October 16, 1938, hand colored as a gift for Gilbert Seldes

THE KRAZY KAT THAT WALKS BY HIMSELF

Krazy Kat, the daily comic strip of George Herriman is, to me, the most amusing and fantastic and satisfactory work of art produced in America today. With those who hold that a comic strip cannot be a work of art I shall not traffic. The qualities of *Krazy Kat* are irony and fantasy—exactly the same, it would appear, as distinguish *The Revolt of the Angels;* it is wholly beside the point to indicate a preference for the work of Anatole France, which is in the great line, in the major arts. It happens that in America irony and fantasy are practiced in the major arts by only one or two men, producing high-class trash; and Mr. Herriman, working in a despised medium, without an atom of pretentiousness, is day after day producing something essentially fine. It is the result of a naïve sensibility rather like that of the *douanier* Rousseau; it does not lack intelligence, because it is a thought-out, a constructed piece of work. In the second order of the world's art it is superbly first rate—and a delight! Since 1914, daily and frequently on Sunday, *Krazy Kat* has appeared in America; in that time we have accepted and praised a hundred fakes from Europe and Asia—silly and trashy plays, bad painting, woeful operas, iniquitous religions, everything paste and brummagem has had its vogue with us; and a genuine, honest native product has gone unnoticed until in the year of grace 1922 a ballet brought it a tardy and grudging acclaim.

Herriman is our great master of the fantastic, and his early career throws a faint light on the invincible creation which is his present masterpiece. For all of his other things were comparative failures. He could not find, in the realistic framework he chose, an appropriate medium for his imaginings, or even for the strange draftsmanship which is his natural mode of expression. *The Family Upstairs* seemed to the realist reader simply incredible; it failed to give him the pleasure of recognizing his neighbours in their more ludicrous moments. *The Dingbats*, hapless wretches, had the same defect. Another strip came nearer to providing the right tone: *Don Kiyoti and Sancho Pansy;* Herriman's mind has always been preoccupied with the mad knight of La Mancha, who reappears transfigured in *Krazy Kat.* And—although the inspirations are *never* literary—when it isn't Cervantes it is Dickens to whom he has the greatest affinity. The Dickens mode operated in *Baron Bean*—a figure half Micawber, half Charlie Chaplin as man of the world. I have noted, in writing of Chaplin, Mr. Herriman's acute and sympathetic appreciation of the first few moments of *The Kid.* It is only fair to say here that he had himself done the same thing in his medium. Baron Bean was always in rags, penniless, hungry; but he kept his man Grimes, and Grimes did his dirty work, Grimes was the Baron's outlet, and Grimes, faithful retainer, held by bonds of admiration and respect, helped the Baron in his one great love affair. Like all of Herriman's people, they lived on the enchanted mesa (pronounced: macey) by Coconino, near the town of Yorba Linda. The Baron was inventive; lacking the money to finance the purchase of a postage stamp, he entrusted a love letter to a carrier pigeon; and his "Go, my paloma," on that occasion, is immortal.

Some of these characters are reappearing in Herriman's latest work: *Stumble Inn.* Of this I have not seen enough to be sure. It is a mixture of fancy and realism; Mr. Stumble himself is the Dickens character again—the sentimental, endearing innkeeper who would rather lose his only patron than kill a favorite turkey cock for Thanksgiving. I have heard that recently a litter of pups has been found in the cellar of the inn; so I should judge that fantasy has won the day. For it is Herriman's bent to disguise what he has to say in creations of the animal world which are neither human nor animal, but each *sui generis.*

That is how the Kat started. The thought of a friendship between a cat and a mouse amused Herriman and one day he wrote them in as a footnote to *The Family Upstairs.* On their first appearance they played marbles while the family quarreled; and in the last picture the marble dropped through a hole in the bottom line. An office boy named Willie was the first to recognize the strange virtues of *Krazy Kat.* As surely as he was the greatest of office boys, so the greatest of editors, Arthur Brisbane, was the next to praise. He urged Herriman to keep the two characters in action; within a week they began a semi-independent existence in a strip an inch wide under the older strip. Slowly they were detached, were placed at one side, and naturally stepped into the full character of a strip when *The Family* departed. In time the Sundays appeared—three quarters of a page, involving the whole Krazy Kat and Ignatz families* and the flourishing town of Coconino—the flora and fauna of that enchanted region which Herriman created out of his memories of the Arizona desert he so dearly loves.

In one of his most metaphysical pictures Herriman presents Krazy as saying to Ignatz: "I ain't a Kat...and I ain't Krazy" (I put dots to

---

*I must hasten to correct an erroneous impression which may have caused pain to many of Krazy's admirers. The three children, Milton, Marshall, and Irving, are of Ignatz, not, as Mr. Stark Young says, of Krazy. Krazy is not an unmarried mother. For the sake of the record I may as well note here the names of the other principals: Offissa Bull Pupp; Mrs. Ignatz Mice;

indicate the lunatic shifting of background which goes on while these remarks are made; although the action is continuous and the characters motionless, it is in keeping with Herriman's method to have the back-drop in a continual state of agitation; you never know when a shrub will become a redwood, or a hut a church)... "it's wot's behind me that I am ... it's the idea behind me, 'Ignatz' and that's wot I am." In an attitude of a contortionist Krazy points to the blank space behind him, and it is there that we must look for the "Idea." It is not far to seek. There is a plot and there is a theme—and considering that since 1913 or so there have been some three thousand strips, one may guess that the variations are infinite. The plot is that Krazy (androgynous, but, according to his creator, willing to be either) is in love with Ignatz Mouse; Ignatz, who is married, but vagrant, despises the Kat, and his one joy in life is to "Krease that Kat's bean with a brick" from the brickyard of Kolin Kelly. The fatuous Kat (Stark Young has found the perfect word for him: he is crack-brained) takes the brick, by a logic and a cosmic memory presently to be explained, as a symbol of love; he cannot, therefore, appreciate the efforts of Offissa B. Pupp to guard him and to entrammel the activities of Ignatz Mouse (or better, Mice). A deadly war is waged between Ignatz and Offissa Pupp—the latter is himself romantically in love with Krazy; and one often sees pictures in which Krazy and Ignatz conspire together to outwit the officer; both wanting the same thing, but with motives all at cross-purposes. This is the major plot; it is clear that the brick has little to do with the violent endings of other strips, for it is surcharged with emotions. It frequently comes not at the end, but at the beginning of an action; sometimes it does not arrive. It is a symbol.

The theme is greater than the plot. John Alden Carpenter has pointed out in the brilliant little foreword to his ballet that Krazy Kat is a combination of Parsifal and Don Quixote, the perfect fool and the perfect knight. Ignatz is Sancho Panza and, I should say, Lucifer. He loathes the sentimental excursions, the philosophic ramblings of Krazy; he inter-rupts with a well-directed brick the romantic excesses of his companion. For example: Krazy, blindfolded and with the scales of Justice in his hand, declares: "Things is all out of perpotion, 'Ignatz.'" "In what way, fool?" enquires the Mice as the scene shifts to the edge of a pool in the middle of the desert. "In the way of 'ocean' for a instinct." "Well?" asks Ignatz. They are plunging head down into midsea, and only their hind legs, tails, and words are visible: "The ocean is so innikwilly distribitted." They appear, each prone on a mountain peak, above the clouds, and the Kat says casually across the chasm to Ignatz: "Take 'Denva, Kollorado' and 'Tulsa, Okrahoma' they ain't got no ocean a tall—" (they are tossed by a vast sea, together in a packing case) "while Sem Frencisco, Kellafor-nia, and Bostin, Messachoosit, has got more ocean than they can possible use"—whereon Ignatz properly distributes a brick evenly on Krazy's noodle. Ignatz "has no time" for foolishness; he is a realist and Sees Things as They ARE. "I don't believe in Santa Claus," says he; "I'm too broad-minded and advanced for such nonsense."

But Mr. Herriman, who is a great ironist, understands pity. It is the destiny of Ignatz never to know what his brick means to Krazy. He does not enter into the racial memories of the Kat which go back to the days of

Kristofer Kamel; Joe Bark the moon hater; Don Kiyoti, that inconsequential heterodox; Joe Stork, alias Jose Cigueno; Mock Duck; Kolin Kelly the brick merchant; Walter Cephus Austridge; and the Kat Klan: Aunt Tabby, Uncle Tom, Krazy Katbird, Osker Wildcat, Alec Kat, and the Krazy Katfish.

Cleopatra, of the Bubastes, when Kats were held sacred. Then, on a beautiful day, a mouse fell in love with Krazy, the beautiful daughter of Kleopatra Kat; bashful, advised by a soothsayer to write his love, he carved a declaration on a brick and, tossing the "missive," was accepted, although he had nearly killed the Kat. "When the Egyptian day is done it has become the Romeonian custom to crease his lady's bean with a brick laden with tender sentiments . . . through the tide of dusty years" . . . the tradition continues. But only Krazy knows this. So at the end it is the incurable romanticist, the victim of acute Bovaryisme, who triumphs; for Krazy faints daily in full possession of his illusion, and Ignatz, stupidly hurling his brick, thinking to injure, fosters the illusion and keeps Krazy "heppy."

Not always, to be sure. Recently we beheld Krazy smoking an "eligint Hawanna cigar" and sighing for Ignatz; the smoke screen he produced hid him from view when Ignatz passed, and before the Mice could turn back, Krazy had handed over the cigar to Offissa Pupp and departed, saying "Looking at 'Offissa Pupp' smoke himself up like a chimly is werra werra intrisking, but it is more wital that I find 'Ignatz'"—wherefore Ignatz, thinking the smoke screen a ruse, hurls his brick, blacks the officer's eye, and is promptly chased by the limb of the law. Up to this point you have the usual technique of the comic strip, as old as Shakespeare. But note the final picture of Krazy beholding the pursuit, himself disconsolate, unbricked, alone, muttering: "Ah, there him is—playing tag with 'Offissa Pupp'—just like the boom compenions wot they is." It is this touch of irony and pity which transforms all of Herriman's work, which relates it, for all that the material is preposterous, to something profoundly true and moving. It isn't possible to retell these pictures; but that is the only way, until they are collected and published, that I can give the impression of Herriman's gentle irony, of his understanding of tragedy, of the *sancta simplicitas*, the innocent loveliness in the heart of a creature more like Pan than any other creation of our time.

Given the general theme, the variations are innumerable, the ingenuity never flags. I use haphazard examples from 1918 to 1923, for though the Kat has changed somewhat since the days when he was even occasionally feline, the essence is the same. Like Charlot, he was always living in a world of his own, and subjecting the commonplaces of actual life to the test of his higher logic. Does Ignatz say that "the bird is on the wing," Krazy suspects an error and after a careful scrutiny of bird life says that "from rissint obserwation I should say that the wing is on the bird." Or Ignatz observes that Don Kiyoti is still running. Wrong, says the magnificent Kat: "he is either still or either running, but not both still and both running." Ignatz passes with a bag containing, he says, birdseed. "Not that I doubt your word, Ignatz," says Krazy, "but could I give a look?" And he is astonished to find that it is bird-seed, after all, for he had all the time been thinking that birds grew from eggs. It is Ignatz who is impressed by a falling star; for Krazy "them that don't fall" are the miracle. I recommend Krazy to Mr. Chesterton, who, in his best moments, will understand. His mind is occupied with eternal oddities, with simple things to which his nature leaves him unreconciled. See him

Krazy Kat, original for a daily strip, July 22, 1935, hand colored as a gift for Gilbert Seldes

entering a bank and loftily writing a check for thirty million dollars. "You haven't that much money in the bank," says the cashier. "I know it," replies Krazy, "have you?" There is a drastic simplicity about Krazy's movements; he is childlike, regarding with grave eyes the efforts of older people to be solemn, to pretend that things are what they seem; and like children he frightens us because none of our pretensions escapes him. A king to him is a "royal cootie." "Golla", says he, "I always had a ida they was grend, and megnifishint, and wondafil, and mejestic...but my goodniss! It ain't so." He should be given to the *enfant terrible* of Hans Andersen who knew the truth about kings.

He is, of course, blinded by love. Wandering alone in springtime, he suffers the sight of all things pairing off; the solitude of a lonesome pine worries him and when he finds a second lonesome pine he comes in the dead of night and transplants one to the side of the other, "so that in due course, Nature has her way." But there are moments when the fierce pang of an unrequited passion dies down. "In these blissfil hours my soul will know no strife," he confides to Mr. Bum Bill Bee, who while the conversation goes on, catches sight of Ignatz with a brick, flies off, stings Ignatz from the field, and returns to hear: "In my Kosmis there will be no feeva of discord...all my immotions will function in hominy and kind feelings." Or we see him at peace with Ignatz himself. He has bought a pair of spectacles, and seeing that Ignatz has none, cuts them in two, so that each may have a monocle. He is gentle, and gentlemanly, and dear; and these divagations of his are among his loveliest moments; for when irony plays about him he is as helpless—as we are.

To put such a character into music was a fine thought, but Mr. Carpenter must have known that he was foredoomed to failure. It was a notable effort, for no other of our composers had seen the possibilities; most, I fear, did not care to "lower themselves" by the association. Mr. Carpenter caught much of the fantasy; it was exactly right for him to make the opening a parody—The Afternoon Nap of a Faun. The "Class A Fit," the Katnip Blues were also good. (There exists a Sunday Krazy of this very scene—it is 1919, I think, and shows hundreds of Krazy Kats in a wild abandoned revel in the Katnip field—a rout, a bacchanale, a satyr-dance, an erotic festival, with our own Krazy playing the viola in the corner, and Ignatz, who has been drinking, going to sign the pledge.) Mr. Carpenter almost missed one essential thing: the ecstasy of Krazy when the brick arrives at the end; certainly, as Mr. Bolm danced it one felt only the triumph of Ignatz, one did not feel the grand leaping up of Krazy's heart, the fulfillment of desire, as the brick fell upon him. The irony was missing. And it was a mistake for Bolm to try it, since it isn't Russian ballet Krazy requires; it is American dance. One man, one man only can do it right, and I publicly appeal to him to absent him from felicity awhile, and though he do it but once, though but a small number of people may see it, to pay tribute to his one compeer in America, to the one creation equalling his own—I mean, of course, Charlie Chaplin. He has been urged to do many things hostile to his nature; here is one thing he is destined to do. Until then the ballet ought to have Johnny and Ray Dooley for its creators. And I hope that Mr. Carpenter hasn't driven other composers off the subject. There is enough there for Irving Berlin and Deems Taylor to take up. Why don't they? The music it requires is a jazzed tenderness—as Mr. Carpenter knew. In their various ways Berlin and Taylor could accomplish it.

They may not be able to write profoundly in the private idiom of Krazy. I have preserved his spelling and the quotations have given some sense of his style. The accent is partly Dickens and partly Yiddish—and the rest is not to be identified, for it is Krazy. It was odd that in *Vanity Fair's* notorious "rankings," Krazy tied with Doctor Johnson, to whom he owes much of his vocabulary. There is a real sense of the color of words and a high imagination in such passages as "the echoing cliffs of Kaibito" and "on the north side of 'wild-cat peak' the 'snow squaws' shake their winter blankets and bring forth a chill which rides the wind with goad and spur, hurling with an icy hand rime, and frost upon a dreamy land musing in the lap of Spring," and there is the rhythm of wonder and excitement in "Ooy, 'Ignatz' it's awfil; he's got his legs cut off above his elbows, and he's wearing shoes, and he's standing on top of the water."

Nor, even with Mr. Herriman's help, will a ballet get quite the sense of his shifting backgrounds. He is alone in his freedom of movement; in his large pictures and small, the scene changes at will—it is actually our one work in the expressionistic mode. While Krazy and Ignatz talk they move from mountain to sea; or a tree, stunted and flattened with odd ornaments of spots or design, grows suddenly long and thin; or a house changes into a church. The trees in this enchanted mesa are almost always set in flower pots with Coptic and Egyptian designs in the foliage as often as on the pot. There are adobe walls, fantastic cactus plants, strange fungus and growths. And they *compose designs*. For whether he be a primitive or an expressionist, Herriman is an artist; his works are built up; there is a definite relation between his theme and his structure, and between his lines, masses, and his page. His masterpieces in colour show a new delight, for he is as naïve and as assured with colour as with line or black and white. The little figure of Krazy built around the navel, is amazingly adaptable, and Herriman economically makes him express all the emotions with a turn of the hand, a bending of that extraordinary starched bow he wears around the neck, or with a twist of his tail.

And he has had much to express, for he has suffered much. I return to the vast enterprises of the Sunday pictures. There is one constructed entirely on the bias. Ignatz orders Krazy to push a huge rock off its base,

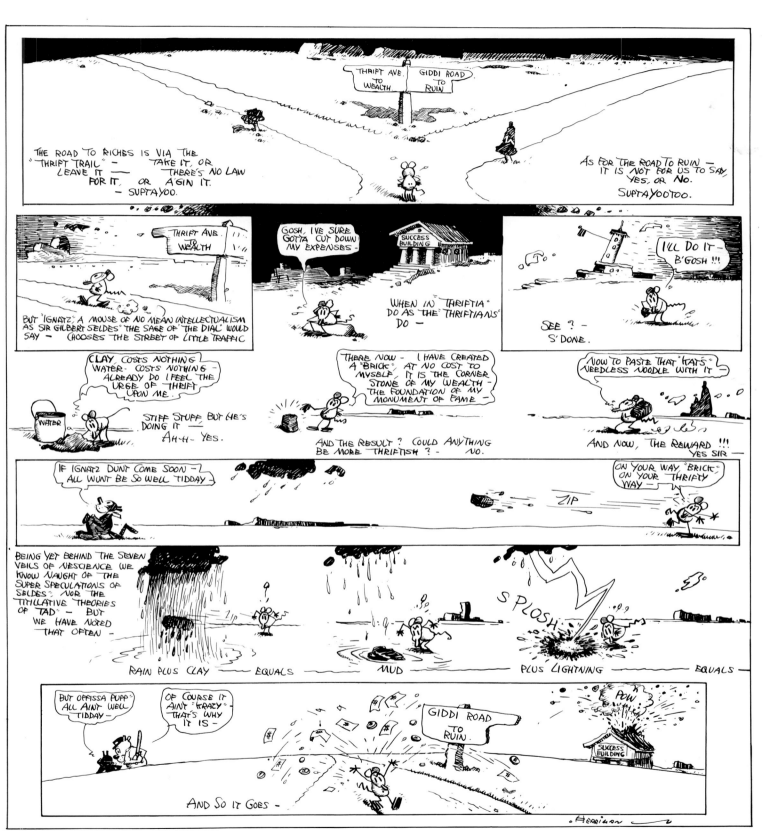

Krazy Kat, original for a Sunday page, October 15, 1922

then to follow it downhill. Down they go, crashing through houses, uprooting trees, tearing tunnels through mountains, the boulder first, Krazy so intently after that he nearly crashes into it when it stops. He toils painfully back uphill. "Did it gather any moss?" asks Ignatz. "No." "That's what I thought." "L'il fillossiffa," comments Krazy, "always he seeks the truth, and always he finds it." There is the great day in which Krazy hears a lecture on the ectoplasm, how "it soars out into the limitless ether, to roam willy-nilly, unleashed, unfettered, and unbound" which becomes for him: "Just imegine having your 'ectospasm' running around, William and Nilliam, among the unlimitliss etha—golla, it's imbillivibil—" until a toy balloon, which looks like Ignatz precipitates a heroic gesture and a tragedy. And there is the greatest of all, the epic, the Odyssean wanderings of the door:

Krazy beholds a dormouse, a little mouse with a huge door. It impresses him as being terrible that "a mice so small, so dellikit" should carry around a door so heavy with weight. (At this point their Odyssey begins; they use the door to cross a chasm.) "A door is so useless without a house is hitched to it." (It changes into a raft and they go down stream.) "It has no ikkinomikil value." (They dine off the door.) "It lecks the werra werra essentials of helpfilness." (It shelters them from a hailstorm.) "Historically it is all wrong and misleading." (It fends the lightning.) "As a thing of beauty it fails in every rispeck." (It shelters them from the sun and while Krazy goes on to deliver a lecture: "You never see Mr. Steve Door, or Mr. Torra Door, or Mr. Kuspa Door doing it, do you?" and "Can you imagine my li'l friends Ignatz Mice boddering himself with a door?") His li'l friend Ignatz has appeared with the brick; unseen by Krazy he hurls it; it is intercepted by the door, rebounds, and strikes Ignatz down. Krazy continues his adwice until the dormouse sheers off, and then Krazy sits down to "concentrate his mind on Ignatz and wonda where he is at."

Such is our Krazy. Such is the work which America can pride itself on having produced, and can hastily set about to appreciate. It is rich with something we have too little of—fantasy. It is wise with pitying irony; it has delicacy, sensitiveness, and an unearthly beauty. The strange, unnerving, distorted trees, the language inhuman, un-animal, the events so logical, so wild, are all magic carpets and faery foam—all charged with unreality. Through them wanders Krazy, the most foolish of creatures, a gentle monster of our new mythology.

Gilbert Seldes

Krazy Kat, Sunday page, February 28, 1943

Self-portrait. *Judge* magazine, October 21, 1922

KRAZY KAT: THE ART OF GEORGE HERRIMAN

George Herriman was a small, slight, handsome man with twinkling gray eyes and curly close-cropped black hair. The hair was hidden under a Stetson hat which he wore indoors and out. A vest, suspenders, a piece of Navajo jewelry, and a shirt with the sleeves rolled up were distinctive features of his daily attire. In the shirt pocket was a pouch of Bull Durham tobacco with the pull cord hanging out. Herriman could roll a cigarette with one hand. Describing himself in his characteristically self-effacing way, he wrote, "A squint at me may give you a laugh—I'm a funny looking monkey—"

A lover of solitude, he was an extremely private and modest person. If it had been up to Herriman, this book would not have included any biographical material. He would quickly have put a halt to such attention. Perplexed by a fan letter, he answered his admirer, "... Your strange interest in my efforts sure has me in a quandary—yes sir I can't add it up at all—It must be something *you* give to it...."

Herriman could usually be found seated at the drawing table amid crowquill pens, watercolor brushes, India ink, and bristol boards. There this gentle artist spent a lifetime creating magic for the newspapers of America.

Herriman's history is the history of the comic strip. His career started in 1897, when the new medium was in its infancy. He helped define it with the fantastical worlds he penned, inhabited by enchanting characters such as Major Ozone, Acrobatic Archie, Professor Otto, Cincho Pansy, Gooseberry Sprigg, and E. Pluribus Dingbat. These creations alone would have been noteworthy, but with the introduction of

Krazy Kat in 1913 Herriman took the comic strip to its zenith.

Krazy Kat is a painterly and poetic work of art. That it appeared in William Randolph Hearst's newspapers, not particularly noted for their espousal of art or poetry, adds to its wonder. It continued to be published through World War I, the Roaring Twenties, the Great Depression, and World War II—a run of thirty-one years. Among comic strips it is a certifiable masterpiece. In the world of art and literature it is an innovation.

The comic-strip medium was perfect for Herriman because he was equally adept at manipulating verbal and pictorial elements. It is therefore not surprising that he was appreciated by both artists and writers. In a 1944 article, *Art News* called Herriman "... one of the greatest innovators of the comic strip.... Hailed as one of the first surrealists, Herriman counted artists and intellectuals among his most constant readers." Elaine de Kooning recalled, "When I first met Bill [de Kooning], I remember he and Edwin Denby would wait for the newspapers to come out and latch on to the newest *Krazy Kat* cartoon. They were particularly struck by the fanciful landscapes ('like Utah,' Bill remarked) and the intense, blunt style of drawing. Bill had read somewhere that even Picasso was 'crazy' about *Krazy Kat*." The Kat's image has been paid homage in the canvases of Oyvind Fahlstrom, and countless other painters have admired Herriman's artistry. Scarcely a cartoonist has failed to call Herriman a major influence. Walt Disney, who may have profited most from Herriman's creation, wrote to Mabel Herriman after her father's death, "As one of the pioneers in the cartoon business, his contributions to it were so numerous that they may well never be estimated. His unique style of drawing and his amazing gallery of characters not only brought a new type of humor to the American public but made him a source of inspiration to thousands of artists."

The many writers and critics who have analyzed and hailed the strip include H. L. Mencken, Gilbert Seldes, whose essay introduces this book, Deems Taylor, and e. e. cummings. Jack Kerouac said *Krazy Kat* was an immediate progenitor of the Beat Generation and its roots could be traced back to "the glee of America, the honesty of America, its wild self-believing individuality." Herriman has been labeled a genius, and deservedly so.

n the simplest terms, *Krazy Kat* is the triangular love story of a cat (Krazy), a mouse (Ignatz), and a dog (Officer Pupp). Krazy, a saintly cat of indeterminate gender, is in love with Ignatz, a unsentimental egotist of a mouse. Krazy says of him, "S'no use with a 'Romeo' like 'Ignatz' I'm a

heppy, heppy 'Julius'. . . . I will sit here to kontemplate upon the blissful mysteries of the soul's sublime pession." Ignatz, who despises all cats, derives pleasure from "beaning that Kat's noodle" with a brick, an obsessive act he attempts to perform every day. Krazy, blind with a love that springs, perhaps, from "racial memories of an Egyptian past," awaits each brick with joy, considering the hurled bricks "missils of affection." Officer Pupp, unrelenting enforcer of law and order, is in love with Krazy and seeks to protect "that dear Kat" from "sin's most sinister symbol," Ignatz's brick.

This unlikely love triangle, with each participant mindless of the others' passions, was played out with endless tragicomic variations daily for more than three decades in the shifting deserts of Coconino County. Krazy once asked a fellow Coconinan, "Do you think, Mr. Bee, that what heppened yesterday will heppen again?" The bee answered, "It most certainly will Krazy. History, events, accidents, thoughts, jokes, you, I, anything and nothing each must repeat itself, everything is just nothing repeating itself—ashes to ashes is the best repeating act we do—so don't worry it'll happen—"

This major theme was woven into such unlikely comic-strip subjects as the forces of nature, the magic of science, the creation of art, the wonder of mysticism, and the power of spirituality. On the funny pages of our newspapers Herriman and his Kat gallantly explored the honesty of unabashed love. "In my Kosmis there will be no feeva of discord . . . all my immotions will function in hominy and kind feelings."

Herriman's drawing has a spontaneity and looseness that imbues each pen stroke with a life of its own. A *Krazy Kat* page has a wholeness in its design that you can enjoy from a distance of ten feet without reading a word or recognizing a character. Up close, the characters have a comical freshness and vitality. Always depicted as full-length figures, their small size is calculated to admit the sweeping perspective of a kaleidoscopic landscape—the deserts of Coconino County, Arizona. The background changes from one panel to the next, but the inhabitants of Coconino are oblivious to the desert's constant state of flux.

As fanciful as his art was Herriman's language, the ramblings of a singularly whimsical psyche that produced the illiterate-literate Joycean patois of Krazy Kat some years before *Finnegans Wake*. Herriman was trilingual, and then some—a master of dialects. His characters shifted from the highest elocution of Victorian prose to the lowest street slang, from English to Spanish to French, from the alliteration of Navajo names to the onomatopoeia of comic-strip language—the words all working, bouncing, and playing off one another, often in the same sentence, veering from a bop rhythm to a dazzling poesy. These juxtapositions produced Herriman's uniquely mellifluous dialogue—and a good laugh—all the more pleasurable when read aloud: "The 'klock rock'

of Kaibito peals the 'media noche' and its echoes quiver on the krimson kliffs of Kayenta—and the moonbeams in the pond of Oljeto ruffle into a thousand riffles—and the shifting sands of Shanto dance to its dizzying din—in other words, 'It's Midnight.'" While Herriman's words soared to maddening heights, they were still tethered to earth. As Ignatz Mouse said, "Plain language, but in a higher plane."

Krazy Kat succeeded artistically, poetically, metaphysically, and—most often overlooked—humorously. Herriman was first a *comic* artist. With the arrangement of his panels, the spacing of the word balloons, the characterization, and the ability to draw "funny," he could direct and deliver a gag with a unique timing and phrasing indigenous to the comic strip. The humor, like everything else in *Krazy Kat*, was implemented in many different ways and worked on many levels. The innocent Gracie Allen logic of Krazy was in counterpoint to the cynical sarcasm of Ignatz, which gave the sweetness an edge. *Krazy Kat* was a brilliant work of nonsense, farce, and whimsy, touched with heart. As Herriman stated in a strip of 1912, "We deal in 'gentle humor'—not that we are in any way sprouting pin-feathers of angel-hood, all we can say is that this is but the first symptom of our becoming a chronic uplifter of the 'age'—that's all—"

Like the plots, many of the jokes were cumulative. They could be set off with the merest sidelong glance or subtle innuendo, leading to the POW of the punch line. A sense of intimacy grew between artist and reader, endearing *Krazy Kat* to his followers and bewildering the newcomer.

The esoteric qualities that captivated the imagination of the intelligentsia were the very qualities that made *Krazy Kat* inaccessible to a larger audience. Herriman once wrote to a friend, "K. K. hasn't so many followers—he's not big enough to stand out in the crowd—so he just bums around along the Baseboards—"

Untold wonders awaited those who bummed along the baseboards with him.

Krazy: Ah, what wundafil day-drims I've had today—be still my heart, flutta not so—I wunda is it "love"

Herriman (as narrator): "Krazy" wonders if it's "love" and we wonder if you do—and maybe you wonder if we do—and then again maybe you're not "wondering" at all—how should we know.

In a frequently quoted panel, Herriman mused on his creation:

As the Kat once explained, "It's wot's behind me that I am...."

Krazy Kat, Sunday page, May 4, 1919

George Joseph Herriman entered the world on Sunday, August 22, 1880, at 348 Villere Street in New Orleans, Louisiana. He was the first child of George Herriman, Jr., who was thirty years old and a tailor at that time, and Clara Morel Herriman, who was twenty-five.

Herriman's lineage has been the basis of conjecture. Previous biographical information describes Herriman as either Greek or French. The theory of Greek descent most surely stemmed from his good friend and fellow cartoonist, Thomas Aloysius "Tad" Dorgan, who dubbed Herriman "The Greek" because "We didn't know what he was." On his death certificate, Herriman's daughter Mabel wrote that his parents had been born in France, his father in Paris and his mother in Alsace-Lorraine. However, on Herriman's birth certificate he is classified as "colored." The census of 1880 listed his mother and father as mulattoes and indicated that his parents and grandparents on both sides were natives of Louisiana. The always private Herriman, who never publicly divulged any information about his personal life or background, once told a close friend he was Creole, and because his hair was "kinky" thought he might have had some "Negro blood."

There were two groups of Creoles in New Orleans at the end of the nineteenth century. The first was of entirely French or Spanish descent; the second referred to themselves as "colored" Creoles. They were, for the most part, of mixed French, Spanish, and West Indian ancestry. A small, tight-knit, predominantly Catholic group, they were mainly French-speaking, though conversant in English and the Creole dialect as well. This established, sophisticated elite were descended from "free persons of color." They were a generally prosperous, well-educated (some studied in Paris), petit bourgeois element of local society. Most were proprietors of businesses and professionals who owned property; some were poets and writers.

The occupational opportunities for these people narrowed as the century closed. Segregation, on the increase since the end of Reconstruction, was by 1890 a firmly established condition of life. The segregation laws multiplied rapidly and it was not long before people with any black ancestry whatever found themselves classified with the ex-slave population. Consequently, those with even a modicum of black blood sought a means of escape from the indignities of racism and prejudice. Some moved north, others migrated to California.

Herriman's father, a strong-willed entrepreneur, sought a better opportunity for himself and his family in the West. Sometime after 1883, when the Southern Pacific Railroad connection between California and New Orleans was completed, the elder Herriman and his wife took George and the three younger children, Henry, Ruby, and Pearl, across the country to Los Angeles. Mr. Herriman was a man of many occupations. At various times out West he operated a barbershop, owned a bakery, and dabbled in astronomy.

George was happy in California and throughout his life he considered Los Angeles his only home. Between the years 1891 and 1897 he attended St. Vincent's College, a small Catholic secondary school for boys, whose motto was Pursue the Truth. There he received a rigorous, well-rounded, and spiritual education, which is reflected in his highly literate and philosophical work. Herriman also assisted after classes in his father's barbershop, later commenting that the only part of the trade he had learned was the singing. He subsequently put this talent to good use when he serenaded his future wife beneath her window, accompanying himself on the mandolin.

Herriman held various odd jobs while at school. Following a stint as a grape-peddler, he worked in a dairy on the outskirts of Los Angeles, where his duties consisted of "...exhorting the lacteal fluid from the reluctant kine...." Also employed as a painter of murals, signs, and houses, he eventually fell off one ladder too many carrying a bucket of paint, and was prompted thereafter to deal "with smaller quantities of coloring matter."

Toward the end of his school days, George was inducted into his father's latest business, a bakery. This entailed helping with the baking, and driving the horse-drawn wagon. George evidently found baking no more to his taste than barbering, and he purportedly salted a batch of doughnuts, consumed too many cream puffs, and buried a dead mouse in a loaf of bread. Shortly thereafter he was relieved of his bakery duties. Herriman spent his newly acquired leisure dashing off pictures on the pavements of the business section of Los Angeles, an endeavor that cost his father a $2.50 fine and nearly lost the budding artist his free room and board at home, where schoolboy pranks were not tolerated. Nor did Herriman find parental support for his creative aspirations. "Our father tried to tell us in his learned way, not to forsake the bakery for art. 'Bread,' he said, 'the world will forever cry for; but art...still allays neither hunger nor thirst.'"

While Herriman was busy with school, chores, and "forsaking the bakery," a new indigenous American art form was stirring in its beginnings: the comic strip. The first continuing-character newspaper cartoon, *California Bears*, was created by James Swinnerton in 1892 for William Randolph Hearst's initial newspaper, the *San Francisco Examiner*. In 1895 *The Yellow Kid*, an imaginative cartoon series by Richard Outcault centering on the adventures of a gamin, appeared in Joseph Pulitzer's *New York World*. Hearst quickly perceived the popularity of *The Yellow Kid* and hired Outcault away from Pulitzer for his newly acquired *New York Journal*. This comic character in a long yellow gown was the source of the phrase, "yellow journalism," coined by critics of the sensationalism in Hearst's newspapers. The continuing rivalry between Hearst and Pulitzer bred fierce competition between the nascent comic syndicates and did much to ignite the comics explosion. Soon comic strips were popping up as circulation builders in newspapers throughout America; they could not have escaped the notice of Herriman.

After completing school in 1897, Herriman got his first break. That year he sold a sketch of the Hotel Petrolia in Santa Paula to the *Los Angeles Herald* and was hired as an assistant in the engraving department at a salary of two dollars per week. In due time he was entrusted with occasional assignments that were more demanding and began drawing advertisements and political cartoons. However, his experience was not yet sufficient to make him eligible for the position of staff cartoonist.

Krazy Kat, daily strip, May 12, 1915

Three years later, at the age of twenty, Herriman decided that career opportunities would be better in New York, the hub of the publishing world, where the most important newspapers, magazines, and comic-strip syndicates were based. The cartoonists' star was in the ascendant. These independent journeymen routinely traveled from newspaper to newspaper, building their careers. Herriman, too, was a published cartoonist, and it was time to trade up to another, better showcase for his talents. In search of his American dream he stole a ride on a freight train eastbound. He never forgot this experience, and later in life would humorously refer to the time he rode the rails as a "hobo."

New York was a town of horse-drawn cabs and barefoot youths plodding to and from corner bars with buckets of ale. Times Square was way uptown. Milch goats grazed in the pastures of Harlem, and the Bronx was a whistle-stop. When he was unable to attain immediate success in the Big City's newspaper business, Herriman was again forced to rely on his ingenuity. For a Coney Island sideshow he painted what were termed "grotesque" billboards and held the supplementary job of barker for a snake act. Twenty years later he could still rattle off the pitch, filled with the flair and flummery of an Officer Pupp speech.

Bosco, the wonderful!
Bosco, the Silurian Senegambian Snake Eater!
He eats them alive!
He bites their heads off!
He grovels in a den of loathsome reptiles!
An exhibition for the educated!
And a show for the sensitive and refined!

The sideshow career proved to be blessedly transitory, for the editors of *Judge*, one of the preeminent humor magazines of the time, began to buy the cartoons he submitted. These first efforts were competent though somewhat derivative, with a good deal of cross-hatching, a technique typical of magazine cartoons of the period. Herriman's themes were generally of a historical or pastoral nature. Eleven of his cartoons appeared between June 15 and October 26, 1901. At *Judge*, he found himself in the company of some of the great illustrators of the day including Arthur Burdett Frost and James Montgomery Flagg.

Herriman often used multiple panels in his *Judge* cartoons, choosing sequential images to tell comical stories—the usual format of newspaper comic pages. And soon his work made its way onto those pages when various syndicates began to buy his comic strips on a noncontractual basis. On September 29, 1901, the Pulitzer newspapers started publishing half- and full-page strips by Herriman, as "one-shots"—not part of a series. On the same date, Herriman had also contributed to the first and subsequent supplements of the Philadelphia North American Syndicate. Starting on October 20, Herriman drew comics that appeared in color for the T. C. McClure Syndicate. These strips were part of comic supplements which usually ran on Sundays, although in some papers they appeared on other days of the week. Herriman's comics were, for the most part, set in the country and focused on the doings of hoboes, farm animals, and cowboys. The broad appeal of the comic strip and his success in this field so captivated Herriman that he eventually gave up

Cartoon,
Judge magazine,
July 20, 1901

A TICKLISH QUESTION.

LITTLE ABEL—"Every time ma scratches herself pa gets a laughing fit and seems to be tickled to death over something."

CAIN—"Gee! wouldn't it tickle you, too, if your rib was being scratched?"

contributing cartoons to magazines and concentrated exclusively on syndicated work.

In 1902, for the Pulitzer newspapers, Herriman developed his first continuing-character comic strips: *Musical Mose*, launched February 16; *Professor Otto and His Auto*, March 30; and *Acrobatic Archie*, April 13. From the start, his strips were about compulsive eccentrics and the troubles their compulsions caused. *Musical Mose*, of which there were three episodes, portrayed the plight of a poor black musician who performed songs at various ethnic gatherings, each time masquerading as a person of that particular nationality. Each time his ruse was discovered, Mose was besieged by the incensed audience. Returning home, he would tell his wife he was swearing off any more "impussinations." This is an intriguing strip in light of Herriman's clouded ethnic background.

Acrobatic Archie was Herriman's first stab at the popular "kid strip" genre. Archie was a hyperactive little boy exhibiting remarkable energy, physical prowess, and nerve as he bounced, juggled, tumbled, and stumbled around the countryside. His gymnastic feats were usually intended to impress a little girl, but he invariably ended up destroying property, hurting himself, and enraging his parents.

Professor Otto could well have been Archie grown up and behind the wheel of a dangerous automobile. The professor drove only at "scorching" speeds, terrorizing neighborhoods with his stunts. Unlike Archie, however, the mad professor rarely paid for his deeds, and in the last panel was always seen, undaunted, rushing off to the next disaster.

Santa Claus Finds Changes in the Children.

One-shot comic, *Pulitzer Syndicate*, December 13, 1903

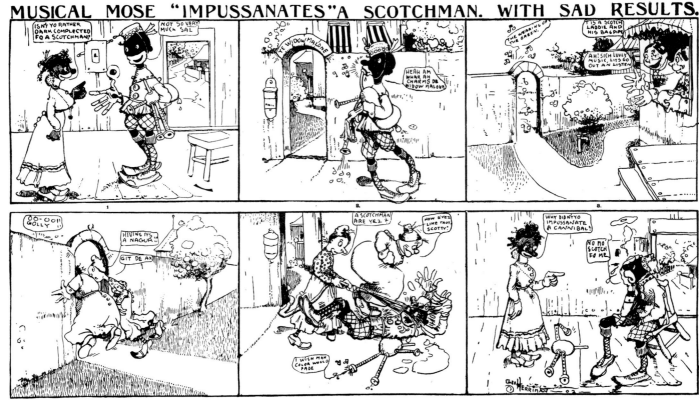

Musical Mose, February 16, 1902

George and Mabel's
wedding portrait,
July 7, 1902

Even these unpolished early efforts show an attention to backgrounds, an ear for dialects, and a penchant for bizarre humor.

In 1902, now a successful cartoonist confident of a continuing career, Herriman caught a train to Los Angeles—this time as a paying passenger—to marry his childhood sweetheart, Mabel Lillian Bridge, on July 7. Immediately following the wedding, the groom returned to New York with his new bride. That fall, just two years after first setting foot in New York, Herriman was included in the November issue of the literary magazine *Bookman*, a considerable distinction. Here he rubbed elbows with the most important cartoonists of the day, including Swinnerton and Outcault. In his article "The American Comic and Caricature Art," La Touche Hancock praised the young Herriman: "Art combined with poetry is the characteristic of George Herriman. Were his drawings not so well known one would think he had mistaken his vocation." A quote from Herriman appears in the article:

Inspiration! Who ever heard of a comic artist being inspired? Take him out into a field where the green grasses, swept by caressing zephyrs, bend and nod in rapt delight, dodging the nibble of the frisky, hungry lamb as it gambols hither and thither, and see if he (the artist not the lamb) can see in this any blissful clutch, grasping heart, mind, and soul in a grip of steely delight. No! He'll draw a lamb all right—a lamb so distorted that the green nodding field will rise in disgust to smite him. What does he know of the inspiration to be obtained from blue, azure, turquoise skies with fleecy clouds riding on and on, whither no one knows. Now take the clouds and skies of which I speak, blend them with the green grass and gamboling lambs, and a few trees, a few red-roofed barns, little hamlets in the distance, a lake, a creek, a rustic bridge, a nestling home amid clinging vines, and lots and lots of other things so dear to an artist's heart, place them in full view of the inspired one and see the light of imagination fire him. They never will. His mind and soul have lost that delicate sense of the poetic and artistic, which one would naturally think were indigenous and he will turn away with a sigh, sit down at his desk and continue to worry out idioticies for the edification of an inartistic majority.

At the ripe old age of twenty-two, Herriman was already feeling the confines of the comic-strip medium as well as the restrictions of commercialism. He had bigger dreams and wanted to do more with comic art, the kind of art that he would realize in *Krazy Kat*.

With his popularity increasing, Herriman frequently produced full front-page color strips for the Pulitzer Syndicate supplements. *Two Jolly Jackies*, first printed on January 11, 1903, was the tale of a pair of unemployed sailors and their misadventures on land and at sea. These overenthusiastic braggart seadogs were always looking for a good time and a bit of excitement and, simpletons that they were, found only trouble. *Two Jolly Jackies* nicely displayed Herriman's inventive wit and the strip continued for nearly a year.

In early May 1903 George and Mabel's first child, Mabel (nicknamed Toodles and later known as Toots) was born. The following month Herriman landed his first staff position on a newspaper, the *New York World*. Although legend has it that the billboards he had painted for the Coney Island sideshow had somehow attracted the attention of the editors of the *World*, more likely it was his consistently fine comic drawings that drew their notice. At the *World*, writer-editor Roy McCardell and Herriman worked together as a team of "geographical surveyors." "Professor Herriman, the Topographer," as his teammate called him, spiced up McCardell's commentary with his illustrations of various events in and around the city. On June 28 their first collaboration appeared in the Sunday Metropolitan section and continued to the end of the year.

While working for local New York newspapers Herriman still submitted strips to the syndicates. For the World Color Printing Company he created *Major Ozone's Fresh Air Crusade*. *Major Ozone*, which first appeared on January 2, 1904, introduced Herriman's most colorful and eccentric character to date. The Major was an older gentleman in constant search of the cleanest of air. His quest sent him off in hot-air balloons, on ocean voyages, on mountain ascents, and to the top of tall chimneys. As happens with all of Herriman's characters, Major Ozone's dreams go up in smoke, sometimes quite literally. His zealous nature renders the Major ecstatic just to "revel in ozoniferous persiflage" with a party of fellow "savants." The fantastic drive of this early health nut and his own unique brand of poetic English set *Major Ozone and His Fresh Air Crusade* apart from its predecessors. In the Major's own words, "Poetry!! Ah! That adds charm to a healthy mind and noble soul."

Herriman moved from the *New York World* to the *New York Daily News* in January 1904. At the *Daily News* he was used much more extensively, and the range of his work was more varied. As a staff cartoonist he recorded sports and political events. Herriman also experi-

Acrobatic Archie, September 21, 1902

Professor Otto and His Auto, December 28, 1902

Grandma's Girl—Likewise Bud Smith, February 17, 1906

(It's always interesting to learn things about people, especially people you know but never have met.

Looking over and laughing at the comic pages of The Call every day, you get the feeling that you know the chaps who tickle you in the ribs via the optics and cause cachinnations.

We reproduce here a cartoon by that famous San Franciscan, Tad, in Circulation, together with some close-up stuff about George Herriman. Cartoon and close-up are by Tad, who expresses himself with equal facility through medium of india ink or typewriter ribbon. There are six popular cartoonists in the cartoon.)

This Is About Garge Herriman
By TAD

HERRIMAN. That's the monicker you see signed to the Stumble Inn drawings in The Call. His first name is George, but the boys calls him Garge, because that's the way he pronounces it himself.

Now I'm not going to sit here and chuck the swell about that guy, I'm going to tell the truth.

Garge came from somewhere out West, we think it's Los Angeles. He came here on a side door Pullman. Of course, he wouldn't want me to say so if he was here, but it's a fact just the same. He hangs around with a lot of painters, poets and authors these days, but when I first saw him he still had grease from the box cars on his pants.

He looked like a cross between Omar the tent maker and Nervy Nat when he eased into the art room of the New York Journal twenty years ago. We didn't know what he was, so I named him the Greek, and he still goes by that name.

Garge is short and wide, like the door of a safe, and as Johnny Dunn, the announcer. used to say of his wrestler, "He is strong. He can bend 'irun' bars with his naked hands."

Garge also has a peculiar way of drawling. He is never in a rush as he drawls his words. He calls garden "gordon," he calls harness "horness," he calls cigars "cigors," and so on.

He always wears a hat. Like Chaplin and his cane, Garge is never without his skimmer. Hershfield says that he sleeps in it.

Garge has three hobbies. They are Arizona Indians, chili con carne and boxing gloves. He once knocked a guy cold on the elevated station at Forty-second street, New York City, and has been living on the "rep" ever since.

No one has ever found out what this knocked out gent did to Garge, but it must have been something awful, because he has never once lost his temper with us and he has been through some tough afternoons and evenings. No matter what happens Garge is always the same. You can steal his pens, but he only smiles. You can knock California, but he merely smiles. You can cut up rubber in his tobacco pouch and he'll smoke it just to let you laugh. He is like the old rye the guy told of. Not a hard word in a barrel of it. There never was a smoother tempered gent. I'll bet right now that if you asked Garge what the brick that hits Krazy Kat was made of he'd say velvet. Then he'd add, "You don't think I'd want the poor lil' cat to be hurt, do you?" Garge is a great reader and a great movie fan. His favorite author is "Chorles" Dickens and his favorite movie guy is "Chorles" Chaplin.

He will sit by the hour and talk of them. That is, he used to before the soda stores took the places once held by the Pilsner peddlers.

He brags about his favorites, Garges does, but never about himself.

The violet imitated Garge when it assumed that attitude of shyness.

He thinks he's the rottenest artist that ever got behind a pen, and no matter how many boosting letters he gets he's of the same opinion still. Of course, we know better.

Half the guys that never get a boosting letter admit that they're good. Garge doesn't and never will. He is always last. He laughs, though. Yes, he gets his giggles. When he laughs you'd think he had just taken a sniff of snuff. It isn't a laugh, it's a sort of internal explosion.

Article by fellow cartoonist Tad Dorgan, c. 1920

mented with a weekday continuing-character comic strip entitled *Home Sweet Home*. It lasted just four days—February 22, 23, and 26, and March 4—and predates what is considered to be Herriman's first *daily* comic strip. Herein the artist tells the tale of newlyweds who rise above their little spats to live in continued wedded bliss, punctuated by the philosophic comment of the family's black cat (a progenitor of Krazy Kat): "It's human nature."

Bubblespikers, a feature in the style of Herriman's earlier collaboration with Roy McCardell, initially appeared that spring. With reporter-writer Walter Murphy, Herriman would record the special features and oddities of various Manhattan neighborhoods. In their own words, "'Whenever you see a bubble, spike it!' is the short and simple slogan of the Metropolitan section's doughty team of truth hunters. . . . If you hear it from the Bubblespikers, believe it."

Herriman's stint at the *Daily News* was short. Rudolph Block, editor of Hearst comics, stole this bright new star away from the rival newspaper by offering him "a salary commensurate with his talents." Commencing April 22, 1904, Herriman, now on the staff of Hearst's *New York American*, drew sports cartoons. At this paper he worked with cartoonists Frederick Burr Opper (*Happy Hooligan*) and James Swinnerton (*Little Jimmy*), and in the shadow of the great sports cartoonist Tad.

Unlike today's cartoonists, who often work at home, the pioneers in this field reported to the newspaper's art room every day, and put in eight (or more) hours side by side at their drawing tables. They were newspapermen in the true sense of the word. A spirit of camaraderie, affection, and understanding linked these early artists, and they would often make joking references to one another in print. They were celebrities of the day and lived their lives to the fullest in the high style they could well afford. Newspaper work was like the era, exciting and expansive. Hearst's ace photographer Harry J. Coleman, who was destined to head the combined photography and art departments of the *New York American*, described these fun-loving artists in his witty and insightful book *Give Us a Little Smile, Baby*.

Artists lived high in that don't-blow-out-the-gas-era. We were all flush, well able to step out, finance our uneducated palates and graze with high society. One night you would find us all duded up, eating in the Bohemian charm of strumming guitars, crocks of Chianti, and lovely women at the subterranean Cafe Boulevard. Next night, we might join the mackerel-snappers at the Fulton Market. . . . We even put on the swell and rode through Greeley Square to the gathering place of artists and writers, the exclusive Gilsey House, where "Diamond Jim" Brady was accustomed to entertain. . . . I had acquired a temperament and pearl gray spats, trimmed my hair chrysanthemum style, carried a portfolio and sported a flowing Windsor tie. These were the trademarks of early-day artists. . . .

Tad was the premier sports cartoonist and writer for Hearst's *New York Evening Journal*, the *American*'s more widely read companion paper. The staffs of the twin papers faced each other across a narrow table which stretched down the center of the art room; thus, Herriman and Tad were well acquainted. They often went on assignments together, each covering the story for his respective paper. Coleman recalled an occasion when he, Tad, and Herriman were assigned to cover *The Village Blacksmith*, a play starring the former boxing champion Robert Fitzsimmons:

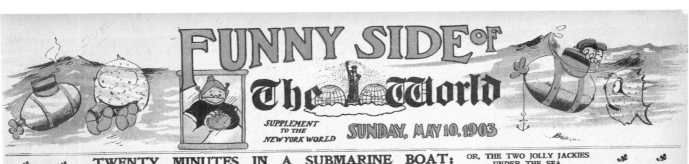

Two Jolly Jackies, May 10, 1903

The Two Jolly Jackies Pose as Mermaids.

Two Jolly Jackies, July 26, 1903

Robert Fitzsimmons, the spindle-pinned piebald conqueror of [Jim] Corbett, was certainly no matinee idol. The former blacksmith lacked sex appeal in any degree and his head was almost completely nude. Nevertheless... he was being starred....

Our sports editor assigned me to make some flashlights.... Two cartoonists went along to sketch the humorous sidelights: George Herriman... and... Tad, whom Herriman always greatly admired.

We were ushered, on the house, into the choicest box seats as the opening curtain rolled up on the first scene.... We noted that [Fitzsimmons's] bald pate was hidden beneath a sheep-dog coiffure of resplendent artificial red hair....

When the curtain fell compassionately on the first act, we hurried to the star's dressing room for an interview and a session of backstage, between-the-acts picturing. Temptingly near the door, perched on a stand, was "Ruby Robert's" flaming red wig. The inevitable happened.

Act Two.... But Robert appeared to be late. Letitia gave him the cue again and again while the audience tittered.

Suddenly... the missing swain flounced on stage.... He wore a highly polished stove-pipe skimmer, slid well down over his red, horizontal ear tips. A hat rack stood waiting, as he entered, but Bob arched an eyebrow in our direction and made no use of it. Instead he stumbled through his love-making lines with all the enthusiasm of a condemned man and completely floored Letitia by doing it with his hat on, while he directed his ardent gaze, not at her, but toward our box. Tad winked at Herriman and me and pointed to his side pocket. We were shocked to see a bright portion of the wig protruding from it.

By this time.... The peanut gallery had begun to heckle....

At the New York
Evening Journal,
top row: Gus Mager,
Charles Wellington,
George Herriman;
bottom row: Harry Hershfie
Ike Anderson,
and Tad Dorgan,
January 31, 1911

Fitz was stopped cold. His jaw dropped and it appeared to us that, at any moment, he might step out of his dramatic role entirely and climb into our midst, even though he was a practical joker of reputation in his own right. We took prudent steps by retreating through a fire exit. Tad passed the wig to an usher, who rushed it backstage in time to save the old homestead.

Tad and George, who had great mutual respect for each other's work, struck up a close friendship. In a 1924 letter to Tom MacNamara, cartoonist of *Us Boys*, Tad wrote, "I still think that George is one of the best sporting artists in the world, and can't understand why he doesn't do that sort of thing." They were an unlikely duo—Herriman, quiet and reserved, and Tad, the self-assured gregarious prankster. Tad's favorite watering hole was Jack's at Sixth Avenue and Forty-third street, and he liked to coerce one or more of his buddies into having lunch there. Once, when Herriman returned to his drawing board considerably under the influence of Jack's nickel beers, his associates put him on top of a filing cabinet, covering him with newspapers, and there he slept the rest of the day.

Herriman's sports cartoons appeared regularly in the *New York American* until April 25, 1905, after which they were inexplicably absent for a month. Then his work was used sparsely until June 2, when a final cartoon appeared—unsigned. Apparently there had been major changes at the paper and Herriman was quite unhappy about them. His discontent may have been compounded by the fact that the *New York American* did not publish any daily comic strips as did the *Evening Journal*. In any case, Herriman left.

Following his departure from the *American*, Herriman headed back to California. From there he continued to mail strips to the World Color Printing Company. He revived *Major Ozone's Fresh Air Crusade* and combined two earlier World Color Printing strips into *Grandma's Girl—Likewise Bud Smith*. He also started *Rosy Posy—Mama's Girl*. The last two were made-to-order "kid strips," in the same manic vein as *Acrobatic Archie*. The brilliance of Herriman's talent is evident even in such minor works.

He did not work for another newspaper until 1906, when he again became a staff cartoonist, this time for the *Los Angeles Times*. His first piece, on January 8, contained an oblique anti-Hearst remark. The affront probably escaped Hearst's notice, for he was still impressed enough by Herriman's work to lure the cartoonist away from the rival paper to his own *Los Angeles Examiner* in August of that year. Herriman's art soon dominated the paper, appearing on nearly every page. Sales increased greatly and Hearst must have felt some degree of indebtedness to Herriman. By the end of October, Herriman was confident enough of his position at the *Examiner* to give up working for the World Color Printing Company.

A few hundred miles to the north, at the *San Francisco Chronicle*, cartoonist Harry Conway "Bud" Fisher began on November 15, 1907, what many acknowledge to be the first six-day-a-week, consecutive daily comic strip. *A. Mutt*, the story of a racetrack gambler, appeared on the sports page. It was an immediate success and greatly improved the paper's circulation. Probably reacting to the *Chronicle*'s success, the *Examiner*, on December 10, 1907, launched its own saga of the antics of a gambler who played the horses. The strip, *Mr. Proones the Plunger*, was developed by George Herriman. Racetrack atmosphere and slang were given the unique Herriman touch, but although similar in theme to *A. Mutt*, it did not enjoy the original's longevity, lasting only from December 10 to December 26. Herriman would not get the chance to do another strip until 1909.

Meanwhile, *A. Mutt* went on to become a major hit for Fisher's new boss, none other than William Randolph Hearst, who had hired him away from the *Chronicle*. Fisher later added Jeff to the strip, a character who bears a remarkable resemblance to the short-lived Mr. Proones, and as *Mutt and Jeff* the strip enjoyed a long and successful run into the 1980s.

In a letter written May 5, 1908, to cartoonist Ralph "Pincus" C. Springer, formerly of the *Los Angeles Examiner* but at that time working in Denver, Herriman comments on how things are going back at the *Examiner*, mentioning several of their colleagues, including H. M. "Beanie" Walker, sports editor of the *Examiner* at that time; Charles Owens, who later became a well-known sketch artist at the *Los Angeles Times;* George Parmenter, who was head of the art department at the *Los Angeles Examiner;* and Foster Coates, a stormy man, blazing with vitality, an expert in "muscle" journalism. Coates, Hearst's general manager and troubleshooter, had run the show at the *New York Evening Journal* and had apparently come to Los Angeles to institute some changes. Herriman and P. C. Springer had become very close and would remain so for the rest of their lives.

Major Ozone's Fresh Air Crusade, April 21, 1906

Major Ozone's Fresh Air Crusade, September 29, 1906

Original sports cartoon with early appearance of Gooseberry Sprig, *Los Angeles Examiner,* c. 1909

Dear ole Punkus—

Well may you howl old sox, and with much cause, I have sorrowfully neglected you with my letters, but the old heart is still in the same place, "know you that much," anyway.

That diminutive missive of yours just received serves but to awaken me to my duty to you, and here goes—. . . .

Foster Coates is out here for a while and is busy revising things, to begin with he slams me a few, like this, and mind you to me face, "You know Herriman—Tad's the big man, we pay him big money, and we've got to use him, I say, that's right Mr. Coates, "humble like," then says he, Herriman, you are only a rank imitation of Tad, now and you know it, I say, I know it Mr. Coates, "very umble." Then why, by the immaculate tit of Josephine, do we want to use the spurious article, when we can git the genuine goods? Why? and my "umble" echo echoes, "why?"—goodnight says he, goodnight says I, and as I leave him, I can hear him shout to Beanie, thusly—Mr. Walker, see if you have a Tad cartoon, and use it for tomorrow, Herriman's a punk German carpenter—Beanie says something about "shit" and I beat it to the art room and pour forth woe upon woe, and wail me life's young blood away to water, but then N.Y.'s the place, from which all great editorial wit floweth and the tide has come this way, but my humble soul is resigned it's nothing new to me, to sit in daily communion with myself while great editors flourish overhead—amen—

○○○○○○○○○○○○○○○○○○○○○○○○○○○○ gloom ○○○○○○○○○○○○○○○○○○○○○○○○○○○○○

It was like a breath of new air when that Elephantine Mass of bull dung blew into town, my ribs are still a bit awry, and my kidneys are gradually returning to their proper places, and outside of that, what's left of me is joyful that he came—but he sighed for Denver and Denver came back to her own—

Wait till you see his masterpiece, it's a wonder, "Dick" they call him, I predict, that said Dick, will someday be a great Sporting Editor—

Mrs. Herriman was all swelled up over the line of Bull you handed her about Billie Burke, Punkus, if I'm still within the deadline of your affection please don't spring anything like that on me, Lord, she did everything but express a desire to go on the stage, I asked her if I wasn't as good as John Drew, but she shrivelled me with a look of scorn, she said the best she could do was to *try* to imagine that she was *trying* to imagine that I was John Drew and it was the hardest kind of imagination work she'd ever done, I humor her by saying she's the leading lady of the Herriman show, at least—I'm afraid Toodles and

Mike [possibly a pet] will get the fever, then all that will be left for me to do, would be Harri Karri—

Next time you write say that you saw 10 nights in a barroom and the leading lady looked like her, savvy—

Mike is fine now he was over that scratch a long while ago—and Toodles celebrates her fifth birthday, Sunday—

Chas. Owens wants to know how much you'll take for the paint box you left with Parmenter—? he's anxious to get his Hooks on it—

Tad's married, and to a Greek girl at that "good luck to him" nothing's too good for them Irish, not even the Greeks—

Well Punkus old boy, here's to you. I will try to come through oftener with a letter but whether I write or not you know that I'm there with a heart full for you—

Our paths may lead apart for a while but someday the "old Gouros" will all meet at some crossing, then the jubilations.

Regards from all the boys here—and pass the good word along to the boys around there—in the meanwhile keep your nuts in the middle of your pants, and behave yourself—

Thine—
G.

Feeling a sense of stagnation, Herriman longed to graduate to bigger and better things. The change he sought would elude him until late 1909, when he entered an extremely productive period, creating three new comic characters for Hearst—Baron Mooch, Mary (*Mary's Home from College*), and Gooseberry Sprigg—and one real-life character, Barbara (Bobbie), his second child.

On October 12, he introduced *Baron Mooch*, a strip about a tall, overweight freeloader who spent his time attempting to crash theatrical and sporting events. Herriman himself appeared in one episode to bail the flimflammer out of jail.

Following the *Baron*'s run, Herriman tried his hand at a completely different type of strip, *Mary's Home from College*, first printed on December 20. It was the tale of a teenage girl coping with her parents, and vice versa. This experiment, which lasted for only a few strips, is worth noting because it was the forerunner of a spate of "girl strips" such as *Polly and Her Pals* and *Merely Margie*, by other artists years later.

More exciting and important was the short strip life of one *Gooseberry Sprigg*, which first appeared three days after *Mary's Home from College*. Gooseberry Sprigg was "the Duck Duke," a small, stubby, cigar-smoking bird adorned with bow tie and top hat. Named after Hen Berry, a manager of the Los Angeles Angels baseball team, he had originally appeared clowning around in Herriman's early *Los Angeles Examiner* sports cartoons. The duck proved popular enough with creator and public to show up thereafter as a wisecracking commentator at the bottom of the *Baron Mooch* strips. As a comic strip, *Gooseberry Sprigg* was a full-fledged animal fantasy with a large cast of wacky birds that included Joe Stork. The drawing showed the control of a veteran cartoonist, yet the cartoon was fresh, with an originality that set it apart from all of Herriman's previous work. Similar in style, atmosphere, and spirit to the future *Krazy Kat*, it was a veritable *tour de force*. *Gooseberry Sprigg* expressed the new sophistication at Herriman's command, and it came to an end on January 24, 1910, much too soon.

Bobbie, Mabel, George, and Toots, c. 1915

Baron Mooch, original for a daily strip, December 14, 1909

Unpublished
original drawing
of Gooseberry
Sprig, 1910

Concurrent with these Hearst strips, the World Color Printing Company ran two strips by Herriman, *Alexander the Cat*, first printed on November 7, 1909, and *Daniel and Pansy*, which first appeared November 21. These Sunday strips were in color, unlike those in the Los Angeles *Examiner*.

Alexander was a white, long-haired house cat, with no human attributes, who unintentionally and invariably frustrated one of its owners, Charlie (who looked very much like Baron Mooch), while being a constant source of enjoyment for Charlie's wife, Leila, who doted on it.

Daniel and Pansy was Herriman's first purely animal strip, predating *Gooseberry Sprigg* by about a month and *Krazy Kat* by several years. The sly Daniel Coyote attempted to outwit the simple pig Cincho Pansy in the strip's three episodes. Unlike *Gooseberry*, which had a cosmopolitan "hip" quality and was geared to the male readership of the Hearst sports page, *Daniel and Pansy* had a more rustic "Uncle Remus" feeling and spoke to the younger, general audience of the World Color Printing Company comic supplements. Herriman would not forget Daniel, Pansy, Gooseberry, or Joe Stork, who were subsequently to become member's of *Krazy Kat*'s Coconino cast.

Animals were an integral part of Herriman's imagery, and he frequently used them as commentators. In one of a series of articles addressed to young art students, Herriman later wrote: "Animals are of great importance to a cartoonist, no matter what kind of strip he is drawing. Almost any strip needs an animal in it once in a while, to add human interest, emphasize the reactions of the characters, to make the strip more realistic." Herriman himself was devoted to animals, and by 1934 his household numbered five dogs and thirteen cats.

Alexander the Cat, *Daniel and Pansy*, and *Gooseberry Sprigg* were, each in its own way, precursors of *Krazy Kat*.

mpressed with Herriman's California work, the sports editor of the *New York Evening Journal* summoned him to come back East, apparently to handle Tad's work load while the latter covered the biggest sports story of the year: the Jim Jeffries–Jack Johnson fight in San Francisco.

Gooseberry Sprig, January 10, 1910

Herriman immortalized his journey in his first cartoon and an article for the *Evening Journal* on June 14, 1910, "Herriman, Cartoonist, Tells of Trip from Coast."

A few days agone and I could have staked the family pottery that I would be chin deep in rosin watching the Jeffries limited heave a load of anthracite off the championship main line.

I had it all doped out centrifugally, centripetally and in the fourth dimension, when bing! comes word to come to the big village in the shadow of the Metropolitan Tower.

It was a separation, most bitter and acrimonious, as the gentleman said when he emerged from a swim in the old brook to find that his entire garmenture, from top coat to chest protector, was guarded by what he had at first taken to be a gentle cow, but what proved to be the bossy's two-year-old brother.

However, the trip was a thirty-six-hundred-mile conversation on the results of the big soiree in the breeze-blown bay burg on the next birthday of our great nation. . . .

Perhaps this excursion to "the big village in the shadow of the Metropolitan Tower" was the chance Herriman had been waiting for. Here he would work with the greats of the industry: Frederick Burr Opper, Tad Dorgan, and James Swinnerton (with whom he had toiled before), Rudolph Dirks (*Katzenjammer Kids*), Harry Hershfield (*Abie the Agent*), Gus Mager (*Sherlocko the Monk*), Winsor McCay (*Little Nemo*), and Cliff Sterrett (*Polly and Her Pals*). This stellar fraternity would help inspire Herriman to create a unique strip, while New York would afford him the exposure that would ensure its endurance.

Just six days after his arrival, Herriman's first comic strip for the *Evening Journal* appeared. *The Dingbat Family*, starring E. Pluribus Dingbat, was the story of an office clerk; his wife, Minnie; their children, Imogene, Cicero, and Baby; and the family cat. A routine vehicle for gags about the misfortunes of a family man, this strip did not start off with a bang. It was amusing enough but had no drive and seemed to be another "experiment" destined for a quick demise. But destiny took a turn when the Dingbats and their cat were invaded by Herriman's imagination in the form of two "neighbors," the family upstairs and the mouse below.

On July 26, the Dingbat's cat was hit on the head by what might have been a piece of brick. The cat's assailant was surely Ignatz Mouse. The mouse's target was not cat, but "Kat." Thus began comic art's finest hour.

Daniel and Pansy, December 4, 1909

It is likely that the first Kat and Mouse confrontation was drawn at the bottom of *The Dingbat Family* page simply because Herriman had time left in his eight-hour day and, remembering the success of *Gooseberry Sprigg,* wanted to add a bit more to the strip. In Herriman's words, *Krazy Kat* was created "to fill up the waste space."

This humble beginning and simple comic role reversal, a play on the old cat and mouse game—mouse chases cat, or more accurately, mouse clobbers cat—were the start of a major opus. Hearst's readers delighted in the brave fight of this small mouse, the would-be emancipator of the rodent kingdom "from the rule of despotic Kats." The Kat popped up everywhere, at "masque" balls and beauty contests, in barrels of sugar and baked pies, angering the surprised mouse, who proceeded to "bean" the Kat with anything he could get his long, thin claws on. The poor noodle of Krazy, as she was now labeled by her tormentor, was subjected to baseball bats, bottles, bombs, exploding cigars, and one-hundred-pound bricks. Pure slapstick, but about to become slapstick with a heart—poetic Punch and Judy.

After a month or so of these repeated beanings, Krazy gently crept over to the sleeping Ignatz and laid a kiss upon his brow (SMACK). Ignatz, awakened, declared, "I dreamed that an angel kissed me." Krazy,

Alexander the Cat, January 9, 1910

stealing away, purred, "sweet thing." Herriman had added a gentle touch of irony. The Kat had fallen in love with her enemy. Every brick Ignatz (Krazy's "li'l aingil") now bounced off her bean was interpreted as a message of love. Ignatz, however, would never be aware of the Kat's love and he would continue, literally, to try to knock some sense into that "fool Kat."

Krazy's gender was uncertain right from the beginning, for Herriman might refer to the Kat as either "he" or "she." The artist once replied thus when questioned about the Kat's sex:

I don't know. I fooled around with it once; began to think the Kat is a girl—even drew up some strips with her being pregnant. It wasn't the Kat any longer; too much concerned with her own problems—like a soap opera. Know what I mean? Then I realized Krazy was something like a sprite, an elf. They have no sex. So that Kat can't be a he or a she. The Kat's a spirit—a pixie—free to butt into anything. Don't you think so?

The characters looked different in those early strips, almost marginal doodles and more animal-like. Ignatz was all arms and legs, with a squat body topped by a teardrop head. He gradually changed, growing fuller and taller, but his obsessions remained the same. The early Kat was taller and leaner, with a more button-like nose. Her looks, too, would alter, but through the years her heart and soul remained the same. Their comic-strip home was cramped into that shallow space below *The Dingbat Family*, hardly allowing Herriman's pen room to swing a cat. Despite the cramped quarters, he still managed to add many idiosyncratic details to the comparatively stable backgrounds. Chinese pagodas, Alaskan totem poles, Turkish minarets, cacti, and assorted pen-stroke vegetation became part of the *mise-en-scènes* for the Kat and Mouse. The cast was small, with such old friends as Gooseberry Sprigg and Joe Stork as members. Bull Pupp was there, not yet Officer, not yet part of the triangle as he chased either Mouse or Kat in fits of rage.

"*Krazy Kat* was not conceived, not born, it jes' grew," its creator commented, using the same phrase Harriet Beecher Stowe chose in

Historic first "beaning" of Kat by Mouse at bottom of *The Dingbat Family*, July 26, 1910.
Note Herriman's brief experimental use of type in word balloons

The Family Upstairs, original daily strip with Kat and Mouse below, November 22, 1910

The Family Upstairs, July 18, 1911

Krazy Kat, original for daily strip, December 24, 1917

Uncle Tom's Cabin to describe Topsy's origins. The mysteries, and intricacies, and joys of *Krazy Kat* evolved naturally, the idea developing from a sense of play in the hands of a master player, a rare case where the creation is as much in command as the creator, one feeding the other. *Krazy Kat* was never a plan laid out and carefully adhered to; rather it was the improvisation of a truly creative and self-trusting imagination.

After the Kat had made a few appearances, it is said that Willie, an office boy at the *New York Evening Journal*, suggested to Herriman that he make the Kat and Mouse regulars. Willie even may have provided a few ideas for their antics. A few days later, Arthur Brisbane, the great editor of the *Evening Journal*, took note and encouraged Herriman to "keep that Kat and Mouse going." With or without Willie's and Brisbane's encouragement, Herriman's elaboration on the pair persisted.

While the Kat and Mouse skirmish developed in the space below the strip, a battle was in the making in the strip itself. *The Dingbat Family* was retitled *The Family Upstairs* on August 1, 1910, when a maddening, mysterious, unseen family moved into the flat directly above the Dingbats at the "Sooptareen Arms." With this family came the farcical dementia that elevated the strip to new heights and changed a domestic strip into a fantasy strip. The new twist above, along with Krazy below, gave Herriman a genuine hit for the Hearst Syndicate.

Mr. Dingbat was incessantly enraged by the rambunctious doings of his noisy neighbors. With a monomaniacal drive reminiscent of Major Ozone, he tried desperately to evict, or at least get a glimpse of, his tormentors upstairs, stopping at nothing to satisfy his desire for revenge. Throughout the year Dingbat hired detectives, cowboys, hypnotists, crooks, Turkish wrestlers, Scottish bagpipers, the Mexican navy, boxers Jack Johnson and Bob Fitzsimmons, Desperate Desmond (a comic character of Harry Hershfield's), and even Bosco (you remember, the Snake Eater) to put a scare into his neighbors. Every scheme backfired. Unlike Ignatz, Mr. Dingbat was unable to express his aggression. In the strip, Herriman narrated:

Now—oyez—oyez—giving vent to a few bon mots, Mr. Dingbat wishes to announce to the public, that, as they all will admit, he has in this last year, battled with much fervor and

Krazy Kat, Sunday page, in which Herriman extols the virtues of "artists" Rudolph Dirks, Gus Mager, James Swinnerton, Tad Dorgan, and Dan Smith, March 4, 1928

courage to wrest the laurels of peace from the sands of war. Every day his love of solitude and quiet has been blasted by the noisy war hoof of the family upstairs and at each agitation he has manfully responded with all the force of his mighty cerebral dynamo, but, the fates refused him success—the old year dies, but Dingbat's courage lives on—t'is a fight to the end—

Obsession is a major theme of Herriman's work: Major Ozone's fixated search for fresh air; Mr. Dingbat's attempts to uncover and evict the family upstairs; Acrobatic Archie's dedication to his calisthenics; and Ignatz's drive to "crease that Kat's bean with a brick." Obsession is a very neat device for an artist-writer who must meet the challenge of telling a story every day of the year. Herriman was a genius at developing infinite permutations.

Mr. Dingbat's obsession ended November 15, 1911, when the entire apartment building was demolished to erect a department store. The Dingbats moved to Yorba Linda, and *The Family Upstairs* reverted to its original title and concept. As the Kat and Mouse shenanigans gained popular support, a ruled line divided them from *The Dingbat Family*. The bottom strip had occasionally replaced *The Family Upstairs* and *The Dingbat Family* and at those times was titled *Krazy Kat and Ignatz*. At last on October 28, 1913, *Krazy Kat* ran vertically down the side of the comics page as a completely independent strip.

The Dingbat Family came to an end on January 4, 1916, making way for Herriman's new strip, *Baron Bean*, which had its debut the following day. The hero of this strip was a down-on-his-luck English nobleman who, due to a lack of funds, was reduced to the role of a tramp. In flavor and characterization, this strip pays homage to Herriman's two favorite "Chorles's," Chaplin and Dickens. On the clever appellation of the major characters, Herriman wrote in a letter: "Baron Bean was the name of that Strip—'Baron Bean'—a bit of a pun—His good wife—"punnier" —was named Lucinda Bean—the stubby jobby in the outfit—was GRIMES—the Baron's Valet—"

The Baron and his faithful retainer and dupe, Grimes, connived and used their wits to survive. Despite his lowly state, the Baron maintained his dignity and sense of noblesse oblige, a twist on the popular rags-to-riches story line as portrayed in cartoonist George McManus's *Bringing up Father*. Later in the strip, the wives of both the Baron and Grimes appeared. Although some of the principal characters' original traits were retained, with the introduction of their wives the Baron Bean cartoons became another domestic strip. Near the end of its run Herriman's boredom with it became apparent as *Krazy Kat* characters began to invade the Baron's panels as "walk-ons."

On January 22, 1919, *Baron Bean* was retired, to be replaced on April 23, 1919, by *Now Listen Mabel*. This was the story of the courtship of a lovesick young man and a fickle woman. In the first episodes Mabel would find her beau, Jimmy, in some innocently compromising situation, whereupon Jimmy would try to explain to a huffish Mabel, "Now listen Mabel...." By the close of the year, both their courtship and the story line were strained, and Mabel and Jimmy were terminated on December 18.

As a daily strip *Krazy Kat* was progressing from slapstick to a more vaudevillian humor. The Kat and Mouse team exchanged quips, usually a play on words or a wacky observation, the upshot of which was Ignatz stoning the Kat for what he considered a bad joke. The mad dance of the backgrounds began. Herriman sent Krazy and Ignatz on a rollercoaster ride from panel to panel. Not missing a conversational beat, they would begin by sitting in the desert, shift to a boat in the ocean, and end up perched on a half-moon. These visual cues give a hint of the phantasmagoric work to follow.

The first Sunday full-page *Krazy Kat* appeared on Saturday, April 23, 1916. Printed in black and white and placed in the weekly arts and drama section, it introduced the strip to a new audience, one that ordinarily shunned the comics. The development of *Krazy Kat*'s small but faithful following ensued.

Expanding within the increased space allotted to a Sunday page, the strip exploded with vivacity and excitement. Not having had a full page to play with since his World Color Printing days, Herriman cut loose, filling the *Krazy Kat* strips with dazzling pictures and intoxicating words. His spatial sensibility unfurled, and there was no timidity in the way he took the whole page and broke it up as he wished; his innovations quickly set him apart from other comic artists working at that time. His

Krazy Kat and I. Mouse, daily strip which lasted

for a short period while The Dingbats were on vacation.

July 2, July 5, July 15, July 16, 1912

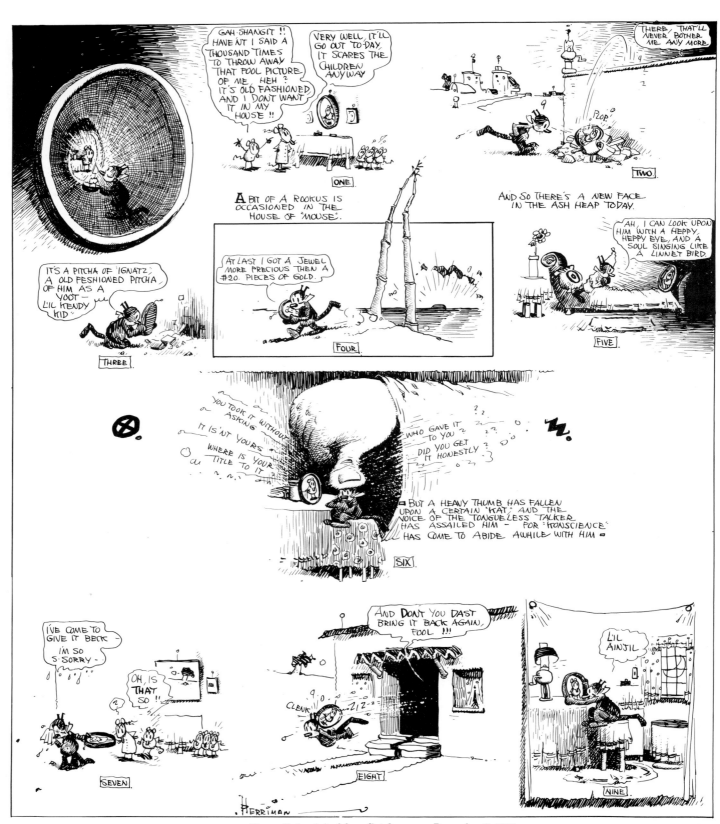

Krazy Kat, original for a Sunday page, December 9, 1917

Krazy Kat, original for a daily strip, January 6, 1918

gift for masterful composition is visible in the overall diagonal or horizontal design of the pages. One particular shape often stands out—a circle, or a high vertical tree or pole. Sometimes Herriman placed many variations of the same shape in an arresting pattern. Though impeccably composed, these images seem to flow spontaneously from the pen onto the page, filling the space kinetically. These comic-strip explorations coincided in time and place with the revolution in the art world brought about by the famed Armory Show of 1913.

George Herriman also knew how line could be subtly used to produce an effect; how a few sparse scratchings could become a lonely tree or cactus; how more complex cross-hatching and more static lines could become the vast sea. His pen line at this time was thinner and more delicate and sensitive than in the later strips. Dark and light areas were interspersed to break up the page and introduce variations in the action. Transitions from black to white panels added to the dynamic movement of a strip and enhanced the story. The quality of Herriman's blacks is striking, sometimes very opaque, at other times more translucent. These are works where opposites attract in a harmony of black and white, a story dramatized by chiaroscuro, enlivened by typical Herrimanesque touches—little banners, an irrelevant picture of Mount Fujiyama as an "intermission" in the strip, or a "hole" in the page with Mock Duck's head popping out as he proclaims, "And now for the display."

A *Krazy Kat* of December 9, 1917, exhibits many of these graphic and expressive qualities. In the upper half, a hand-drawn oval, meticulously shaded, contrasts with a single-ruled, rectangular panel. The clean line of the top border of the panel is interrupted by two strikingly rendered "trees." The free-floating central vignette is embellished on both sides by two of Herriman's major emblems, the *x* in a circle, and the zigzag. A trompe l'oeil panel in the lower right corner is a subtle jest that fills out the strip.

Early *Krazy Kat* Sunday pages often read like a mini-novel. At times reminiscent of *Aesop's Fables* or Kipling's *Just So Stories,* they were how-and-why parables. Herriman told "how" the rattlesnake got his rattle, "how" mice lost their fur, "how" the robin got his red breast, "why" cats are afraid of water. As the strips of 1916 grew rich and complex in

Krazy Kat, daily strip, May 4, 1918

Krazy Kat, daily strip, December 25, 1919

design, they also burgeoned in narrative and language. The early *Krazy Kats* have an unstudied linguistic freedom that is akin to the unconstrained feeling of the hand-drawn circle on page 60. Depending on Herriman's whim or how a story evolved, the dialogue of a strip would either crowd the page or be spattered lightly on it. Sometimes there was no dialogue at all. In his early strips, the author-creator often interjected himself into the story as narrator, usually to add a touch of ironic humor or to set the stage for the scenes to follow.

Herriman was a poet. He loved shapes and colors, but he also loved the sound and feel of a word, the rhythm and pace it could set in motion. The words set the tone of the story; they were the point of departure, but at the end there was always a detour to the denouement of the climactic brick. These words were an outrageous alphabet soup of Coconino patois, Spanish, French, Brooklyn Yiddish, onomatopoetic juxtapositions—and almost anything else that came to Herriman's mind. The lilting voices of the inhabitants of the capricious Kat world were perhaps nascent in a boyhood spent in the Creole quarter of New Orleans. Certainly the rhythm of the speech in these strips carries a strong suggestion of that patois.

During *Krazy Kat's* early years as a full-page cartoon, the scenario was populated with a cast of diverse characters. Bull Pupp was now an officer of the law, an upstanding public servant. However, the intense triangle of Krazy, Ignatz, and Officer Pupp was in its embryonic stage; Bull Pupp was still but a secondary player, while his jail was barely in evidence.

The supporting cast was made up of Joe Stork, who lived on top of the Enchanted Mesa and was "purveyor of progeny to prince and proletariat"; Gooseberry Sprigg, "the Duck Duke"; Don Kiyoti (originally Daniel Coyote), "psalmsinger of the Desierto Pintado," and his sidekick pig, Sancho Pansy (originally Cincho Pansy); Walter Cephus Austridge, "the Kalaharan Dickey-Bird"; Mock Duck, "Launderer Deluxe and Sage of the Orient"; Kolin Kelly, "Dealer in Bricks"; Mr. Wough Wuph Wuff, "Bone Trust Magnate"; Mr. Bum Bill Bee, "a Pilgrim Peregrinating the Highway of Dreams"; Pauline Parrot, "the Town's Most Prolific Prattler and Pragmatical Propagandiste"; from "The House of Mouse," Ignatz's wife, Matilda, and sons Irving, Marshall, and Milton; innumerable Katfish and Katbird Kousins; and a wide assortment of other members of the animal kingdom.

Herriman was a master of characterization. One of the most endearing qualities of *Krazy Kat* is the delineation of the characters' personalities. They are not "cute" in a forced or static way; they are captivating

Baron Bean, daily strips, 1916, 1917

because those tiny scratchy ink drawings are so alive. The trio of Mouse, Kat, and Pupp still had atavistic animal traits such as sometimes walking on all fours, but their more human qualities had become dominant. In a deceptively simple way Herriman manipulated their facial expressions and body postures to convey the subtlest innuendoes. Two black dots for eyes, a thick line for a nose, and a thin one for a mouth could be arranged in infinite variations to convey any emotion. He had the innate ability when drawing a body to create kinesthetic illusion. Ignatz's brick-throwing posture is perfectly represented; one can sense the physical exertion of the little mouse as he throws the brick and the impassioned joy of the Kat as she is hurled forward by its impact. Each character has its distinctive gait, and much can be read into every movement. But beyond personality and expression, the characters are imbued with an enigmatic quality that makes them linger in the mind long after the strip has been read.

The expressionistic landscape of Herriman's beloved Southwest, Coconino County, became an integral part of the strip. Lunatic cacti, mesas, buttes, and slivers of moon shift and change like mirages in the desert. This, and Herriman's playful emphasis on the limitations and nature of the comic-strip medium itself created a unique world for *Krazy Kat*.

William Randolph Hearst, among other things a fervent patron of the comic strip and possibly the sole reason *Krazy Kat* continued through its later, less popular years, was a great fan of George Herriman's. On one occasion, after reading a Sunday *Krazy Kat*, Hearst gave a direct order to raise his employee's salary. Herriman sent back the extra money, claiming he wasn't worth the increase since *Krazy Kat* "took so little work from one week to the next." Hearst remained firm and Herriman was forced to accept his raise.

At the height of its popularity, *Krazy Kat* was translated into different mediums. In 1916 the International Film Service (IFS), an offshoot of Hearst's International News (Wire) Service (INS), produced *Krazy Kat*, the world's first animated-cartoon cat film. Although Herriman was not personally involved in making this or any subsequent animated cartoon, the *Krazy Kat* character, akin to the original in name only, was used by many animation studios through the 1960s (Bray, Winkler, Columbia, and King Features Television).

John Alden Carpenter wrote the score for a jazz-pantomime ballet, *Krazy Kat*, choreographed by Adolph Bolm. It was fitting that the Kat and comrades should be eulogized in choreography, for freedom and joy of movement permeate the comic-strip pages. The verve and rhythm of the strip evoke the sound of early jazz. Krazy Kat is a dilettante of the arts—music, dance, painting. It is no wonder that choreographer-dancer Bolm was inspired by Herriman's work. The ballet was first performed in Town Hall, New York City, on January 20, 1922, by Ballet Intime. The scenery was based on Herriman's strip, and he designed the costumes, wrote the scenario, and illustrated the libretto. The ballet was

KRAZY KAT AND IGNATZ MOUSE GO INTO THE MOVIES

Promotional piece for *Krazy Kat* animated cartoons, *Photoplay*, July 1916

not very well received, but critics Stark Young and Deems Taylor gave it favorable reviews. In the *New Republic*, Young described the ballet with perceptive enthusiasm.

The light is so managed that the cartoons at the back, turning on rollers and changing every two or three minutes against the action in front of them, the costumes in black and white, the walls, the grayish trees on either side, take on a strange pearl color, as if we were seeing in some crazy dream the fantastic action of these fabled creatures whose human traits are all turned now to flickering inclinations and fragile passions and the shadows of whims. And meanwhile the music has about it a kind of added light that shines on this laughing unreality; it is bright, dramatic; it has also vaguely underneath its animation something very grim and pathetic and comic and original.

Herriman later wrote to a friend, "Yes sir John Alden—sure let himself loose on music—there—and you're right about the notes—he sure bought out the store."

Recognition beyond the newspaper world came for Herriman with Gilbert Seldes's article in the May 1922 issue of *Vanity Fair,* "Golla, Golla the Comic Strip's Art." This was the basis for the chapter on *Krazy Kat* in Seldes's book *The Seven Lively Arts,* in which he praises the best in popular culture, placing Herriman in the company of Charles Chaplin, Al Jolson, Irving Berlin, and George Gershwin. His panegyric, "The Krazy Kat That Walks by Himself," is the most celebrated essay on *Krazy Kat.* Seldes's circle included the renowned literary figures F. Scott Fitzgerald, e. e. cummings, James Joyce, Ernest Hemingway, and H. L. Mencken, all of whom were introduced to *Krazy Kat* by Seldes. Once when Seldes was leaving on a trip, Fitzgerald, cummings, and the critic Edmund Wilson sent him this Herrimanesque telegram: "A happy bon voyage from Ignatz and Krazy with hope that you may do somethink monimountit lil embessioer of the mewses."

Herriman and Seldes corresponded infrequently. Herriman would write to thank Seldes for his praise of *Krazy Kat* or to present Seldes or one of his colleagues with a drawing, in his inimitable style:

It's sure nice, folks like me—getting letters from folks like you—even though it was meant for that Kat—et al—wish we knew how to render you the thanks it all deserves—but—no sobby—

Further kudos followed Herriman's induction into the *Vanity Fair* Hall of Fame in April 1923, "...because he has invented in his comic series, *Krazy Kat,* a nonsense creation which, for humor and originality is comparable only to *Alice in Wonderland....*" *Krazy Kat* was also featured in *Vanity Fair* on three occasions.

After nearly three years of producing only *Krazy Kat,* Herriman developed a new strip, *Stumble Inn.* The first daily was printed on October 30, 1922, and the first Sunday page on December 9. It appeared in the comic supplement in color, unlike the black-and-white Sunday *Krazy Kat* page.

Stumble Inn is the story of Mr. Uriah Stumble and his wife, Ida, who rent out rooms to a mixed bag of Herriman oddballs. Regulars at the inn were Joe Beamish, the ultimate loafer (a character who showed up in many Herriman strips, including *The Dingbat Family* and *Baron Bean),* and the ineffective house detective, Owleye. A very imaginative

Rare pencil sketch for *Krazy Kat* ballet, c. 1922

strip with many surreal touches, it showed Herriman at his most loquacious, with some Sunday pages looking like illustrated text. Although the daily strip lasted only a few months, the Sunday page continued for three years.

Hearst had given Herriman a lifetime contract with King Features Syndicate, providing him with security and the privilege of working wherever he pleased. *Krazy Kat* would always have a home in the Hearst papers, and Herriman enjoyed the freedom to continue his somewhat esoteric strip without the restrictions of commercialism.

With his wife and their two teenage daughters he moved back west about 1922. They established themselves in Hollywood, California, in part because of its proximity to Herriman's beloved Arizona, where he could now visit frequently.

erriman was truly enamored of the Southwest. He said, "That's the country I love and that's the way I see it. I can't understand why no other artists ever use it. All those Indian names mean something to me and they 'fit' somehow whether or not the readers understand their meaning. I don't think Krazy's readers care anything about that part of the

Krazy Kat, daily strip, September 23, 1940

strip. But it's very important to me and I like it nearly as well as the characters themselves."

There can be no true understanding of George Herriman, and only a limited understanding of *Krazy Kat*, without some knowledge of the Navajo country, which includes the settlement of Kayenta as well as Monument Valley and straddles Arizona and Utah. Herriman took artistic license when he included this Navajo country in Krazy's Coconino County, since the real Coconino County is a bit further southwest.

Monument Valley is an elevated desert, a land of hogans, mesas, and buttes, dogs herding sheep, wild horses grazing, and tumbleweed blowing across the land. Majestic orange-colored corrugated rock formations stand in awesome stillness, casting purple shadows across the vast expanse. Only the whirling wind whistling through the monuments disrupts the quiet and hallowed serenity. One feels as if one were on sacred ground where time stands still. Like *Krazy Kat*, this valley exists in its own "world" and is a geographic counterpart of Herriman's peaceful spirit.

Kayenta, approximately twenty-five miles from Monument Valley, was founded as a Navajo trading post by John and Louisa Wetherill when in 1910, two years before Arizona was granted statehood, they pitched their tents there in the snow. Hosteen John (Mr. John) and Asthon Sosi (the Slim Woman), as they were known by the Indians who loved and trusted them, had been traders and explorers in Navajo country for ten years. Kayenta was farther from a railroad than any other "white" settlement in the United States. To keep the trading post alive, John Wetherill and his brothers had to ride their horses across two hundred miles of sand and arroyos to pick up supplies in Gallup, New Mexico.

In 1913, shortly after his term as president, Theodore Roosevelt visited Rainbow Bridge, near Kayenta, and stayed at the Wetherill ranch. On his return he wrote in *Outlook* magazine:

Next morning we journeyed on, and in the forenoon we reached Kayenta, where John Wetherill, the guide and Indian trader, lives. . . .

Mrs. Wetherill has made an extraordinarily sympathetic study of the Navajos and to a less extent the Utes; she knows, and feelingly understands their traditions and ways of thought, and speaks their tongue fluently; and it was she who first got from the Indians full knowledge of the [Rainbow] Bridge. . . .

She not only knows their language; she knows their minds; she has the keenest sympathy not only with their bodily needs, but with their mental and spiritual processes. . . .

Stumble Inn, Sunday page, January 7, 1923

Painting made as a gift for Ernest Pascal, Herriman's son-in-law, c. 1932

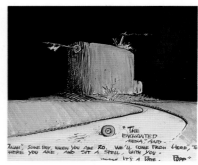

Small watercolor with personal message for granddaughter Dinah, c. 1940

The publicity that ensued brought a few brave adventurers to this remote place. A close friend and frequent guest of the Wetherills' was George Herriman. It is not known exactly when he first visited the Navajo lands. It may have been after Roosevelt's account was published or before, on the occasion of one of Herriman's early cross-country trips. Most likely he learned of Monument Valley from his friend James Swinnerton, who was probably the first of several cartoonists to venture into northern Arizona. (In 1903, Swinnerton, who was thought to be dying of tuberculosis, was sent by his doctor to Arizona, where the dry air might help to prolong his life. This prescription worked. Swinnerton lived for seventy-two more years, dying at the age of ninety-eight.) Herriman made references to Coconino County in his strips as early as 1911, and renderings of that landscape appeared there in 1916. Whenever Herriman first laid eyes on Navajo country, once there he was hooked: "Those mesas and sunsets out in that ole pais pintado . . . a taste of that stuff sinks you—deep too—"

The Mittens, Monument Valley, Arizona

Mrs. Betty Zane Rodgers, adopted daughter of the Wetherills, remembers Herriman in Kayenta:

To my knowledge, George Herriman found out about Kayenta through articles of the pack trips and knowing it was a ranch of serenity. He visited in the summer for at least twenty years. His stay was to escape from his routine in the city and he visited, relaxed, and did a little work when he felt like it.

George's wife . . . did not expect us to wait on her in any way. She helped us in the kitchen and was a very sweet person.

His daughter, nicknamed Bobbie, was about sixteen when she first came to Kayenta.

Mailing envelope
and souvenir photo
of Tom MacNamara
and George Herriman
at the Grand Canyon,
c. 1924

She was somewhat of a practical joker, teasing the cowboys after they'd returned from a long trip, ragged and dirty. She used to put a big wad of chewing gum in her palm and then shake hands with them. She enjoyed herself immensely.

Mr. Herriman rarely talked of his work.... George was concerned about the Navajo people and listened while my mother, Mama Lu, talked of the Navajo. He often went to the ceremonials with my folks.

He was very generous. He sent a movie projector to the T.B. sanitarium in Kayenta, as a gift. Then he arranged for films to be sent every Friday. Those were the first "talkies" in Kayenta.

In 1923 Harry Goulding and his young wife, "Mike," set up their trading post in Monument Valley. Goulding was responsible for introducing director John Ford (*Stagecoach, She Wore a Yellow Ribbon, My Darling Clementine*) and the movie industry to the area, thus making Monument Valley emblematic of the American West. Swinnerton became a close friend of the Gouldings', and subsequently stayed with them at their lodge, built in the late twenties and still in operation. Mike Goulding wrote:

We first met Jimmie and Gretchen Swinnerton at a Navajo sing, in Monument Valley some time in the thirties, he was staying at the Wetherills. Hardly any one knew we had a spare bedroom!

Jimmie Swinnerton did field sketches when he stayed in the valley with us, did a beautiful oil of our old trading post and home....

I really don't know if Jim brought George to the Indian Country or if he like so many of us just ventured—we met George Herriman in Kayenta, he always stayed with Mr. John, and was very interested in the Navajo people, and wanted them to know some of the things we did out in the world, so sent in the first movies they had ever seen. Once a week at the old sanitarium we could all gather and see Tom Mix or some kind of movie. Great fun, the Navajos always laughed at the sad scenes!

Through the years a group of adventurous writers, painters, and photographers made their way to the valley, and the trading posts became somewhat like artists' colonies. Getting there was no easy task. Mike Goulding said that Tonalea (Red Lake), about fifty miles from Monument Valley, was the weeding-out point: "Anyone who got past there was of good stock." Cartoonist Rudolph Dirks showed up once in a while to paint landscapes with Swinnerton, some of which made their way into Herriman's personal collection. Dirks insisted that Herriman try his hand at capturing the landscape in paint, and although he obliged with two small paintings, he was less interested in the job of recording the monuments on canvas than in the joy of observing their beauty.

In describing the "world" of *Krazy Kat*, many writers have called the locale surreal. e. e. cummings called it "a strictly irrational landscape," and the Italian author Umberto Eco writes of "certain surrealistic inventions, especially in the improbable lunar landscapes." Herriman's Coconino County may seem irrational and improbable, but most of the backgrounds are realistic depictions of the rocky outcroppings and vegetation of the valley. The perpetual metamorphosis of Herriman's settings can, in part, be attributed to the changing light playing over the huge rock formations. These "sculptures," though unchanged for millennia, appear to alter in color and shape with each blink of the eye as they pick up every gradation of the rays of the sun, passing across the heavens from dawn to dusk.

Self-portrait for the Wetherills in thanks for their care during a stay in Kayenta, c. 1930

The best-known monuments and those most often used in *Krazy Kat* are the Mittens. Like two huge fingerless hands they point to the sky. According to the Navajos, the Mittens are the Big Hands, representing a great power once present upon the earth but now dormant. One day, the legend goes, the power will return again to rule from Monument Valley.

Also finding their way onto the pages of *Krazy Kat* were the Totem Pole (Thunder Needle), Rainbow Bridge, the volcanic rock Agathlan (1,225 feet high), the Enchanted Mesa, Joshua trees, Oljeto (Place of Moonlight Water), the wind witches of Wunanji, the blue bean bush, Chuckawalla Butte, the echoing cliffs of Kaibito, the Desierto Pintado, Pika Mesa, the Mesa Dedo del Pie Grande, and the Elephant's Feet. The Elephant's Feet stand outside Monument Valley near Tonalea. Today a road goes around the two seventy-foot-high monuments, but Mike Goulding remembered that "in the old days we'd just drive right between them!"

Professor Wough Wuph Wuff explained the mysteries of the monuments to Ignatz "in a moment of erudite effluvium" in the May 16, 1926, *Krazy Kat* strip: "It is only sandstone, Mr. Mouse and so, but a baby, a mere child—ten, maybe twelve million years of age—shaped by the nimble fingers of nature in a moment of play."

Not only did the images of the rocks of Monument Valley appear in *Krazy Kat*, but the images of the Indian culture were also prevalent. A quiet, private people who venerate nature, the Navajos are superb crafters of silver and turquoise jewelry, respecting the earthly origins of the metal and stone. They are, as well, skilled weavers of blankets and rugs from shearings of the sheep they herd. These native Americans were a source of inspiration to Herriman. In *Krazy Kat* he made extensive use of their designs and motifs, which may appear on a piece of pottery, as elaborations on the border of a strip, as the ornamental trim on a house, as the decorations on the mesas and the foliage of the trees, and also as the overall design of a Sunday page. Navajo "storm pattern"

Monument Valley, Arizona

rugs from time to time decorate the houses of the inhabitants of Coconino. A Sunday page of December 11, 1938, depicts Krazy sleeping next to a traditional Navajo loom, on which she has just woven a "febric" in a design of Ignatz's creation—a brick, centered on the rug. A strip dated October 28, 1928, shows Krazy making a sand painting of Ignatz, saying: "Well if he can't be here in person, he can be here in pitcher—I'll draw him in the sand."

The philosophy of *Krazy Kat* often reflected that of the Navajos. Herriman's comic strip reveals the artist's respect for the mystical forces of nature. As much of Navajo life revolved around the elements and their whims, so do many of the *Krazy Kat* strips. Rain, windstorms, snowstorms, thunderstorms, lonely clouds, half-moons, moon rings, moonbeams and buckets of moonlight, cyclones, zephyrs, and gravity play a pivotal part in many of the strips.

Navajo customs and beliefs are occasionally in evidence throughout *Krazy Kat*, as for example in the following soliloquy of Officer Pupp, dated Sunday, November 11, 1938.

> *Officer Pupp:*
> Today my world walks in beauty.
> Beneath me a good earth—
> A gracious glebe, lies in beauty—
> Shifting sands dust its cheeks in powdered beauty—
> And now will I turn my eye to the empyrean—
> where stars' gleam moon's beam—
> and sun's sheen abides in beauty . . .
> So—I'll nap in beauty.
> *The Brick (off in the distance):*
> ZIP—
> *Ignatz Mouse:*
> Today—my world walks in beauty.
> *Officer Pupp:*
> HIS world—Yaaaa

Original drawing of *Krazy Kat* and friends discussing Agathelan in Monument Valley, c. 1925. Gift to H. P. Raleigh

Compare it with the following lines from the Navajo ceremonial Yeibichai, the Night Chant:

> With beauty may I walk.
> With beauty before me, may I walk.
> With beauty behind me, may I walk.
> With beauty above me, may I walk.
> With beauty below me, may I walk.
> With beauty all around me, may I walk.

Herriman never lost his affinity with the ways of the Navajo people, and he once told Gilbert Seldes he would like to be reincarnated as an Indian. He always wore a silver Navajo bracelet and owned many books about American Indians. On trips down to Navajo country he would bring a huge five- or ten-gallon jar of hard candy for the Indian children. In appreciation of Herriman's kindness and his concern for them, the Navajos sent him a handsome handmade book of photographs of Monument Valley, taken by photographer Josef Muench. The women loomed him a rug in black, white, and gray with his name woven across it: GEO. HERRIMAN. He treasured these gifts and displayed them prominently.

To this day there is no post office in Monument Valley. No doubt, if the mails had been better Herriman would never have left Kayenta.

Mabel and George in Hollywood, c. 1930

The Herrimans took up residence in Hollywood in a white, two-story, Spanish-style dwelling at 1617 North Sierra Bonita, then known as the Outpost Estates. Now Herriman was closer to some of his California-bred friends and to others from the East who had already moved westward. Although generally quite a private person, Herriman did enjoy seeing his friends, and he could be a wonderfully entertaining host. Poker was his favorite sport, and he especially liked to play with fellow cartoonists. At times, however, he might sit through social gatherings without saying a word, or he might be found alone in the kitchen doing the dishes, an activity which he claimed helped him think.

In Hollywood Herriman developed ties with the movie industry. Two old newspaper cronies were now working for the studios, Tom Mac-Namara and Beanie Walker, Herriman's closest friend. Walker was head writer for Our Gang Comedies at the Hal Roach Studio, and in the early twenties Herriman occasionally drew his Hearst strips there, possibly because he missed working in the middle of all the action of a noisy office. Or perhaps he needed to get away from the activity at home. Whatever the reason, he enjoyed drawing at the Roach Studio, and the creative people who worked there enjoyed his company as well as his work. Krazy Kat appeared as a stuffed toy in the Our Gang Comedy *Fire Fighters* and in Harold Lloyd's film *I Do*. Herriman was paid a small tribute in the 1934 Laurel and Hardy version of *Babes in Toyland* (later reissued as *March of the Wooden Soldiers*) when the cat in "the cat and the fiddle" was hit with a brick thrown by a mouse. On the Roach lot Herriman met many celebrities, including Will Rogers and the writer of the Laurel and Hardy comedies, Carl Harbaugh. At their request, the generous Herriman presented each with a hand-colored drawing.

At the Hal Roach Studios Herriman met director Frank Capra, who in his autobiography, *The Name Above the Title*, wrote of Herriman:

Another fascinating professional I met at Roach's was cartoonist George Herriman, the creator of one of my favorite comic characters, Krazy Kat, that lovable combination of wisdom and innocence who tilted cat whiskers at inhumanities against the ever-changing Arizona backgrounds of Coconino County. Herriman was one of the first intellectual philosophers to comment entertainingly and shrewdly on life's frustrations through the medium of the comic strip.

I don't remember where this talented man lived, but he worked quietly in a studio bungalow in the middle of the Roach lot—"Because," he said, "Krazy Kat feels right at home with all these crazy comics."

I spent many an hour watching this shy humorist draw.

> Capra later described George Herriman as "one of my heroes."
>
> Surrounded by the movie industry, and having great admiration for Charlie Chaplin's films, Herriman reviewed *The Gold Rush* for the October 1925 issue of *Motion Picture Classics* magazine.

There is no question of why he is here, slipping, sliding or scampering over the ice, no talk of the danger all about, depths below, heights above, bears behind, and ice all about—and we following, following, ever following. We have waited long to katch this sprite at play, so let no one stay our step while we have him—we will follow—whither he wills until he loses us in the mists and we flounder back to earth again. Rich man, poor man, beggar man, thief—leveled to a kommon denomination. . . .

Let all the kobblers of earth fashion flat shoes, all awry—and all the tailors trim trousers as loose as gunny sacks, put all the reeds of the world into kanes, and let the hatter go mad making Derbies—then pour into them the genius of another Chaplin. It is as easy as writing kriticism—mes amis—Twice as easy!!!!

And now, Ignatz!! The BRICK!!!

Krazy Kat,
daily strip,
October 15, 1918

Starting in August 1925 and continuing until September 1929, the freedom of design of the *Krazy Kat* Sunday page was sacrificed to the convenience of printing. King Features forced the strip into a layout that gave each newspaper the option of continuing to print *Krazy Kat* as a whole page or running it as two four-panel daily strips. The full page now conformed to a format with three panels on top, two panels in the middle, separated by an unrelated free-floating drawing, not used when the page was broken up to be printed as dailies—and three panels across the bottom. All panels were of equal dimensions. Despite these restrictions, Herriman took liberties with the design of the individual panels, but the new format surely constricted the rhythm and artistry of his experimental storytelling.

He felt keenly the limitations of conventional spacing, and claimed that a real comic page would allow him to create images and decorative effects that the present page could never accommodate. "The people don't know what they want. And if they get an entirely new taste of something that's good, they'll want it until they find something better. But we've got to give them the initial taste before they start clamoring for more."

This compositional straightjacket denied Herriman the space to continue the fantasy elaborations and storybook fabrications of the earlier Sunday pages. The scope of the strip was pared down to fit the space, but with this paring down came a sharper focus on characterization. It was in the twenties that the notorious triangle began to be fully explored and defined.

Officer Pupp came into his own with the declaration (made only to himself) of his love for Krazy. It was a secret love, an unrequited love from afar. "Oh, would that I were klown instead of kop oh, would that my forte be komedy instead of the konstabulary—that I might bring a smile to the wan, wasted, wistful pan of that dear Kat." We now have the kat who loves the mouse who hates the kat, and the dog who, in turn, hates the mouse and loves the kat. Whereas the cycle formerly ended with Ignatz beaning Krazy with the brick, it now concluded with Pupp putting Ignatz in jail for the evil act. A triple dose of irony transformed every strip into, in the words of e. e. cummings, "meteoric burlesque melodrama."

Ignatz now reached new heights in his obsessive scheming. Each brick thrown became a work of art; he never threw the same brick twice. Every detail—time, place, brick acquisition—was carefully plotted, although he wasn't above improvisation when the opportunity arose.

Ignatz: I've had this scheme in my mind for some time—it should work fine, it has such a dramatic appeal to it.

Officer Pupp, oblivious both to Krazy's love for the mouse and Ignatz's artistry with the brick, thinks, "He's just a 'mouse'—so how could he be 'Esthetic'?" and imprisons mouse and impounds brick. Ignatz, in a classic exchange from October 9, 1927, pleads his case to his jailer:

OP: I saw you toss that brick at that "Kat," you wen—and don't tell me it was the you in you that did it—it was you just you—
IM: T'was truly I who did it, "Officer Pupp" but it was the me in me that willed it.
OP: And it's the you in you that I should arrest, is it?
IM: Sure, it's the me in me that's to blame. So it's the me in me that you should arrest.
OP: All right, I'm arresting the you in you.
IM: —But you're also arresting me—
OP (*with* IM *in jail*): Well, if you can get away from the you in you, you are a free mouse.

Through Krazy's ingenuous eyes Ignatz and Officer Pupp appear "like lil innisint childrens they play togeda."

In his work of the late twenties, Herriman's drawing line was at its scratchiest and sketchiest, in marked contrast to the delicate, detailed style of the teens and not yet possessing the graphically strong quality of the mid-thirties and forties, which ushered in a new phase. The "rushed" look of some of these late twenties strips may have resulted from the layout imposed on Herriman as well as his now frequent vacations in Arizona. It has been noted that he did only a little work while in Kayenta, and one can surmise that he got the jump on his deadlines by producing a large batch of work in Hollywood before escaping to the desert.

Just as Monument Valley was now playing a larger part in Herriman's life, it was also playing a bigger one in Krazy's. Gone are the little country houses, stores, and trees that occasionally appeared in the earlier strips. From now on, the *Krazy Kat* drama would be acted out entirely in the Navajo desert. The unrelated center drawing of the Sunday page gave Herriman a new place to play. At first he treated his readers to beautifully rendered, realistic Arizona landscapes, but later he used the space for one-panel *Krazy Kat* jokes and abstract vignettes of the trio.

During the winters of 1924–28, Herriman spent time in Mexico with

Original watercolor, c. 1925. Gift to Carl Harbaugh

the Wetherills, who conducted trips across the border from a ranch in southern Arizona. During this period there is a strong Mexican influence in the artist's work. Along with the Navajo designs, Mexican pottery, architecture, and ornate decorations are now placed along the edges of the strip, and animal characters from Vaca Blanca and Toro Verde make their way into Coconino. The Spanish language is sprinkled liberally throughout the narration and sometimes bursts forth from Kat and guitar in the lyrics of songs.

Herriman was also busy with changes in his other strips. When

IT'S ONE OF THOSE SILLY IDEAS SOME SIMP SENT IN, IT'S AWFUL, BUT I'LL FIX IT UP —

EMBARRASSING MOMENTS

HAVING UNLOADED THIS PRETTY PATTER, YOU FIND THAT THE PERSON YOU ARE ADDRESSING IS THE ONE WHO SENT THE "IDEA" IN. 8-9

Embarrassing Moments,
one-panel cartoon,
August 9, 1930

Illustration for
Archie and Mehitabel

THEY TASTE ALIKE TO ME.

THEY DO, HEH?

Stumble Inn ended, on January 9, 1926, he produced *Us Husbands,* printed from January 16 until December 18, along with *Mistakes Will Happen. Us Husbands,* the saga of the tribulations of a married couple that harks back to Herriman's first daily strip, *Home Sweet Home,* was the most domesticated of Herriman's domestic strips. *Mistakes Will Happen* was the topper (a self-contained smaller strip running above the main feature) for *Us Husbands.* At one point it involved a husband and wife in medieval times. Here Herriman has fun with "olde English": "Sniff it well 'Arbutus,' get thee a heaping nose full of its aroma—then get thyself hence in search of its owner—my husband and thy master."

In 1928 Herriman began working on a one-panel cartoon entitled *Embarrassing Moments.* Originating in 1922, it had been drawn intermittently by various cartoonists in the years that followed. *Embarrassing Moments*—the title is self-explanatory—is based on a simple idea, but when Herriman took it over he brought to it his own special touch. In the first months some embarrassing moments concerned Kayenta, Indian pottery, scottie dogs, and even the trials of a cartoonist. Herriman turned his *Embarrassing Moments* into the panel *Bernie Burns.* The theme was the same, but a central character, Mr. Burns, endured all the embarrassments. Neither panel appeared in many papers, and those that carried them did so sporadically. *Bernie Burns* slowly faded and by 1932 *Krazy Kat* was the sole strip Herriman drew until his death.

In addition to *Krazy Kat,* the only work Herriman took on in the thirties was illustrating Don Marquis's book of verse *archy and mehitabel.* These jaunty poems about a lower-case cat and a cockroach are in the same vein as Herriman's comic strips. It was an ideal relationship for an artist well versed in the quirks of the feline character and a poet with a wry and inventive wit. The result was a book so popular it is still in print today. In an unusual gesture Herriman, quite pleased with the sketches for this project, stopped by the *Los Angeles Examiner* to give his old friend "Punkus" Springer a firsthand look at the drawings. In the introduction to one of the editions, E. B. White wrote, "... on George Herriman's part, double-barreled illustration. It seems to me Herriman deserves much credit for giving the right form and mien to these willful animals. They possess (as he drew them) the great soul. It would be hard to take Mehitabel if she were either more catlike, or less. She is cat, yet not cat; and Archy's lineaments are unmistakably those of poet and pest."

The Herrimans moved for the last time around 1930. Herriman himself designed his second Hollywood home, a Spanish-style mansion atop a hill at 2217 Maravilla Drive. On the living-room wall he painted a huge orange zigzag, a throwback to his sign-painting days and a reminder of Navajo culture. Throughout the rooms hung paintings and drawings of Indians and the Southwest by Swinnerton, the illustrator Henry Raleigh, and the painter Maynard Dixon. Herriman was one of the first in Hollywood to pave his yard with flagstones, transforming it into a Mexican garden while avoiding the bother of cultivating a lawn. In his pragmatic philosophy there was "no point in raising something you can't do anything with." Outside he painted decorations on the walls and on large pots blooming with tropical plants and flowers ("azaleas, gardenias and such"). Crowning the house and gently following the "vagrant zephyrs" was a weathervane with the figures of one of Herriman's pet scotties and an angel, guardians of the household. Later he bought the hilly lot across the street and made it into a park. Anyone could stop and rest a while on one of the benches to enjoy the spectacular view.

Herriman sold his first California home, which had cost him fifty thousand dollars, to a friend for forty thousand. This was purely an act of generosity as he had a good head for business and invested his money wisely.

The Herriman daughters, Bobbie and Toots, were part of the Hollywood scene and on May 22, 1932, Bobbie married author-scriptwriter Ernest Pascal, who wrote the screenplay for *Hound of the Baskervilles*. They presented Herriman with his only grandchild, Dinah (Dee). Bobbie held a special place in her father's heart not only because she had inherited his artistic talent, but also, sadly, because she was epileptic.

The thirties were marked with tragedy for George Herriman. On November 14, 1934, his wife died as a result of a car accident. She left her husband with their daughters and numerous dogs and cats. Five years to the day after her mother's death, Bobbie died at the age of thirty. Herriman suffered deeply from the untimely loss of both his wife and daughter and he lived for the remainder of his years as a virtual recluse, focusing himself more than ever on *Krazy Kat*.

In his later years Herriman worked in his living room at an adjustable drawing table in front of a window facing west. The table was covered with random ink doodles of *Krazy Kat* characters and nearby were stored all the proof sheets of his work. There were a piano and radio-phonograph in this room as well. He had done away with his bed and instead slept on a couch next to the drawing table. When he finished with his day's work, Herriman would roll up the *Kat* pages, put them in a mailing tube, and take a long walk to the post office.

In the same way that he had experimented in the teens with full pages, Herriman now began again to push the medium further. His compositions had a more deliberate, resolute feeling because in 1935 a significant newcomer came to Coconino County—color. After appearing for years in black and white, *Krazy Kat* joined the other color comics in the Sunday supplements. Like the actual Coconino landscape, Coconino color changed from panel to panel: readers were now treated to Herriman's painted desert. His use of color was as individual as was his use of line: bright yellow moons dipped over vivid red mesas against pitch-black skies; and purple cacti sprang out of green desert in orange daylight. This artist, who had such strong conviction in his use of line and layout, had the same conviction about the use of color. He had no fear of using a full, bold palette.

With the addition of color, Herriman rethought the design and even the drawing of *Krazy Kat*. He introduced bigger panels with more open space, less cross-hatching in the drawings, panels with huge skies usually at darkest night, and wide open desert, which allowed for expansive masses of color to shine forth. The layouts are boldly graphic,

Herriman and daughter Toots in a playful moment on the California beach, c. 1940

Herriman at the drawing board, c. 1940

Krazy Kat, daily strip, March 8, 1938

not as loose or free-floating as before. The fine detail of the early strips would have been extremely hard to print in color. Gone are the quirky hand-drawn oval panels of the past, and in their place are strong compass-drawn circles placed near bold diamonds, triangles, or diagonals. Each panel is enclosed to contain the printed color; each drawing has a thicker, solid line to hold the color. These Sunday pages are so strongly composed that one could paint the insides of the individual panels black and still enjoy a page as pure design.

The characters, too, have expanded in size and altered in shape to coincide with their surroundings and complement the new-found color. They are at the farthest from their humble animal origins. One cannot imagine this cat and mouse living in Mr. Dingbat's, or anyone else's, apartment. As Coconino is its own world, Krazy, Ignatz, and Pupp are their own entities. In a run of 1938 dailies, Dr. Y. Zowl had to remind the trio of their "atavism."

Coconino's cast shrinks to the mainstays, the eternal triangle, plus Kolin Kelly, Joe Stork, Bum Bill Bee, and occasionally a few others, and there are not as many interlopers as before. Krazy is often seen sashaying about holding an umbrella, a possible reflection of Herriman's memories of his early days in New Orleans. Mrs. Kwak Wak emerges, taking the place of Pauline Parrot as town gossip and society's conscience. She played a large role during the last years, most often teaming up with Officer Pupp in their assault on Ignatz.

In these later pages Herriman played with variations on the *Krazy Kat* logo, no two alike. From 1938 on he added a thin horizontal runner panel along the bottom of the page. Like the center vignettes of the twenties, these drawings were idea sketches which often commented on the story line above.

More than ever the man was in total control of his art. After almost thirty years of daily variations on the triangle theme, a joke could be set off by the slightest glance, action, or word. While he continued to include the customary long poetic discourses, many of the later Sunday speeches have a tightened language, haiku-like in their brevity. Herriman, the perspicacious master, was completely confident in his mature work, and everything went like clockwork.

In spite of the renewed vigor of the strip, it was appearing in fewer and fewer papers. By 1944 *Krazy Kat* could be found in only thirty-five papers, not a large number compared with a strip like *Blondie*, which ran in over a thousand.

Weathervane designed
by Herriman for
his house on
Maravilla Drive

Original drawing of Coconino characters, c. 1940. Gift to E. B. Crosswhite

Krazy Kat, daily strip, June 24, 1936

Krazy Kat, daily strip left unfinished on Herriman's drawing table, April 1944

From the twenties and continuing into the thirties, the *Krazy Kat* dailies were filled with longer narratives, continuing story lines, some of which lasted for months. These included the arrival of Krazy's Uncle Tomm Katt, Mimi, a French poodle schoolteacher who wreaked havoc on the male population, and suave Mr. Kiskidee Kuku, another French poodle who briefly won Krazy's affection, generating jealous rages in Ignatz and Officer Pupp who joined forces in their hatred of the new paramour. This suitor vanished when his wife and children showed up in Coconino. Another rather long story line had Krazy adopting a little kitten; the perplexed Krazy wondered if the kitten should call her Mommy or Daddy. The kitten, taking after its adoptive parent, soon fancied being beaned with a brick by its own little mouse, Marmaduke. Kitten Kat turned out to be the lost child of millionaire Mr. Meeyowl, the katnip king. Mr. Meeyowl also played a role in the longest continuous story in *Krazy Kat*, the 1936 opus known as "Tiger Tea." Here Krazy leaves Coconino only to return mysteriously with the world's most powerful katnip. Tiger Tea is "Tunda in a tea-potz," capable of giving the meekest worm the confidence of a "King Kobra" chasing after the early bird. The tea turned Coconino upside down for two years, causing many twists and turns.

The very last years took Herriman's scratchy style to its extreme. Perhaps because of his arthritic condition, instead of drawing, he actually scraped or knifed out a good portion of the whites from the black-inked surface. Those areas on the originals resembled woodcuts or scratchboard drawings in effect. There is a precious frailty in these last drawings which is in marked contrast to the energy of the overall design.

Herriman's years of living an almost reclusive life heightened his saintly nature. Always a sensitive soul, he was eager to help anyone in need, and in memory of his early struggles he gave liberally, often anonymously, to many charities. Believing animals to be superior to people, he was practically a vegetarian, varying his diet only when it made him feel too weak. Once, while he was driving with P. C. Springer on the desolate roads to the Navajo country, a bee flew in the open window of the car. Herriman insisted that Springer stop the car so he could carefully shoo it out, explaining, "Everything has a right to live, even a bee!"

Herriman's house was overrun with thirteen adopted stray cats. To add to the menagerie, he kept as many as five scottie dogs, some of which were not housebroken. When one of them demonstrated its lack of control, Herriman, not missing a stroke at the drawing board, would deliver in a quiet drawl his attempt at "discipline": "Now stop that, you rascal!" He declared that his favorite activities were reading and walking his dogs Angus, Ginsberg, Shantie, MacTavish, and MacGregor; the latter two occasionally appeared in *Krazy Kat*. During the war years he used almost all of his ration points to feed his pets. Invariably, when leaving a friend's home he would say, "I have to go home and put a leg of lamb in the oven for the dogs."

In accordance with his convictions, Herriman would never ride a horse and for a time would not drive any car but a Ford—or a Ford product. Wilson Springer, the son of P. C. Springer, remembers, "...one Sunday the Herrimans came to our home and picked our family up in a huge, new Lincoln touring car.... George Herriman said he admired Henry Ford so much for his humanitarian policy towards war.... Henry Ford was ridiculed as a pacifist but he had won the respect of George Herriman and later, he said he would never buy anything but a Ford product for transportation."

Later, according to Herriman's granddaughter, he bought his daughter Toots a big cumbersome Buick convertible for her birthday. Each year he would trade in the last year's model for a new one, sometimes black, sometimes white, but always with a red interior.

After his wife's death, Herriman had a close relationship with Louise Swinnerton, first wife of James Swinnerton, and from the late thirties on the two corresponded frequently. On May 13, 1938, after undergoing a kidney operation, Herriman sent this telegram to her from his hospital bed: "I am heading for home tomorrow wish it were right on through to where I could get the sniff of a hogan or the sight of a red butte on the horizon but three little scotch monkeys are waiting for me so will have to forgo that desire for the moment thanks again for everything." During the ten weeks he was in the hospital King Features Syndicate reran old strips.

Herriman sent Louise another letter on June 10 of that same year:

My Dear Louise—
Yes ole man Herriman is getting better—No, I didn't do all that work while I was laid away—it's old stuff they picked out of the morgue and used over again.—my junk is so much the same—y'could use it backwards or forwards—now, or then—and nobody would know the Difference—that's how come I fooled 'em for ten weeks—YOU should have known better—aint you a newspaper gal?—I don't savvy at all why you give a mug like

Letter with
self-portrait,
Toots, and pets,
December 1943,
mailed in
decorated envelope
to Gus Mager

me so much time—writing long letters—looks to me like I'm just an excuse—so you can unload about those mesas and sunsets out in that ole pais pintado—Don't blame you for that—a taste of that stuff—sinks you—deep too—Shux I was more than ½ mad at the Doctors for holding me over—

I was all poised to grab me a set of wings—and blow—

—If your mind can stand it—try and imagine a Kinky headed runt—and four Scotty dogs raising hell in a pool of purple shadow—Would that make the navajos sing "Coyote"—bye bye

—THINE—

ole man Herriman

P.S. this is the longest letter I've ever writ *any*body.—
However I did it—I don't know—G.H.

P.P.S. I hate writing. G.

> Herriman, indeed, wrote very few letters. The ones extant are unlike his strips in their brevity but similar to them in their articulate, though idiosyncratic, expression. The following letter of 1940 to Louise Swinnerton also demonstrates his unassuming attitude.

Amibil—
    Comical artists write comical letters—I'd probably write that kind too—if I writ—only it wouldn't be as funny—not being a comical genius—anyhoo what's a letter—a match can dispose of it—nicely—

> Herriman continued to make frequent trips to Arizona: "Tuesday, which is to be Oct. 1—I get myself going for a wee visit to a trader or two in Coconino County—I will have come back—fate willing about Oct. 8...." Gilbert Seldes recalled that Herriman wanted to end his life in Monument Valley, "lying down on a cactus leaf until he was shrivelled up and blown away by the wind."
>
> In his later years, when Herriman was plagued with arthritis, he had some difficulty in walking. He also suffered from severe migraine headaches; his frequent remark that he liked to lie down in order to think may have been a mask for this ailment. He sometimes stayed in a darkened room for days while Toots cared for him. In the forties, writing to Jack Kent (J. W.), a young fan then and not yet the creator of the *King Aroo* comic strip, Herriman explained:

Didn't answer your letter so soonly—ole man migraine had me down—he jumps me every sunday and holds me down over till monday night—I'm wobbly all day wednesday—so all I've got in days to do my chores is Thurs. Fri. and Sat.—and as my old brain has lost its cunning and my old fingers are stiff—and won't go where I want them to—an old uncle time has heaped a load of years upon me—I'm in a most uncertain state of condition—This is no complaint J. W.—just the wail of the wounded with age—

> George Herriman died quietly in his sleep on April 25, 1944. There was a service at the Little Church of Flowers in Forest Lawn Memorial Park, sparsely attended. Speaking for all who knew him, cartoonist Harry Hershfield said, "If ever there was a saint on earth, it was George Herriman."
>
> As Herriman wished, his ashes were scattered over the sands of Monument Valley. On the drawing table, amid crowquill pens, watercolor brushes, and India ink, were left a week's worth of unfinished *Krazy Kats*.

Krazy Kat, daily strip, March 7, 1919

DAILY STRIPS

January 21, 1918

February 12, 1918

May 24, 1920

August 17, 1920

August 30, 1920

September 21, 1921

September 23, 1921

July 22, 1922

October 6, 1923

November 6, 1930

July 4, 1938

July 5, 1938

July 9, 1938

July 29, 1938

July 30, 1938

September 5, 1938

Krazy Kat, original for a daily strip, October 26, 1935, hand colored as a gift for Jack Kent

September 6, 1938

September 7, 1938

September 9, 1938

September 10, 1938

October 24, 1938

October 25, 1938

October 26, 1938

October 27, 1938

October 28, 1938

October 29, 1938

January 23, 1939

January 24, 1939

January 25, 1939

January 26, 1939

June 13, 1939

June 14, 1939

June 16, 1939

June 17, 1939

November 13, 1939

November 14, 1939

November 15, 1939

November 16, 1939

November 17, 1939

November 18, 1939

September 9, 1940

September 11, 1940

September 12, 1940

September 13, 1940

September 14, 1940

February 10, 1941

February 11, 1941

February 12, 1941

February 13, 1941

February 14, 1941

February 15, 1941

April 26, 1941

June 2, 1941

June 3, 1941

June 4, 1941

June 5, 1941

June 6, 1941

June 7, 1941

July 21, 1941

July 27, 1942

July 28, 1942

July 29, 1942

July 30, 1942

July 31, 1942

August 1, 1942

April 10, 1943

July 1, 1943

July 2, 1943

July 3, 1943

January 14, 1944

January 15, 1944

SUNDAY PAGES

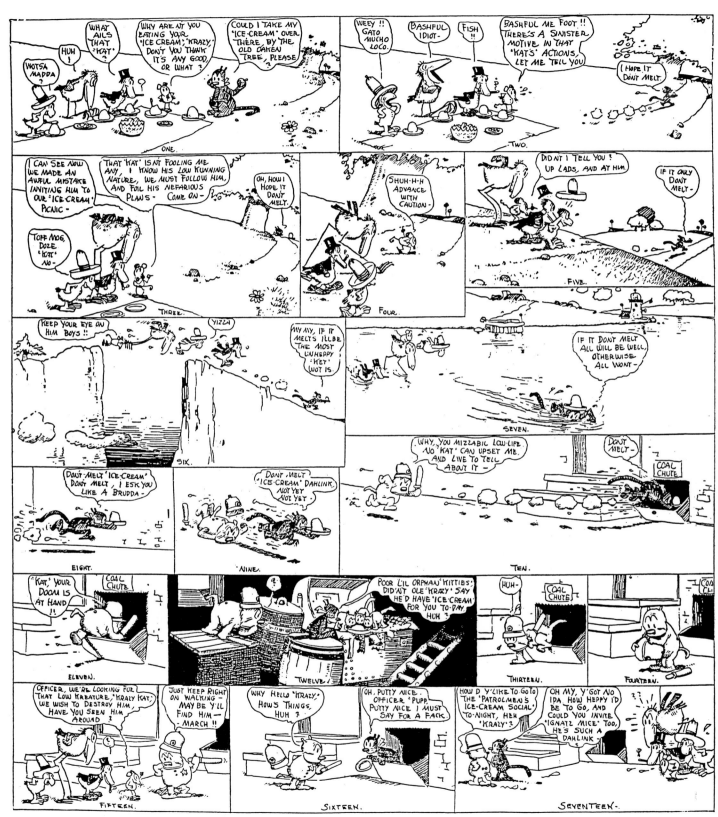

First printed Sunday page, April 23, 1916

April 30, 1916

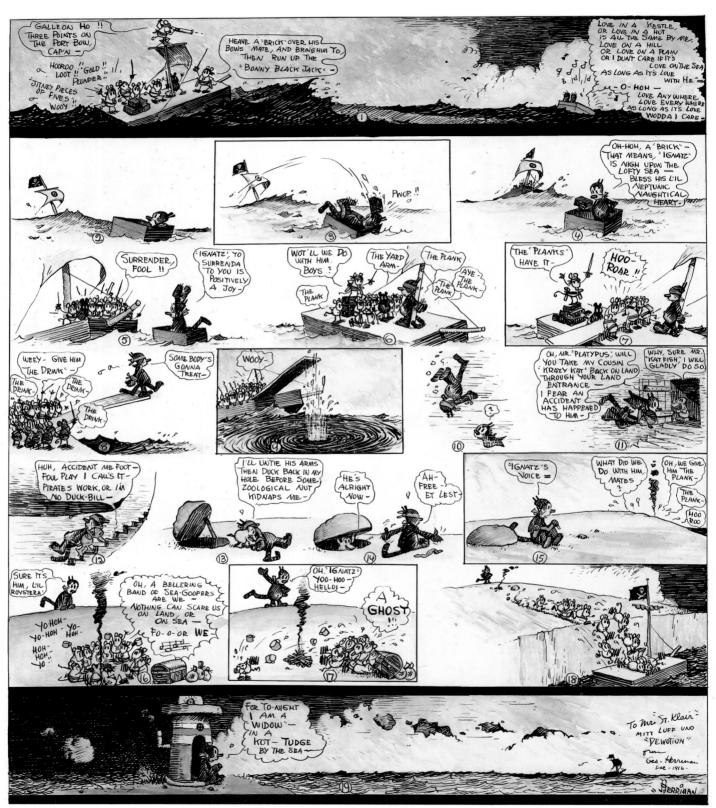

Krazy Kat, original for a Sunday page, December 3, 1916, hand colored as a gift for Rudolph Dirk's sister

Krazy Kat, original for a Sunday page, November 17, 1916, hand colored as a gift for fellow cartoonist, Tom MacNamara

September 3, 1916

September 17, 1916

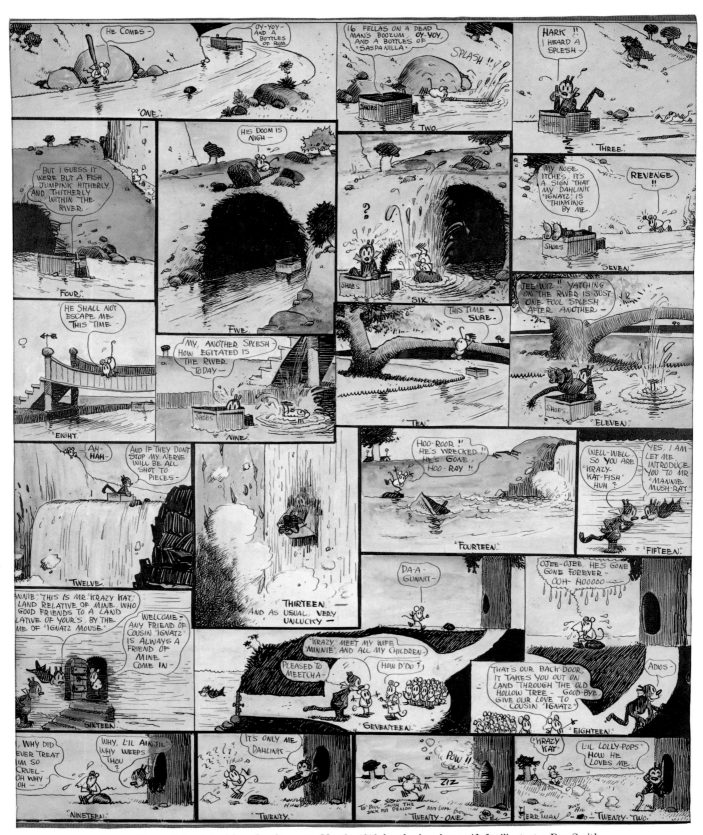

Krazy Kat, original for a Sunday page, May 21, 1916, hand colored as a gift for illustrator Dan Smith

Krazy Kat, original for a Sunday page, August 8, 1936, hand colored as a gift for Jack Kent

October 15, 1916

December 3, 1916

October 17, 1937

March 6, 1938

January 14, 1917

June 17, 1917

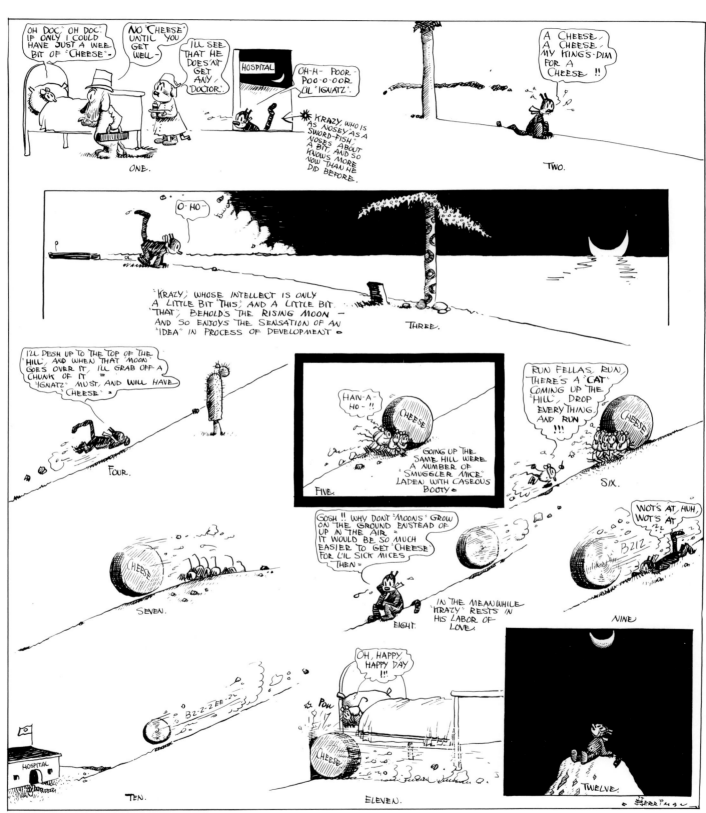

August 19, 1917

September 9, 1917

September 16, 1917

SLEEP RELEASES THE INCORPOREAL SELF, AND AS WE CAN EASILY SEE, TWO IMMATERIAL FORMS PASS QUIETLY OUT INTO THE NIGHT.

AND A GHOSTLY BRICK IS TOSSED FROM ONE TO THE OTHER.

AND WHEN THE SUN'S FIRST SHAFT OF LIGHT RENDS THE VEIL OF NIGHT THE SPIRITUAL MIDNIGHT FROLIC CEASES, AND EACH SEEKS ONCE MORE IT'S CORPOREAL ABODE.

WHILE IN THE FAIR VILLAGE OF "COCONINO", SOMBER SOULS, AND SAD HEARTS RECOUNTED DOLEFUL TALES.

BUT, "MOCK DUCK" HE OF THE OCCULT ORIENT, SAPIENT, AND FULL OF WILE, OBSERVED WHAT HE OBSERVED — AS THE SUN CROSSED OVER THE RIM OF THE MORNING =

September 23, 1917

—125—

March 10, 1940

April 14, 1940

Now !!

November 21, 1917

January 6, 1918

February 3, 1918

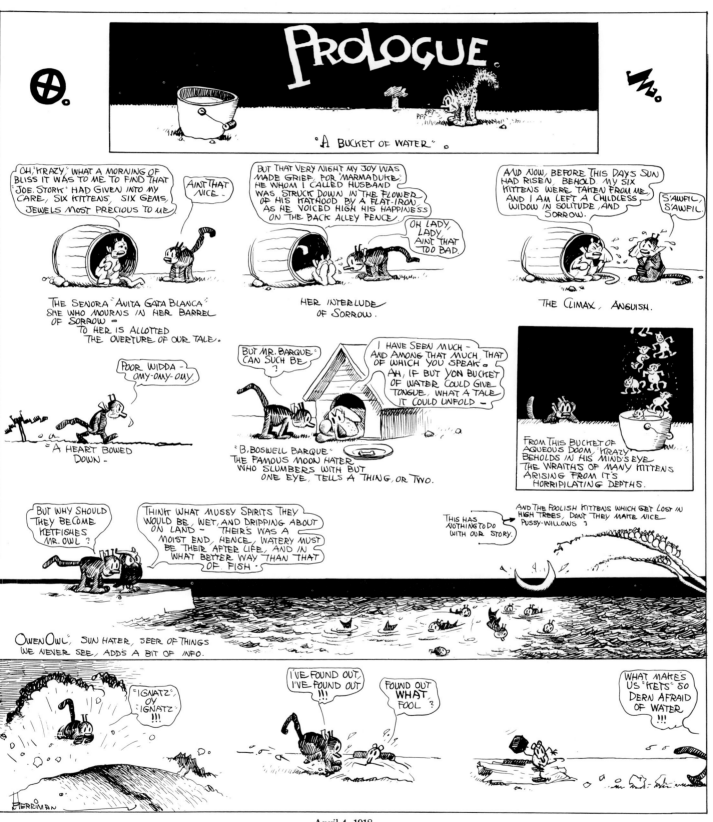

April 4, 1918

May 5, 1918

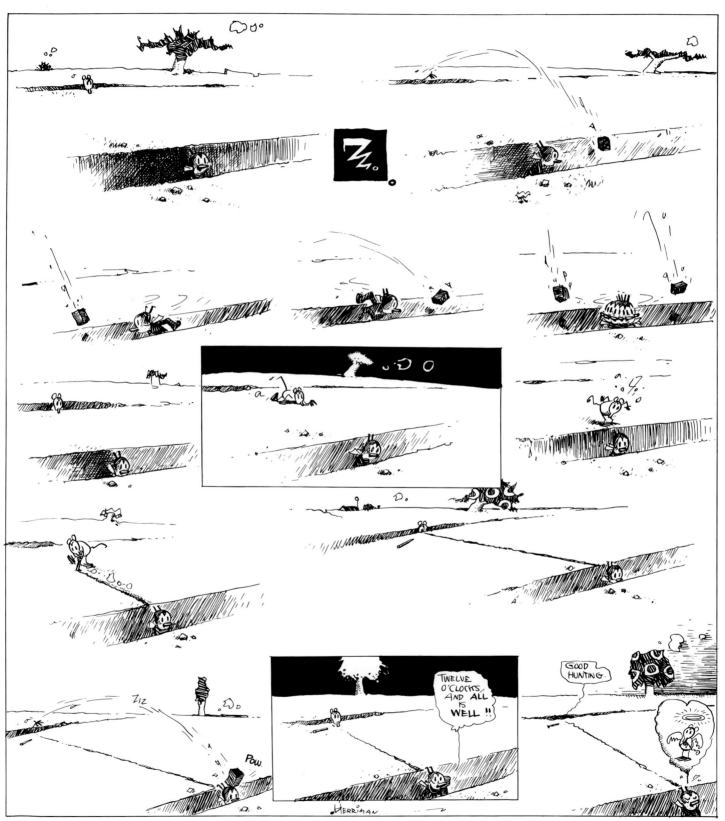

June 3, 1918

July 21, 1918

August 14, 1918

August 25, 1918

September 29, 1918, Courtesy Amon Carter Museum, Fort Worth

April 21, 1940

May 5, 1940

October 27, 1918

—140—

November 10, 1918

June 1, 1940

July 14, 1940

December 15, 1918

January 20, 1918

February 2, 1919

March 9, 1919

March 16, 1919

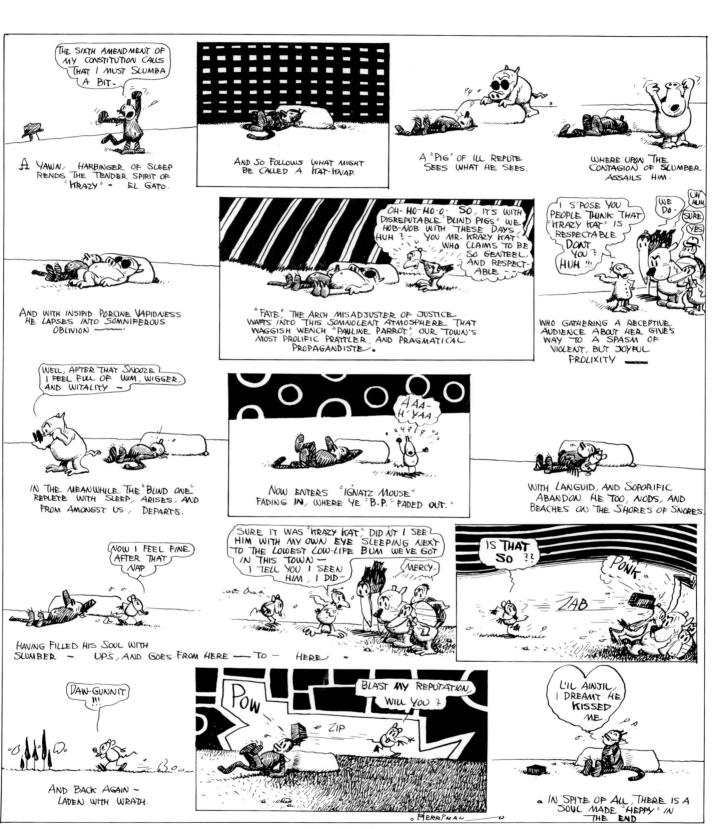

March 30, 1919

October 6, 1940

November 10, 1940

May 18, 1919

July 27, 1919

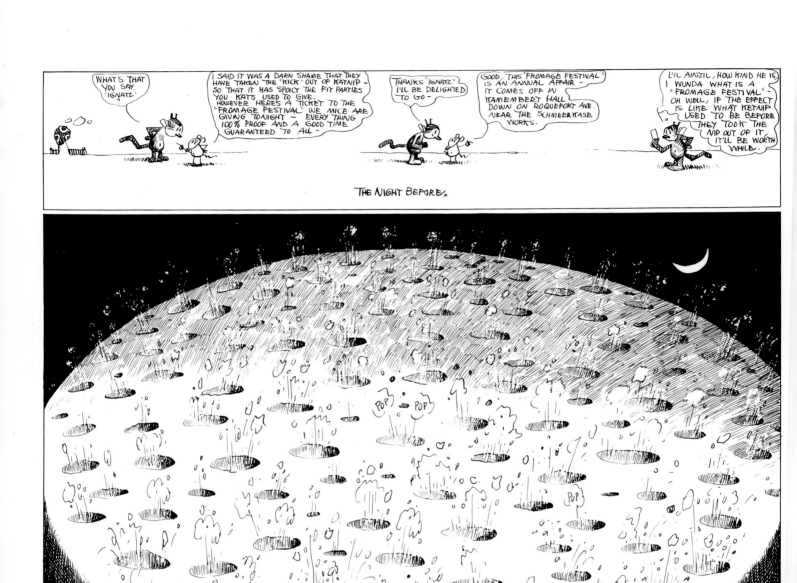

September 7, 1919

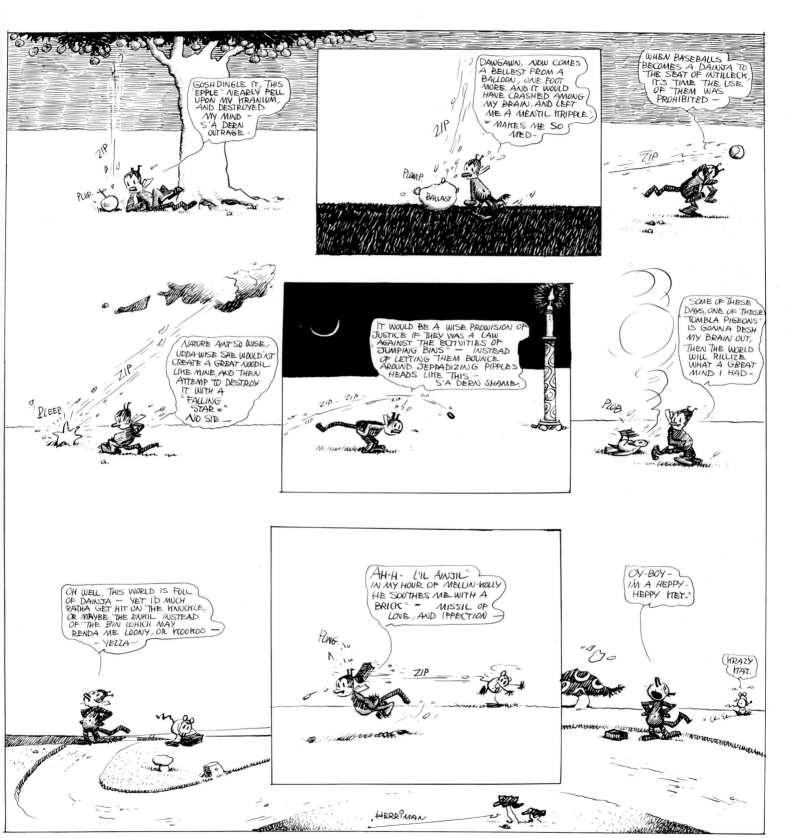

September 28, 1919

SHIPS THAT PASS IN THE NIGHT, WHENCE DO THEY COME, AND WHITHER DO THEY GO?
AND SO "KURIOSITY" IS BORN IN THE PALPITATING BOSOM OF "KRAZY KAT". "KURIOSITY" UNREQUITED,
AND UNSATISFIED AS THE OBJECTS OF HIS INQUISITIVENESS LIE IN AN ELEMENT FORBIDDEN TO KATS —
QUANTITIES OF OCEAN, MULTITUDES OF WATER.

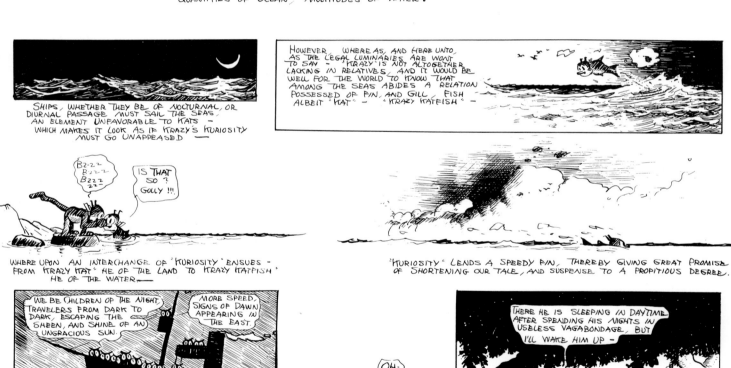

SHIPS, WHETHER THEY BE OF NOCTURNAL, OR
DIURNAL PASSAGE MUST SAIL THE SEAS,
AN ELEMENT UNFAVORABLE TO KATS —
WHICH MAKES IT LOOK AS IF KRAZY'S KURIOSITY
MUST GO UNAPPEASED —

HOWEVER, WHEREAS, AND HERE UNTO,
AS THE LEGAL LUMINARIES ARE WONT
TO SAY — "KRAZY" IS NOT ALTOGETHER
LACKING IN RELATIVES, AND IT WOULD BE
WELL FOR THE WORLD TO KNOW THAT
AMONG THE SEAS ABIDES A RELATION
POSSESSED OF FIN AND GILL, FISH
ALBEIT "KAT" — "KRAZY KATFISH" —

B2-22
B222
B222
22—

IS THAT
SO?
GOLLY !!!

WHERE UPON AN INTERCHANGE OF "KURIOSITY" ENSUES —
FROM "KRAZY KAT" HE OF THE LAND TO "KRAZY KATFISH"
HE OF THE WATER.—

"KURIOSITY" LENDS A SPEEDY FIN, THEREBY GIVING GREAT PROMISE
OF SHORTENING OUR TALE, AND SUSPENSE TO A PROPITIOUS DEGREE.

WE BE CHILDREN OF THE NIGHT,
TRAVELERS FROM DARK TO
DARK, ESCAPING THE
SHEEN, AND SHINE OF AN
UNGRACIOUS SUN.

MORE SPEED,
SIGNS OF DAWN
APPEARING IN
THE EAST.

OWLS
!!

OH·

THERE HE IS SLEEPING IN DAYTIME
AFTER SPENDING HIS NIGHTS IN
USELESS VAGABONDAGE, BUT
I'LL WAKE HIM UP —

HERRIMAN

AND YET THERE BE THOSE WHO BELIEVE THAT KATS
PROWL, AND HOWL AMONG THE HALLS OF NIGHT
IN NEFARIOUS AND SINFUL PURSUIT.

December 7, 1919

December 21, 1919

November 17, 1940

January 12, 1941

MANY THINGS HAVE STALKED THROUGH "COCONINO" AND YET HAVE LEFT BUT LITTLE IMPRESS UPON THAT ASTUTE DEMOCRATIC COMMUNITY – BUT YESTERDAY, "ROYALTY" IN THE SHAPE OF A "KING" STRUTTED INTO THEIR MIDST, AND EVERY SOUL AMONG THEM WAS SHAKEN TO ITS VERY CENTER –

"KRISTOPHER KACKIL" ONCE LEADER OF THE POPULIST TICKET, LETS IT BE KNOWN THAT HE IS NOW IN THE KING'S GOOD GRACES, HAVING BEEN MADE LORD HIGH BREAKFAST ANNOUNCER, AND IMPERIAL KAPON TO THE KOURT –

"MOCK DUCK" NO LONGER DEALS WITH THE PROLETARIAT, BEING NOW THE ROYAL LAUNDERER, AND SHIRT MANGLER TO HIS MAJESTY –

"KOLIN KELLY" DEALER IN BRICKS NO LONGER ATTIRES HIMSELF IN THE EMBLEM OF TRUE REPUBLICANISM THE "BINOCLE" SINCE HIS ATTACHMENT TO THE KING'S PERSON AS CUSTODIAN OF THE IMPERIAL BRICK, HE NOW BASKS IN THE SHEEN OF ROYALTY WITH HIS EYE DECKED OUT IN A SET OF ONE CYLINDER CHEATERS, THE "MONOCLE"

"WALTER CEPHUS AUSTRIDGE" THE KALAHARAN DICKY-BIRD, WHOSE WEARING OF A CELLULOID DICKY HAS LONG PROCLAIMED HIS STAUNCH DEMOCRATIC SPIRIT HAS FALLEN PRONE FOR MONARCHICAL BLANDISHMENTS, AND IS NOW CHIEF PROVIDER OF PLUMES TO THE QUEEN, FOR WHICH HE HAS BEEN DUBBED "KNIGHT OF THE FEATHER".

MENIAL, AND REPUBLICAN FAMILIES WILL WAIT IN VAIN FOR THE THRILL WHICH ATTENDS THE PERIODICAL VISITS OF "JOE. STORK" THAT MOST DEMOCRATIC OF BIRDS – BE IT KNOWN THAT HE IS NOW ALLIED TO THE ROYAL HOUSEHOLD AS SPECIAL PURVEYOR OF PRINCESSES, PRINCES, AND QUINCES TO THEIR MAJESTIES

IGNATZ MOUSE IS NOW LORD HIGH CHAMBERLAIN OF THE ROYAL CHEESE.

OFFICER B. PUPP" IS NO MORE A PUBLIC SERVANT, ENFORCING LAW, AND ORDER, BUT CONSTABLE IN THE KING'S GUARDS.

AND SO IT ALL WENT, UNTIL "KRAZY" THE KAT, WHO HAD TAKEN ADVANTAGE OF THAT GREAT BOON ACCORDED TO KATS, AND HAD LOOKED A LONG WEARY EYE FULL UPON THE KING ———— (CONTINUED PICTORIALLY BELOW.).

WHILE DEMOCRACY TOTTERED ON THE BRINK, AND KINGHOOD THREATENED THE EQUIPOISE OF LIBERTY, "KRAZY KAT" IN HIS OWN SIMPLE WAY SHOWS HIS FELLOW "COCONINONIANS" THAT A KAT MAY NOT ONLY LOOK AT A KING, BUT WITH THE USE OF HIS LONG TAIL, TOMATO-CAN, UMBRELLA, AND THE AID OF A KOUPLE OF KRAZY KITTENS HE CAN LOOK LIKE A KING – A LESSON WHICH CERTAIN PROSELYTES TO ROYALTY (NOT ENTIRELY BEREFT OF INTELLIGENCE) TOOK WELL TO MIND, AND HEART ————.

THAT VERY NIGHT, "ROYALTY" RODE OUT OF "COCONINO" BY RAIL – AIDED BY IT'S LOYAL, (IF NOT ROYAL SUPPORTERS ——.

Herriman

December 28, 1919

c. 1919

January 25, 1941

March 9, 1941

March 21, 1920

April 25, 1920

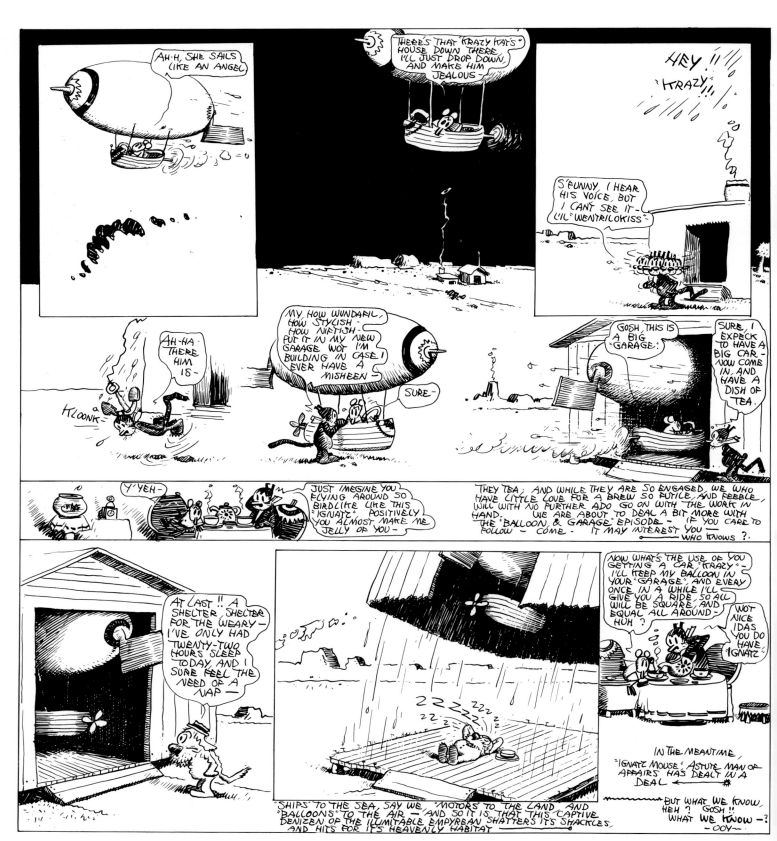

September 25, 1921

February 5, 1922

April 2, 1922

April 16, 1922

March 23, 1941

April 13, 1941

May 14, 1922

June 18, 1922

May 11, 1941

July 6, 1941

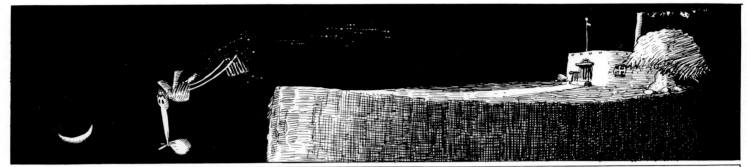

July 16, 1922

July 23, 1922

July 27, 1941

October 5, 1941

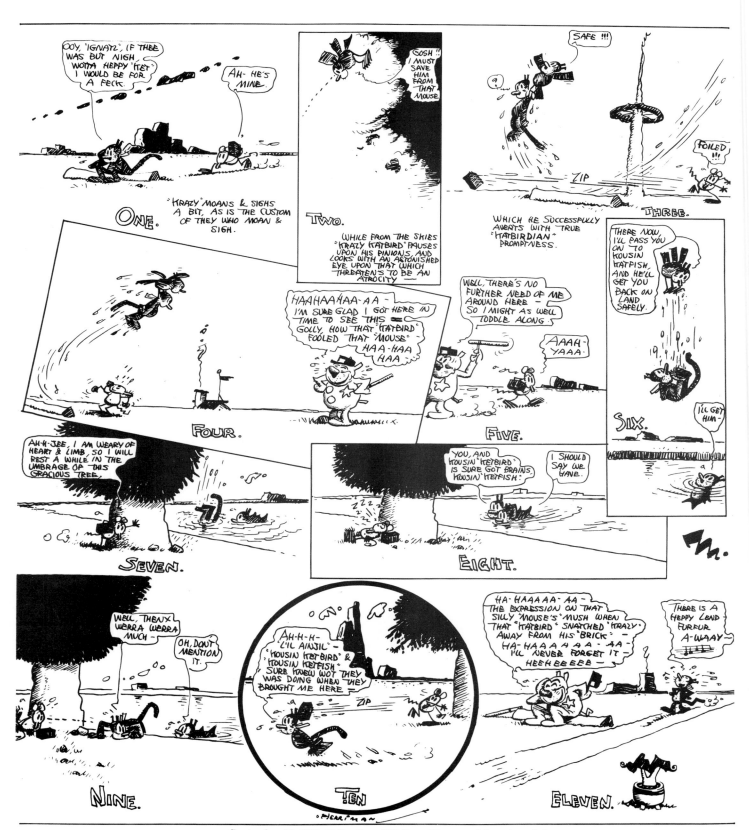

September 10, 1922, Collection of Whitney Museum of American Art

November 12, 1922

November 28, 1920

May 5, 1920

—183—

February 15, 1925

November 22, 1925

October 12, 1941

October 26, 1941

March 7, 1926

May 23, 1926

November 16, 1941

November 30, 1941

July 29, 1929

March 12, 1933

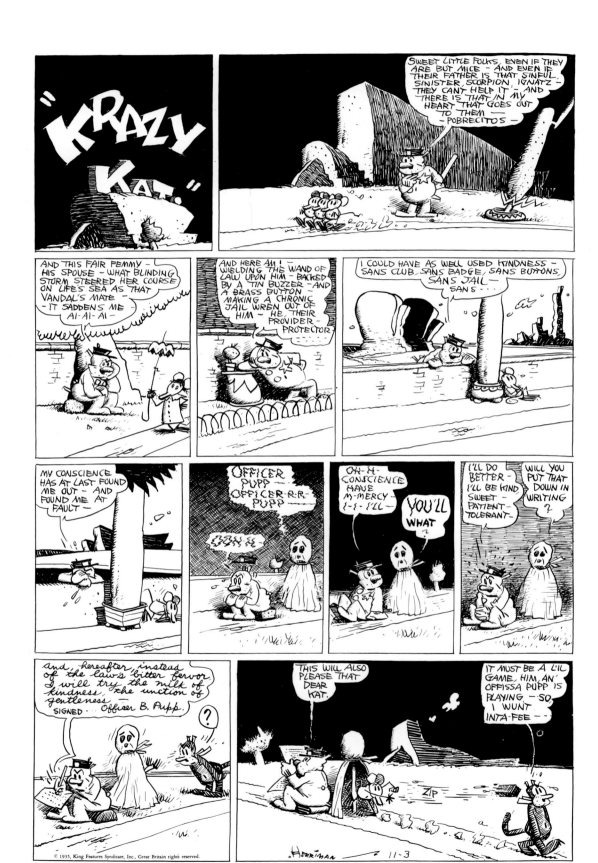

November 3, 1935

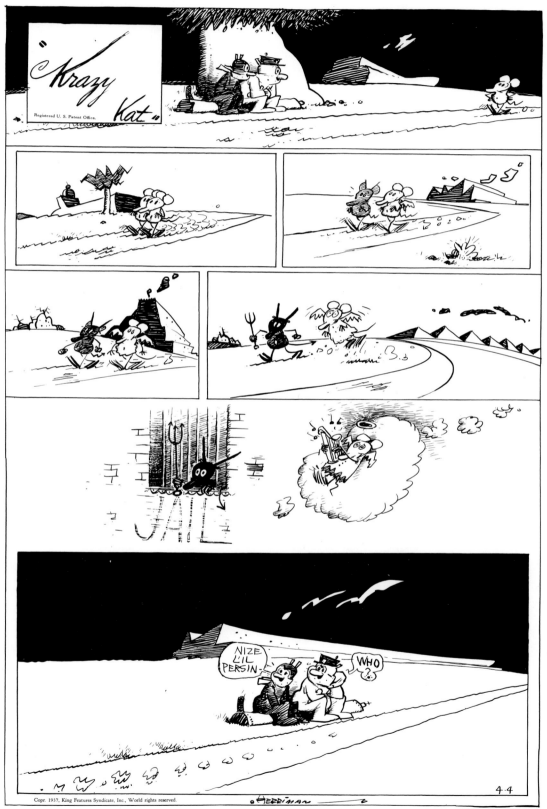

April 4, 1937

May 15, 1938

December 27, 1942

July 2, 1939

July 23, 1939

July 30, 1939

September 8, 1940

November 3, 1940

February 23, 1941

March 7, 1943

April 11, 1943

January 11, 1942

January 25, 1942

September 14, 1943

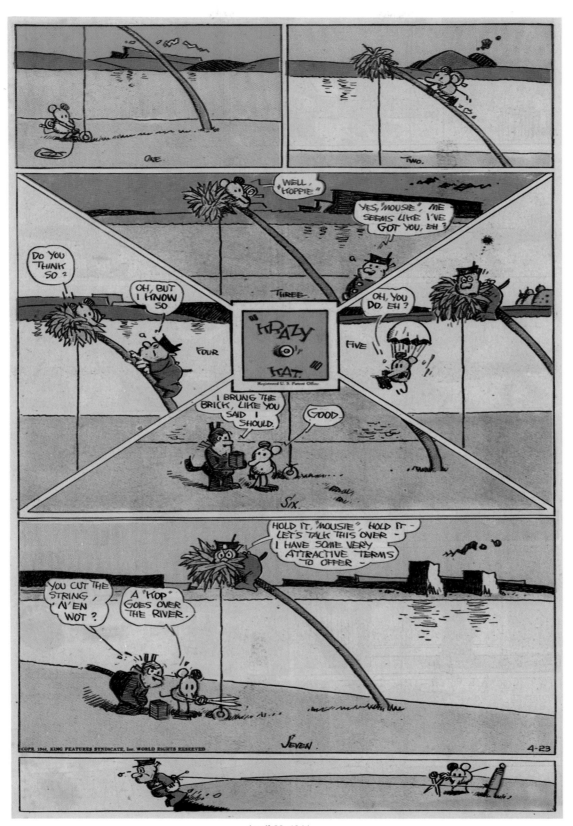

April 23, 1944

February 20, 1944

Krazy Kat, original for a Sunday page, 6/25/44. The last printed Sunday page

Herriman asleep at his drawing board in the art room of the *New York Evening Journal*, c. 1916. A *Baron Bean* strip was in progress

ACKNOWL-EDGMENTS

This book would never have come about were it not for the concern and care of George Herriman's granddaughter, Dee Cox. Her interest in her grandfather's work prompted her not only to preserve it, but also to bring it to the attention of museums and art galleries in order that it might be seen and enjoyed. Her kindness and her cooperation in this venture have been invaluable. We are most grateful to her and her family.

We would especially like to express our appreciation to Robert Graham, whose foresight about its artistic merits led him to exhibit comic art in his gallery more than fifteen years ago. His support of this book was instrumental in its materialization.

For their research and insights and their loan of newspapers from a better time, we are greatly indebted to comic-strip historians Mark Johnson and Cole Johnson. "A missle of affection" to fellow Kat devotees, Bob Laughlin and Brian Nelson.

Our special thanks go to those who have shared their memories of George Herriman with us: Frank Capra, John and Mary Dirks, Mike Goulding, Karl Hubenthal, Jack Kent, Elaine and Willem de Kooning, Otto Messmer, Betty Zane Rodgers, Marion Seldes, Florence Sharp, and Wilson Springer.

We would also like to thank the following persons for their helpful interest: Gordon Campbell, Marge Devine, James Godbout of King Features, Bob Green, Peter Kriendler (who brought this project to the attention of Abrams), Dr. Marie McDonnell, and Professor Robert Quinn.

Our thanks, too, to our publisher, Harry N. Abrams, Inc., where editor Darlene Geis, designer Sam Antupit, and Doris Leath shaped our material into a book that will, we hope, find an enthusiastic audience once again for Krazy, Ignatz, and their friends.

And finally, our gratitude to all the collectors who temporarily parted with their *Kats*. Their names appear in the picture credits on page 223.

P. McD., K. O'C., and
G. R. de H.

Krazy Kat, daily strip, October, 1915

CHRONOLOGY

1880	August 22. George Joseph Herriman is born in New Orleans, Louisiana.
c.1886	Moves with family to Los Angeles, California.
1891–97	Attends St. Vincent's College, Los Angeles.
1897	Sells a drawing to the *Los Angeles Herald* and is hired as an assistant in the engraving department.
1900	Steals train ride to New York City. Works as a barker and paints billboards for a Coney Island sideshow.
1901	June 15–October 26. Eleven Herriman cartoons appear in *Judge* magazine.
	September 29. Pulitzer newspapers first publish "one-shot" comic strips by Herriman.
	September 29–April 27, 1902. Draws one-shots for the Philadelphia North American Syndicate.
	October 20. Begins one-shots for the T. C. McClure Syndicate.
1902	Creates "continuing character" comic strips for the Pulitzer newspapers.
	February 16 and 23, and March 9. *Musical Mose* is published.
	March 30–December 28. *Professor Otto and His Auto* is published.
	April 13–January 25, 1903. *Acrobatic Archie* is published.
	July 7. Marries Mabel Lillian Bridge in Los Angeles. Returns to New York.
	November. Literary magazine *Bookman* gives Herriman early recog-

nition in La Touche Hancock's article "The American Comic and Caricature Art."

1903 January 11–November 15. *Two Jolly Jackies* appears in the Pulitzer newspapers.

May. Birth of the Herrimans' first child, Mabel (Toodles, Toots).

June. Becomes a staff artist for the *New York World*.

July 11–December 26. Herriman's cartoons appear in *Judge*.

September 6–November 15. Takes over the *Lariat Pete* strip for the McClure Syndicate.

1904 Creates new strip for the World Color Printing Company, *Major Ozone's Fresh Air Crusade* (January 2 through July 10).

January 3. Leaves the *New York World* and becomes a staff cartoonist for the *New York Daily News*.

January 10. Final piece for Pulitzer newspapers published.

February. Herriman's first weekday comic strip appears, *Home Sweet Home* (February 22, 23, and 26, and March 4).

April 22. Becomes a staff artist of William Randolph Hearst's newspaper, the *New York American*.

1905 June 2. Herriman leaves the *New York American* and subsequently moves back to California. For World Color Printing Company he revives *Major Ozone's Fresh Air Crusade* (September 10 to October 20, 1906). He draws *Bud Smith* (October 29 to November 19), combines two older strips into *Grandma's Girl—Likewise Bud Smith* (November 26 to May 12, 1906).

1906 January 8. Becomes a staff cartoonist for the *Los Angeles Times* until August 13.

May 19 to September 15. Draws *Rosy Posy—Mama's Girl* for World Color Printing Company.

August 21. Hearst hires Herriman to work for the *Los Angeles Examiner.*

September 22 to October 20. Revives *Bud Smith* for World Color Printing Company.

1907 December 10–26. *Mr. Proones the Plunger* appears in the *Examiner.*

1909 Birth of Herriman's second daughter, Barbara (Bobbie).

October 12–December 19. *Baron Mooch* strip appears in Hearst newspapers.

November 7–January 9, 1910. World Color Printing Company runs *Alexander the Cat*. This was the last work Herriman did for anyone other than Hearst.

November 21 and 28, and December 4. World Color Printing Company runs *Daniel and Pansy.*

December 20. *Mary's Home from College* appears for four episodes in Hearst newspapers.

December 23–January 24, 1910. *Gooseberry Sprigg* is published in Hearst newspapers.

Krazy Kat, daily strip, 1915

1910	William Randolph Hearst's *New York Evening Journal.* summons Herriman back to New York.
	June 14. Draws his first cartoon, "As Herriman Came East," and writes his first article for the *New York Evening Journal*
	June 20. The first *Dingbat Family* appears in the *Evening Journal.*
	July 26. For the first time, the Dingbats' cat is hit on the head with the brick hurled by a mouse and becomes "Kat."
	August 1. *The Dingbat Family* is retitled *The Family Upstairs.* The Kat and Mouse "fill up the waste space" at the bottom of the page.
1911	November 16. *The Family Upstairs* reverts to its original theme and title.
1913	October 28. *Krazy Kat* becomes a completely independent strip under this name.
1916	*Krazy Kat,* the world's first animated-cartoon cat film, is produced by the International Film Service.
	January 4. The last *Dingbat Family* appears.
	January 5. *Baron Bean* begins to run in Hearst newspapers.
	April 23. The first *Krazy Kat* Sunday page appears.
1919	January 22. *Baron Bean* ends.
	April 23–December 18. *Now Listen Mabel* appears in Hearst newspapers.
1922	January 20. *Krazy Kat,* a jazz-pantomime ballet, choreographed by Adolph Bolm and scored by John Alden Carpenter, is performed in Town Hall, New York City.
	May. Gilbert Seldes's article "Golla, Golla, the Comic Strip's Art" appears in *Vanity Fair.*
	Moves with his family to 1617 North Sierra Bonita, Hollywood, California.
	October 30. The first daily *Stumble Inn* appears in Hearst newspapers. It ran until May 12, 1923.
	December 9. The first Sunday *Stumble Inn* appears.
1923	April. *Vanity Fair* inducts Herriman into its Hall of Fame.
1924–28	Spends the winter months on the Mexican border with John and Louisa Wetherill.
1925	August–September, 1929. Layout of the *Krazy Kat* Sunday page suffers restrictions.
	October. Reviews *The Gold Rush* for *Motion Picture Classics* magazine.
1926	January 9. The last Sunday page of *Stumble Inn* is published.
	January 16–December 18. Produces *Us Husbands* Sunday strip for Hearst newspapers.
1928	April 28. Takes over *Embarrassing Moments* for Hearst newspapers.
1931	Illustrates Don Marquis's book of poems *archy and mehitabel.*
	Designs his second Hollywood home, built at 2217 Maravilla Drive.

Photograph of Herriman, which he embellished with drawing of Krazy and Ignatz and presented to Jack Kent, c. 1940

1932	*Embarrassing Moments*, sometimes called *Bernie Burns*, runs until December 3.
	May 22. Bobbie Herriman marries scriptwriter Ernest Pascal.
1934	November 14. Mabel Herriman dies as the result of a car accident.
1935	June 1. *Krazy Kat* first appears in color.
1939	November 14. Bobbie dies at the age of thirty.
1944	April 25. Herriman dies. According to his death certificate, the cause of death was "non-alcoholic cirrhosis of the liver." His ashes are scattered over Monument Valley.
	June 25. The last *Krazy Kat* is printed. Contrary to usual practice, *Krazy Kat* was not continued after Herriman's death.

Krazy Kat, Sunday page, June 11, 1922

SELECTED BIBLIO-GRAPHY

Books

BECKER, STEPHEN. *Comic Art in America.* New York: Simon and Schuster, 1959.

BERGER, ARTHUR ASA. *The Comic-Stripped American.* New York: Walker and Company, 1973.

BONNER, ANTHONY JOHN CAMPBELL. *"George Herriman, His Life and Work."* Unpublished thesis. Syracuse University, Syracuse, N.Y.

CAPRA, FRANK. *The Name Above the Title: An Autobiography.* New York: Macmillan, 1971.

COLEMAN, HARRY J. *Give Us a Little Smile, Baby.* New York: E. P. Dutton & Company, 1943.

GILLMOR, FRANCES, and WETHERILL, LOUISA WADE. *Traders to the Navajos.* Albuquerque, N. M.: University of New Mexico Press, 1953.

HERRIMAN, GEORGE. *Baron Bean, 1916–1917.* Introduction by M. Thomas Inge. Westport, Conn.: Hyperion Press, 1977.

———. *The Family Upstairs: Introducing Krazy Kat 1910–1912.* Introduction by Bill Blackbeard. Westport, Conn.: Hyperion Press, 1977.

———. *Krazy Kat.* Introduction by e. e. cummings. New York: Henry Holt and Company, 1946.

———. *Krazy Kat.* Introduction by e. e. cummings. New York: Grosset & Dunlap, 1969.

HIGHWATER, JAMAKE. *Ritual of the Wind*. Toronto: Methuen Publications, 1984.

KLINK, RICHARD E. *Land of Room Enough and Time Enough*. Albuquerque, N.M.: University of New Mexico Press, 1958. Reprinted Layton, Utah: Peregrine Smith Books, 1984.

MCNALLY, DENNIS. *Desolate Angel, Jack Kerouac: The Beat Generation, and America*. New York: McGraw-Hill, 1980.

MARQUIS, DON. *archy and mehitabel*. New York: Doubleday and Company, 1927, 1930.

NELSON, BRIAN K. "A Krazy Kat Kompanion: A Travel Guide to Coconino County." Unpublished thesis. University of Massachusetts, Amherst, Mass.

O'SULLIVAN, JUDITH. *The Art of the Comic Strip*. pp. 24–27. University of Maryland, Department of Art, 1971.

SELDES, GILBERT. *The Seven Lively Arts*. New York: Harper and Brothers, 1924. Reprinted New York: Sagamore Press, 1957.

SHERIDAN, MARTIN. *Comics and Their Creators*. New York: Luna Press, 1971.

Articles

"Among the Unlimitless Etha." *Time*, May 8, 1944, pp. 94–96.

BLACKBEARD, BILL. "The Forgotten Years of George Herriman." *Nemo*, June 1983, pp. 50–60.

CASKEY, MARIE. "George Herriman." *Dictionary of American Biography*, Supplement 3, 1941–1945. pp. 356–357. Charles Scribner and Sons, New York.

"Death of Herriman." *Art News*, May 1–14, 1944, p. 7.

"First Drawings of Our Biggest Drawing Cards." *Vanity Fair*, December 1930, pp. 72–73.

"A Genius of the Comic Page." *Cartoons*. c. 1916.

"Geo. Herriman Dies; Creator of Krazy Kat." *New York American*, April 26, 1944, p. 1

"George Herriman, Noted Cartoonist." *New York Times*, April 27, 1944, Late City edition, sec. 1, p. 23, col. 5.

"Hall of Fame." *Vanity Fair*, April 1923, p. 72.

HANCOCK, LA TOUCHE. "The American Comic and Caricature Art." *Bookman*, November 1902, pp. 263–74.

KRAMER, HILTON. Review of the *Krazy Kat* exhibition at Graham Gallery. *New York Times*, January 17, 1982.

"Krazy Kat, George Herriman." Catalogue of the exhibition at University of Arizona Museum of Art. November 5–December 3, 1972.

"Krazy Kat's Kreator." *Newsweek*, May 8, 1944, p. 96.

LANDENBERGER, MARY. "Herriman Stumbles on Krazy Kat and Has Been Embarrassed Ever Since." *Nashville Tennessean*, May 1930.

MCCARTHY, TODD. "John Ford and Monument Valley." *American Film*, vol. III, no. 7, May 1978.

Rosemont, Franklin. "George Herriman (Krazy Kat)." *Cultural Correspondence*, no. 10–11, Fall 1974.

Seldes, Gilbert. "Golla, Golla, the Comic Strip's Art." *Vanity Fair*, May 1922.

Strip Scene magazine #12, Summer 1980. "An Early Newspaper Checklist, Part Two," Reverend Kenneth Barker.

Tad. "This Is About George Herriman." *A Collection of Cartoons* by Thomas Aloysius Dorgan. The Museum of Cartoon Art, Port Chester, N.Y.

Tashlin, Frank. "In Coconino County." Review of George Herriman's *Krazy Kat. New York Times Book Review*, November 3, 1946, p. 6.

Warshow, Robert. "Woofed with Dreams." *Partisan Review*, vol. XIII, no. 5, 1946.

Young, Stark. "Krazy Kat." *New Republic*, October 11, 1922, pp. 175–76.

Newspapers

Albuquerque Journal (New Mexico), 1929–1931
Boston American (Mass.), 1909–1910
Los Angeles Times (California), 1906
Louisville Courier-Journal (Ky.), 1905
Mobile Register (Ala.), 1909–1910
Nashville Banner (Tenn.), 1909–1910
New York Journal, 1911–1944
New York Mirror, 1929
New York News, 1904
New York Press, 1901–1903
New York World, 1901–1904
Philadelphia North American (Penna.), 1901–1902
Philadelphia Press (Penna.), 1901–1904
St. Louis Post-Dispatch (Mo.), 1901–1904
St. Louis Republic (Mo.), 1901–1902
St. Louis Star (Mo.), 1904–1923
Washington Times (D.C.), 1922–1932

PICTURE CREDITS

The publisher and authors wish to express their appreciation to the following individuals and institutions who kindly provided original Herriman art. Numbers refer to pages. Letters refer to position of art on page. Amon Carter Museum of Western Art, Fort Worth, 137; Richard Berenholtz, 71c; Knox Berger, 92b; Dee Cox, 68, 71a, 71b, 73, 83a, 85b, 113, 120, 128, 131, 132, 135, 136, 140, 145, 152, 157, 160, 164, 168, 169, 176, 182, 183, 211; Dee and Tom Cox, 154; Mr. and Mrs. Frank Daley, 114; Georgia Riley de Havenon, 122; William and Elaine de Kooning, 181; Jeff Gnass, 74; Graham Gallery, 56, 110, 141, 146, 147, 155; Robert C. Graham, 116; Murray Harris, 79, 111, 202; Karl Hubenthal, 7, 48; Jesse Karp, 148; Jack Kent, 94a, 115, 219; Bob Laughlin, 93b, 93c, 129, 185, 188, 195; Robert Lesser, 173; Patrick McDonnell & Karen O'Connell, 55b, 125, 130, 149; L. Mulrooney, 83b; Al Ordover, 8, 161; Stu and Miriam Reisbord, 50b, 91d, 144, 153, and cover; Alan Rose, 87, 109, 112, 133, 134, 156; Marian Seldes, 14, 19, 21; Art Spiegelman, 198; Garry Trudeau, 60, 117, 165, 166, 167, 172; Whitney Museum of American Art, New York. Lawrence H. Bloedel Bequest, 180; Arthur Wood, Jr., 50a, 75, 192; Granddaughters of Mr. & Mrs. Irving C. Valentine, 6.

Anchored in Hope
devotionals for infertility

Ali Forrest

CONTENTS

Introduction   5

Grounded in Faith   7

Anchored in Hope   14

Strength for Your Inner Superwoman   22

Grace Days   31

While You are Waiting   41

Worry Less; God's Got Your Back   51

Created for Purpose   61

Community: Lean on Your People   70

Rooted in Joy   78

Anger in the Heart   87

Lessons from Pain   96

"P" is for Patience   105

Living with Loss   112

Trust Him Always   121

Contributors   131

Scripture Index   141

Final Note   143

About the Author   144

INTRODUCTION

I was the girl who had her entire life planned out. The plan included two kids by age 30. It did not include having my world turned upside down by infertility. No, that was definitely not in the plan. The life plan did not include an early miscarriage or two failed adoptions. It also didn't include writing and compiling a book on devotionals for women going through the same infertile season of life.

Let's back up here. About a year before I got started on this project, I told very few people (also known as no one) the details of my experiences with infertility. I didn't want people to know. I was embarrassed, ashamed. I didn't want to be different. Hello! Two kids by 30!

I was struggling with faith. I had just quit my job with my cushy 401k and moved to a new state for my husband's job, when BAM! Out of nowhere (literally, out of nowhere), God laid a project on my heart: Write a devotional book for women, just like me, going through infertility. What? Are you crazy, God? Surely you have chosen the wrong woman!

I could never get the project out of my mind. It was nagging me, so I finally said, "Yes" ... one year later. I was so nervous that I was shaking as I hit the send button on my laptop, reaching out to a handful of women to ask if they would be interested in contributing to a zero budget project.

I remember distinctly thinking, *Okay, God. If You brought me to this, I kind of expect You to help make this a reality.*

And you know what? He did! Before I knew it, stories started pouring in from women all over the country. I texted my husband every single time someone responded saying they wanted to help and squealed with giddiness.

That is one of the coolest things about this book. It does include stories and writings from women all across the United States. My story is just one story, whereas infertility is not a one-size-fits-all experience.

Anchored in Hope reflects that. It is a tapestry woven together by the thread of women who understand infertility.

To the women who contributed, thank you! This book would not be possible without you, and because of that, it's dedicated to the 45 women who said "yes" without hesitation.

This is a book for women trying to conceive their first child. This is a book for women struggling with secondary infertility. If you are in the middle of fertility treatments, taking a break, choosing alternate paths, trying to decide whether or not you want to adopt, or seeking deep peace with your situation, this is your book. Maybe you are a friend or family member trying to support someone going through infertility. Perhaps this book can help you understand what they are going through. Whatever your tie to infertility, this book is for you.

The daily readings are rooted in scripture to ensure you stay grounded in God's Word throughout your journey. The devotionals are a collection of insights written by women who have been there. They know exactly what you are going through and what you are feeling. So whenever you feel alone, know you aren't. There is a sisterhood of women who understand where you are in this season.

This book was so encouraging and, dare I say, healing to me while working on it. I truly, truly hope you find encouragement and community within these real, raw pages. Use this book however you want. You can skip around to topics that are most relevant at the time, or you can read it from start to finish. Simply find what feels good.

Finally, my prayer for you, new friend, is that you do stay grounded, smack dab in the middle of God's Word through infertility. Infertility sucks; I get that. It's okay to be unhappy where you are sometimes. This is H-A-R-D stuff we are dealing with, but I pray it does not make you resentful. On the contrary, beautiful stories are created during the wait, not just when the wait is over.

GROUNDED IN FAITH

Now faith is confidence in what we hope for and assurance about what we do not see.
–Hebrews 11:1 NIV

Having faith means believing in something fully. We may not understand His timing or what He is doing, but we can open our hearts fully to God's will. The devotionals in this section remind us God is in control; He is faithful. Our journey with Christ may look different from another's, but know this awesome God we serve is one worth praising and loving through all tribulations and trials.

Father, fill us with faith that moves us to do good works with a pure heart. Amen.

Faith Day One >>> Kelly Evans

I can do all things through Christ who strengthens me. —Philippians 4:13 NKJV

Infertility. I hate that cold, harsh word.

Merriam-Webster Dictionary defines infertility as "not able to reproduce, not able to produce children, young animals, etc." Well, what *Merriam-Webster* doesn't know is that I serve a God who IS ABLE, a God who can do things exceedingly, abundantly and beyond anything we could even ask or think!

I read a great post from a blog not too long ago, and she chose to use the phrase "reproductively challenged." I like that so much better. A challenge is a difficult task or problem; yet, a problem can indeed be solved. It is a temporary thing. I will not allow myself to be defined by infertility. I am ABLE through Christ who strengthens me!

Along this journey, I have met people and read numerous stories of couples who were told they will never be able to bear children. There it is again … infertility … not able … NEVER. What permanency.

Months, years later, upon being surprised with a miraculous pregnancy, they discover that, yes, they are ABLE! Those are the stories filled with so much HOPE! It's hope I feel the word "infertility" could never portray.

So many women and men are given that final word by a doctor: "I'm sorry; there is nothing more we can do. You will never be able to have children."

We put our trust in doctors, treatments, anything that can give us even a sliver of hope to cling to. I know; I've done it myself! That is human nature; it is a need for something tangible we can see and feel. But faith is not something tangible; it is trusting in things unseen.

God is in control. I truly feel there are going to be a lot more joyful, freer days – days when I can openly enjoy blessings that already surround me instead of focusing solely on the blessing we don't have yet.

Nope … we're not infertile, just reproductively challenged and fully ABLE to overcome!

God, how wonderful it is that You are ABLE to overcome all things. You are faithful, and because of You, I can do all things. You are on my side, and I am grateful for Your love, always and forever. Amen.

Faith Day Two >>> Elisha Kearns

But he was pierced for our transgressions; he was crushed for our iniquities; upon him was the chastisement that brought us peace, and with his wounds we are healed. –Isaiah 53:5 ESV

I sat on the edge of my bed taking my blood pressure. As I waited for the reading, I remember thinking to myself that if it was within normal range, then I would finally be healed of this symptom resulting from Polycystic Ovarian Syndrome. However, as numbers appeared and I saw 160/92 on the display screen, I heard a whisper that said, "Not healed yet."

Each morning as I plucked out 15 dark, coarse hairs from my chin, I would hear the same voice whispering, "Not healed today." And as my menstrual cycle went past 50 days for the fourth time in a row, I heard it quietly reminding me that once again, I was not healed.

It wasn't until I looked in the mirror one day, wondering when I would be cured of this dreaded infertility that consumes my entire being, that I heard a different voice … a different whisper. This one said, "By His wounds, you ARE healed." And you know what I did? I laughed!

If I am healed, then why do I still see evidence of PCOS? Why do I still have high blood pressure, excess facial hair, insulin resistance, lack of ovulation and long cycles? *I am not healed … at least not yet.* It wasn't long after thinking those thoughts that I realized the voice I had been listening to – the one telling me I wasn't healed yet, was the enemy. He was feeding me the lie that my healing of PCOS was a work to be completed rather than already finished.

Isaiah 53:5 says that by His wounds we ARE healed. It doesn't say we might be, will be or could be, but that we <u>ARE</u>. God wants us to know that what we desperately want Him to do for us has already been done. Jesus' finished work at the cross satisfied the Father's heart so that from heaven's throne came the pronouncement, "It is done!" in response to Jesus' cry on earth that "It is finished!"

I no longer worry about what I see or feel, or the presence of contradicting reports. These are just lies from the enemy, and though they are *very* real, I know they are temporal and untruthful. God's Word is the truth. When you start believing only what God's Word says about your situation is true, all the lying symptoms carry no weight.

I am living proof. I can testify that once I began ignoring the voice of the enemy and believing the truth that by His stripes I am *already* healed, my cycles suddenly became much shorter and ovulation started occurring naturally. I give all the honor, glory and praise to God. My question to you today is this: What do you see when it comes to your healing? Do you see a

9

finished work, or a work yet to be completed? God the Father says, "It is done!" Jesus says, "It is finished!"

What do you say?

Father, thank you for the words of Isaiah 53:5. By His wounds we are healed! Help me and all women with infertility to draw closer to You and away from the enemy. Amen.

Faith Day Three >>> Elisha Kearns

God is our refuge and strength, a very present help in trouble. –Psalm 46:1 ASV

When you go through deep waters, I will be with you. When you go through rivers of difficulty, you will not drown... –Isaiah 43:2 NLT

Growing up I lived in Florida, and even though we didn't visit the beach much (gasp!), I have many memories from swimming in the ocean. I remember how sometimes I would venture out too far and then become too tired and overwhelmed to swim back to shore--my place of safety. But I also remember that just when I thought I was too exhausted to continue and all looked hopeless, a wave would come and help me.

It would give me that little push...you know, that little help I needed to make it closer to shore. And today as I thought about that memory (and those scary moments), I realized that faith works in the same way. Because sometimes it comes in waves. It scoops us up and carries us just a little further than we thought we could ever go on our own.

And maybe right now you are swimming and treading water in your own deep ocean and feeling hopeless. Maybe you are convinced things will always be this complicated and overwhelming. Maybe you are exhausted from trying to do it on your own. If so, listen to my heart this morning, friend. Because there is hope for you. His name is Jesus and He is our strength. He is our deliverer. And through Him, He will help you get to "your shore"...your place of safety, whatever or wherever that is today.

So friend, right in this moment, allow hope to come in like a wave. Let it swoop you up and remind you that it won't always be like it is right now. Let it remind you that things can change. Things can get better. And that it won't always be this hard, this stressful, or this overwhelming.

Let this hope bring you closer to your shore.

Lord, let Your wave wash over the one reading this book right now. Help her get to "her shore."

Faith Day Four >>> Marianne Jennings

Rejoice in hope, be patient in tribulation, be constant in prayer. —Romans 12:12 ESV

During this infertility journey, it's common to encounter multiple struggles ranging from questioning your faith, jealousy of others or simply anger toward life. We need to remember we must always have hope. In the end, everything will be okay.

Maybe God has chosen this path on purpose to open another door for us. Maybe we are not meant to give birth to a child, but rather, we're meant to adopt a child of God's whom another may not be able to take care of. It is through our prayers that God hears our cries and sees our tears. He does not allow anyone to suffer without a reason. Through all our struggles, we must pray to God to keep us strong and in the light.

Remember, you are not alone on this journey. There are wonderful women and men out there on the same path, wondering and feeling the same things as you. Reach out to the ones who mean the most to you. Not everyone is going to understand what you are going through, and you cannot expect them to. Find someone or even a group of people who keep you feeling positive and know and understand what you're going through.

This road is not always glitter, sunshine and roses. Some days may contain more thorns or rain than you'd like. It is okay to feel troubled, but remember to always keep your faith during your darkest hours, for this is when God is listening. God is sitting right next to you during each emotional roller coaster, which all too unfortunately does not slow down or get easier each time you ride it.

My roller coaster may be faster, slower or have more or fewer twists than yours, but that doesn't make it more or less important than your own ride. And, no doubt the time may come when it leads to an emotional wreck. If it does, it's okay to cry, get mad, scream or throw things, but do not stay in that state of mind for long, and do not blame others. This is no one's fault! We are all in this together and must pray and have hope that our roller coasters eventually come to a halt. Keep your faith in God's timing. He knows what He is doing.

God, I will trust in Your timing, even when I don't understand it. I will put my hope in You, for You have done great things!

Faith Day Five >>> Ali Forrest

And God said to Noah, "I have determined to make an end of all flesh or the earth is filled with violence through them. Behold, I will destroy them with the earth. Make yourself an ark of gopher wood. —Genesis 6:13-14 ESV

Now Thomas, one of the Twelve, called the Twin was not with them when Jesus came. So the other disciples told him, "We have seen the Lord." But he said to them, "Unless I see in his hands the mark of the nails, and place my finger into the mark of the nails, and place my hand into his side, I will never believe." —John 20:24-25

Say my neighbor started building a giant spaceship in his backyard because he claimed God told him to. I would probably think he had gone nuts. *Pack up babe; we're moving!* Then again, I'm also a "Doubting Thomas," someone who would have had a hard time believing Jesus had really risen from the dead. *Jesus saith unto him, Thomas, because thou hast seen me, thou hast believed: blessed are they that have not seen, and yet have believed. —John 20:29*

I mean, really, can you just imagine the strength and faith Noah must have had building that gigantic arc? Whenever I think of this story, I picture him loading up his wife, sons, their wives and all the animals, as if he were getting ready for a road trip. *Got the bears? Check!*

Would you do it? Would you really do it? I can't help but laugh at the thought! There is no way in heck I would. Then again, God hasn't asked me to build a big boat. Thank goodness. However, I have my own set of faith tests to get through, as does everyone, and if ever there was a time for strength, this is it. If you're reading this devotional today, you are likely carrying a similar burden, as well. For whatever reason, we are in the middle of an infertility storm. Let God be our ark, the ark that protects us from rain and wind, whatever those elements might look like in your story. Let Him be our safe harbor, the calming eye of a hurricane.

Just like Noah did when he nailed those first wooden boards together, let's piece our faith together, make it a tenfold stronger and trust this storm will pass. Trust our faith will bring us through. That the ground will dry after the rain, just as it did for Noah. *In the second month, on the twenty-seventh day of the month, the earth had dried out. —Genesis 8:14*

Today, channel your inner Noah. He survived his storm, and you and me, friend? We will survive our storm, too. As we live amidst this tumultuous weather, let's trust God. He is our strength, our refuge and our safe haven. Noah lived this out, while good ole Thomas questioned it. Whose path will you choose to follow?

Help me to trust you, Oh Lord! Through the storm, I will praise You. Amen.

Anchored in Hope

Hebrews 6:19 is my favorite verse in the entire Bible, and it's what the title of this book is based upon. It became my favorite once I began walking the infertility road. *We have this hope as an anchor for the soul, firm and secure.* I love the imagery it conjures. I love the message it sends. Hope changes everything. It anchors us firmly in our faith, and it allows us to keep dreams alive while we wait for the grand finale. Even when you feel like giving up, don't. Don't leave before the miracle appears.

Friends, this section is filled with hope-laden stories from women who embody Hebrews 6:19. Take it away, Elisha, Cassie, Brandy, Nadine and Joanna!

Hope Day One >>> Elisha Kearns

While he was saying this, a synagogue leader came and knelt before him and said, "My daughter has just died. But come and put your hand on her, and she will live." Jesus got up and went with him, and so did his disciples. —Matthew 9:18-19 NIV

Oh Jarius, Jarius! I want to sit here in my comfy chair and roll my eyes at you. Why didn't you go to Jesus before your daughter was too sick? Why did you wait until it was too late and she died? Did you think you had time to try all your own ideas first? Or that it was okay to wait until everyone had given their opinions? No offense, but it seems silly knowing you could have just went and talked to Jesus. Beckoned Him to come and help.

These thoughts enter my mind, but then I shrink back in reflection. I see how I have spent the past four years of my life and realize, yeah, Jarius and me? We are the same. So often during my infertility journey, I waited until it looked hopeless before I, too, went to Jesus for help. It was as though He was my last ditch effort. You know, the one who became my final resort after I had taken matters into my own hands. After I had done all *I* could do.

So, Jarius, while I want to sit here and shake my finger at you for waiting until the situation was impossible to change, I won't. While I wish I could say "tsk, tsk," because you didn't seek His help until all was lost, I can't. I can't because I see myself in you. I am reflected in your thoughts and actions.

But, oh, how amazing your story is because it proves the love our heavenly Father has for you and me. It shows that even when we come to Him at the last minute, after exhausting our own resources and efforts, He still has compassion for us. He still extends His mercy into our lives. And He still pours out His amazing grace into our messy situations.

So, friends, if you are in a position where your situation seems hopeless, don't hesitate. Run to Jesus, because He will always meet you at your point of need. He can change the unchangeable. He, alone, can always do what you can't, which is make the impossible, possible. So, don't waste another second. Run. Run into His open arms and ask Him to restore, revive, mend and change you. Then, have faith to believe He will.

Christ, your mercy and grace is unending, and for that, I am thankful! I'm running to You with open arms; restore and change me so I may stay grounded in hope and Your love. Amen.

Hope Day Two >>> *Cassie Rief*

But he said to me, "My grace is sufficient for you, for my power is made perfect in weakness." Therefore I will boast all the more gladly of my weaknesses, so that the power of Christ may rest upon me. For the sake of Christ, then, I am content with weaknesses, insults, hardships, persecutions, and calamities. For when I am weak, then I am strong.
–2 Corinthians 12:9-10 ESV

It was a few years ago. I was so excited to plant flowers at the house my husband and I had recently bought. I couldn't tell you how many seed packets I bought, enthusiastically anticipating that by mid-July, my yard would be overflowing with vintage, cottage-style flowers. Butterflies and fuzzy bees, I thought, would flit between dense rows of poppies, and a dazzling display of colorful blooms would surely impress all passersby.

Nebraska's unpredictable weather didn't fail to disappoint. Spring was unnaturally chilly – so much so that I couldn't plant my poppies in May and instead, was resigned to patiently wait until the weather warmed in June. The heat brought strong, violent thunderstorms, which swept through the area week after relentless week.

My poppies were just emerging from the ground, delicate seedlings in need of warm sunlight and gentle care. Some turned yellow as they drowned in puddles leftover from strong showers the day before. Others drooped sadly, unable to support the weight of the pounding water each storm gifted. Where even the mulch had washed away, weeds now threatened to overtake the tiny seedlings.

Still, millimeter by millimeter, the poppies determinedly grew.

Spring turned to summer. As I watched my mother-in-law's biannual poppies blossom brilliantly without a care in the world, I was saddened because I knew my own wouldn't have the necessary time to mature and bloom before the end of the season.

Then, leaving for work one morning, a searing yellow – like that of a low-hanging, full harvest moon – caught my eye. Four vibrant petals stretched defiantly toward the sun. A poppy in full bloom. I must have taken a dozen photos of that poppy in my incredulous state.

Throughout the last year, I have fought through painful experiences relating to my infertility. The surgeries, tests, medical expenses, prescriptions, an early miscarriage, overwhelming physical symptoms and fear of the unknown often leave me battered and fragile.

I think of loved ones fighting their own demons: a dear loved one's alcoholism, my friend's own journey through infertility, or my mother-in-law's recurring cancer.

We fight endlessly for our deepest desires. My loved one wages war on his sobriety, one day at a time. It's an endless struggle. My friend yearns for a healthy pregnancy after her first heartbreaking loss. My mother-in-law aches to tend her garden again.

To me, that poppy signified hope. Hope for brighter, happier days ahead. Hope that whatever our crisis – we are not alone. God, our guiding light, is there, gently allowing us to grow and become stronger, even on days when we feel beaten down and defenseless.

We are made stronger with hope, and with the grace of God.

Each day, another poppy rears its beautiful head toward the sun. And as it stands a little straighter, toughened by the sun's rays, I do, too, because I have found strength and resilience in God.

When all seems to be against me, help me remember, Lord, I am not walking this path alone. You are beside me, leading me toward Your wondrous light. You are a beacon of hope for all good things in life yet to come.

Hope Day Three >>> Brandy Miller

Blessed is the man who trusts in the LORD, whose trust is the LORD. –Jeremiah 7:17 ESV

My sophomore year in college, I spent my fall break in Florida visiting some dear friends.

In the middle of my trip, we went to the beach so I could watch the sun set over the Gulf. As we made our way toward the coast, the entire sky was overcast. There were dark, gray rainclouds everywhere, and my friends warned me circumstances were not going to be ideal. I was bummed, of course, but we stood on the beach and waited anyway. As the sun started to set, it could barely be seen peeking through the clouds. Perhaps my friends' omen was correct: it was going to be anticlimactic; there would be nothing beautiful to see after all. Still, we stayed. Am I glad we did!

As the sun sank in the sky, a radiant, orange glow surrounded us. The sun reflected off the clouds and painted the most magnificent sky I've ever laid eyes on. I felt tears begin to well as I stood in awe of our beautiful Creator, who used rainclouds to enhance the beauty of the sunset. And the view only got better.

Right before the sun reached the water, its reflection shifted gear, turning that orange sky into many shades of violet mimicked in the lavender waves. Now, when your local friends claim it was the most beautiful sunset they'd ever seen, that's saying something!

It was one of those God moments where I felt tiny amidst the wonder of His creation.

Even now, I smile when I think about that day. It's such a beautiful reminder of how God redeems the rainclouds in our lives. It's easy to look at a situation sometimes and feel like He is giving you less than His best. It's how I felt when infertility became our journey.

It seemed God was holding out on us, but I knew His character better than that. So, my husband and I waited, holding onto the belief He is ultimately good and loving.

And see enough, little by little, that radiant, orange sky came, and I saw how God was using our journey for His ministry and glory. I saw how He was using this season of waiting to enhance intimacy between not only me and Him, but me and my husband, as well. I saw how He connected me to people who would have never otherwise been part of my life. Finally, I saw how He was giving me such a fierce love for the child I have yet to meet.

Maybe today, you're still waiting for the clouds to break. I encourage you to reflect on the Lord's faithfulness in your life. Meditate on His character, and trust He is not withholding His best from you. Your beautiful sunset amidst the clouds could be starting any day. Trust and see.

Father, let the clouds part and bring a miracle to those awaiting Your redemption. You are GREAT. Let all hearts beat with Your love, grace and mercy. Amen.

Hope Day Four >>> Nadine Easty

Yes, my soul, find rest in God; my hope comes from Him. –Psalm 62:5 NIV

Hope. It's there all the time. Even when you don't want it, it's there. No matter how many years I have had an empty womb, I still believe one day it will be filled with life. That's hope speaking.

I will never forget some nights in this infertility journey when I would cry myself into the early morning hours. My poor and very patient husband would try to comfort me throughout the night. My heart was so overwhelmed. The pain was strong, and I was weak.

I felt alone. My heart and soul were restless, and the pain was relentless. I felt no comfort in anything I did, and although I tried to mask my sadness, there were times the tears would roll down my face so unexpectedly.

Yet still, within all this pain, there was something deep down in me that said, "Have hope." This internal hope had a quiet, small voice, but it was always there. Hope got me out of bed to face the day. It carried me through what seemed like a billion baby showers. It brought me through another loved one's surprise baby announcement. Hope brought me to today. In my darkest hour, when I wanted hope to go away, it remained. There is nothing more steady and faithful then our Father in heaven. He knows how many tears I shed, He has heard every cry, and He has seen my pain. When I felt alone, He whispered hope into my soul.

Those who sow with tears will reap with songs of joy. –Psalm 126:5 NIV

We have this hope as an anchor for the soul, firm and secure. It enters the inner sanctuary behind the curtain. –Hebrews 6:19 NIV

Maybe you have experienced pain and hurt like I have. Maybe you are in your darkest moments today. Maybe you feel alone. I pray that today, you will find rest in Him. I pray that no matter where you are in your journey, you will hear hope spoken to you.

Lord, speak life into those who need a dose of Your hope today. We are not alone, we have You, and that will forever be enough. Amen.

20

Hope Day Five >>> Joanna Nissley

The Lord is good to those whose hope is in Him, to the one who seeks Him.
—Lamentations 3:25 NIV

*"For I know the plans I have for you," declares the LORD, "plans to prosper you and not to harm you, plans to give you hope and a future." —*Jeremiah 29:11 NIV

As my husband and I have ridden the unpredictable and emotional rollercoaster of infertility during the past five years, we've struggled.

In the midst of my pain, God whispers to the innermost part of my being, the part that wants to give up because it hurts to hope and to repeatedly have those hopes dashed. It is as if this verse was written just for me and for this time. It speaks to my heart.

The Lord is good to those whose hope is in Him, to the one who seeks Him.
—Lamentations 3:25

I'm slowly realizing I am blessed.

I find myself fixating on the unfulfilled desire for a child rather than focusing on Jesus to fulfill my deepest longings and desires. However, as I silently listen for His still, small voice to tenderly call my name, asking me to trust Him, to trust His heart, it is then that I can surrender. I can place my hope solely in Him, knowing His plans for my life might not look familiar to me, but they are good.

*"For I know the plans I have for you," declares the LORD, "plans to prosper you and not to harm you, plans to give you hope and a future." —*Jeremiah 29:11

I encourage you to continue to hope, dear friend. And yes, in the midst of striving to hope, there will be grief.

Please take comfort though, for it is in grieving the loss of what might have been that we open our hearts to what may be: the unique and special dream we never envisioned until God planted the seed in our fertile hearts, healed by His gracious, redemptive love. The dream that was far better and more beautiful than we could ever imagine.

Father, thank You for the trust and bond we share! I'm excited to see what lies ahead on this journey, and while I wait, I will keep a hopeful, open heart. Amen.

STRENGTH FOR YOUR INNER SUPERWOMAN

The LORD is my strength and my shield; my heart trusts in him, and he helps me. My heart leaps for joy, and with my song I praise him. –Psalm 28:7 NIV

I think we, as humans, fail to give ourselves enough credit. We are capable of so much more than we imagine. We can push ourselves and test boundaries. Some of the moments when I have faced my fears and mustered up strength I didn't know I had have been the best in my life. In those moments, like the first time I flew on an airplane and was convinced I was going to crash, I prayed. He got me through it! He'll do it every time, too.

With God on your side, nothing is impossible because He is our strength! We all need it, some days more than others. Where we are weak, He is strong. It's wonderful, like having our own, built-in Superman or fairy godmother. Send Him an SOS when you need strength, and let the life-breathing words in this section help you find your footing when you need a reminder that God will bring you to the other side of your troubles.

Strength Day One >>> Ali Forrest

Then Saul clothed David with his armor. He put a helmet of bronze on his head and clothed him with a coat of mail, and David strapped his sword over his armor. And he tried in vain to go, for he had not tested them. Then David said to Saul, "I cannot go with these, for I have not tested them." So David put them off. Then he took his staff in his hand and chose five smooth stones from the brook and put them in his shepherd's pouch. His sling was in his hand, and he approached the Philistine. –1 Samuel 17:38-39 ESV

I have to admit, I often feel like the underdog on my quest to gain the title of mommy. Each month comes with new challenges, but you get that, don't you?

Some of these obstacles include waiting, procedures, medicines, holistic therapies, blood work, doctor's visits or stocking up on pregnancy tests. Others leave you mentally drained as you wonder how much is too much, if you should take a break, or if slapping the bottoms of your feet 36 times will really work (a Chinese remedy, supposedly). Some days, it just flat out feels like you need a knight in shining armor from a fairy tale to save the day.

I'll let you in on a little secret. You have a knight. It's Jesus! So, send an SOS up to the heavens and cue the happy ending music because He's riding down on His white horse right now with arms outstretched, ready to fight the bad guys beside you.

The best part? He's always doing that! Praise God! He is a well of salvation and our abundant source of strength. Halleluiah and hosanna!

And, just like David mustered up the strength to defeat Goliath, I want you to take a slingshot and a stone and show your problem that you are the boss. Dominate it. Rock it. Own it. Strike it down. God's got your back. If He is for you, nothing is against you.

In verses 34-37 of the David versus Goliath match-up, David recognizes the predicaments he's been in as a shepherd, defeating lions and bears. He attributes his victories to the fact God protected him: *The Lord who rescued me from the paw of the lion and the paw of the bear will rescue me from the hand of this Philistine.* –1 Samuel: 17:37

In similar fashion, God will rescue you and me from the trenches in which we fight. And just how will He do that?

Well, we can't predict how our own stories will end; just know God is present. He is cheering for all of us, and He will bring us through our battles. It might not be according to our own will, but isn't His will so much better? Okay, okay. If you're like me, it's hard to think that in the middle of this fight, but I believe He has something great in store for you and me. I

23

can be overly optimistic, but one day, I'd like to think we will be able to look back and see exactly how He pieced our stories together.

Believe. Believe you can do it, whatever your "it" is. Believe you can fight the fight. Believe you can win. Believe and know all this is possible because our good God above blesses and clothes you in strength. Amen to that!

So, what happens if you lose the battle this month? What happens if this isn't the cycle or a month passes without a clear answer? Channel your inner Garth Brooks: Some of God's greatest gifts are unanswered prayers. While you might feel like you have more than you can handle and your heart is overwhelmed, just know He will always give you strength. Let's stand up to our Goliaths, just like David did.

Thank you for being the One who I can always lean on! In my toughest moments, I know I can lean on You and You will be there. In the battle, in the fight, and against all opponents, You are my greatest source of strength.

Strength Day Two >>> Logan Andreotta

Do not fear or worry about this army. The battle is not yours to fight; it is the True God's ... Stand and watch, but do not fight the battle. There, you will watch the Eternal save you. Do not fear or worry. Tomorrow, face the army and trust that the Eternal is with you. —2 Chronicles 20:15, 17 VOICE

Trust in the Eternal One, your True God, not in your own abilities, and you will be supported. —2 Chronicles 20:20 VOICE

In 2 Chronicles 20, Jehoshaphat (king of Judah) finally solidified his throne by fortifying the nation of Judah and appointing regional judges. Now, during a time when his throne should have been secure and the nation should have been able to live in peace, Jehoshaphat learned a *huge* army was planning on attacking him. In his fear, with the eyes of his subjects upon him, he cried out to God, exalting and praising Him (20:6), and asking for His help (20:10).

God responded in a powerful way, with words I sense Him often whispering to my soul: *"Do not fear or worry about this army. The battle is not yours to fight; it is the True God's ... Stand and watch, but do not fight the battle. There, you will watch the Eternal save you. Do not fear or worry. Tomorrow, face the army and trust that the Eternal is with you."* —2 Chronicles 20:15, 17 VOICE

Scripture then tells us Jehoshaphat and all the assembly fell prostrate before the Eternal and worshipped Him. They trusted the Lord completely. Jehoshaphat instructed his people, *"Trust in the Eternal One, your True God, not in your own abilities, and you will be supported."* (20:20)

Jehoshaphat went on to win the battle without lifting a finger to fight. Instead, God fought and won the battle for him.

Although Jehoshaphat was a king committed wholly to God, His reign was not without trials. Likewise, God promises us we will face our own trials. This battle is not the only one Jehoshaphat fought. He fought many and was successful because of his complete reliance on God.

And, not only did God give Jehoshaphat victory over his enemies time and time again, but He also used those battles to give Jehoshaphat greater power. He used them to expand Jehoshaphat's territory ... to give Jehoshaphat more than he could have ever imagined.

We must give our battles to God for Him to claim victory over them. We must unclench our hands and give our dreams, desires and struggles over to the One who loves us. Victory comes when we let go, when we open our hands and give thanks to the Lord for His enduring love. This is what Jehoshaphat did, even upon facing a powerful and quickly approaching enemy. He counted his blessings in the heat of battle, in the face of danger.

God means to heal the holes in our souls. He means to give us victory. But, we must choose to say "yes" to what He freely gives. We must trust Him completely. In the heat of battle, in the midst of shattered dreams or unmet expectations, we must count our blessings and give thanks to the God who loves us and is our salvation.

God, I turn my infertility battle over to you. You are my victory in trials and tribulations and I will lean on You always. Amen.

Strength Day Three >>> Ali Forrest

Then God remembered Rachel, and God listened to her and opened her womb. She conceived and bore a son and said, "God has taken away my reproach." —Genesis 30:22-23 ESV

Raise your hand if you have ever complained about infertility! Rachel, wife to Jacob, can relate. She complained to her husband, saying, "I will just die if you don't give me children!" (Genesis 30:1) Jacob's response? "Am I God? He's the One responsible for you not getting pregnant, not me." (Genesis 30:2)

I can think of a few conversations in my own marriage that mirror that of Jacob and Rachel's. The tears. The anger. The husband who gets worn down by the constant when and why questions. Should I dare mention the ultimatums to God, which never seem to work in my favor, by the way? My heart relates to this two-verse conversation between Rachel and Jacob a little too much because we have been there. We *are* there. In those moments that seem impossible to face, I often think of Isaiah 66:9. I see it almost as a promise of sorts. *"I will not cause pain without allowing something new to be born, says the Lord."*

Good stuff happens on the other side of a painful situation. You might have to look for it sometimes, but it's there. Rachel's story is a big, flashing sign example of this, simply because you can see her go from Point A(nguish) to Point B(aby).

Just know that when you feel centered at your lowest point, you are not there forever. Psalm 23 says, *Even though I walk through the darkest valley, I will fear no evil, for you are with me; your rod and your staff, they comfort me.* We walk *through* the darkest valley. "Through" is the key word here. We walk through our darkest valleys.

God does not have you build a house in the valley of your trials and tribulations. We pass through it to find a place called home. Sure, it may be a crappy camping spot for a bit, but we will get through it. Rachel walked through her dark days. So will you and I.

Heavenly Father, walk with me through my dark valleys. Do not abandon me. Let me see glimpses of Your goodness. Help me to celebrate the smallest of victories and help me to find my strength in You.

Strength Day Four >>> Ali Forrest

Strength and dignity are her clothing, and she laughs at the time to come. She opens her mouth with wisdom, and the teaching of kindness is on her tongue. –Proverbs 31:25-26 ESV

You know the one: First comes love, then comes marriage, then comes a baby...

However, I had to rewrite my own lyrics to that popular nursery rhyme: First comes love, then comes marriage, then comes infertility. Womp, womp. But the thing is, there is so much comparison at any stage of life.

If you're single, people want to know when you're getting a boyfriend or husband. If you're married, people want to know when you're having a baby. If you're married with kids, they want to know when you'll pop out the next kid. Unless you have too many kids ... then they want to know when you're going to *prevent* little ones.

I might be veering off into stereotype-land a little bit here, but you catch my drift, right? Accepting your circumstances means embracing the life you have today, not the one you wish you had. By accepting what we can't change, we can cast our gaze forward and take a leap toward God's plan for us, even if it's hard. Especially if it's hard! Hard doesn't mean bad.

I've learned that God really does redeem your pain. All the verses that talk about how He won't let you suffer without reason are apparently true. Infertility is my pain. No, a life did not grow inside of my body. As I write this, I am in Nicaragua adopting my daughter. I look back and see how I didn't trust God and how I got frustrated when everything seemed to fail. I am now so thankful for every failure, wrong turn and brick wall. I didn't walk confidently with God, yet He was there all along. Hindsight is a bitch, y'all.

That is why today I triple dare you to be confident in your current state of affairs. Proverbs 31 says, strength, dignity and kindness are always in style. Wear them proudly. Open yourself up to the possibility of being vulnerable. Let yourself live out the story you have right now, not the one you hope for someday. Own it. Always be an original. Your story is beautiful. You are a Daughter of Christ. So do it. Accept my triple dare.

Laugh at the future and let the best moments of your life be the ones where you break the comparison model, your plans, and your expectations by walking confidently with a father who walks proudly beside you.

Christ, help us to find our confidence in You when we hit brick walls. I am thankful for Your timing and Your way because it is always perfect. Amen.

Strength Day Five >>> Amber Holmes

Trust in the Lord with all your heart, and lean not on your own understanding.
–Proverbs 3:5 NIV

Have you ever had the Lord speak to you? I feel like sometimes God tickles us with a feather, while other times He smacks us with a 2x4. And, boy, did He get that 2x4 ready for me!

As a little girl, I always dreamed of my future: a good job, wonderful husband, happy marriage and children. Never did I imagine infertility would darken my plans, but that's exactly what happened. My husband and I have experienced it all when it comes to infertility: doctor's appointments, hormone pills, injections, in vitro fertilization, failed tests, heartache and tears.

Halfway through our infertility journey, I began to get angry with God. My prayers turned to begging, and when that didn't work, I stopped praying altogether. I couldn't understand why we couldn't conceive; we did everything we were supposed to and still were barren and childless. I thought maybe God couldn't hear my prayers, and I definitely felt I couldn't hear Him. I was constantly thinking we were doing something wrong. What could I do to fix this? How could I give us a child?

In my despair, I turned to reading my Bible. I found myself constantly returning to Proverbs 3:5: *Trust in the Lord with all your heart, and lean not on your own understanding.* But while my faith seemed to strengthen, I was still unsure and untrusting of the Lord's plan. I would lay my troubles at His feet, and instead of walking away, I would snatch them back up. I was certain I could fix my problems a lot faster than He could.

During our first round of IVF, we had three failed embryos during two frozen embryo transfers. After completing our second round, we found we had only two viable embryos for our final transfer. I was devastated and completely heartbroken, thinking I had failed again.

And that's when it happened. The Lord got His 2x4 ready. As I was crying over our lost potential children and the only two embryos we had, the Lord filled my entire body with an overwhelming sense of calm, during which one thought entered my mind and heart: *I gave you two for a reason.*

WOW! Talk about a game changer. I instantly hit my knees and thanked the Lord for the two miracles He had blessed me and my husband with. I thanked Him for never turning His back on me, even when I turned my back on Him. Through my struggles, I realized it's easy to have faith in the Lord on my timeline and when things are going my way. Absolute faith and trust truly matter when things don't go the way I want. I wasn't sure why God blessed us with those two embryos, if two were all it would take for my husband and I to have a child, or if He had different plans for us, but I know He has perfect timing.

My hope is to have patience to see it through to the end. Our Heavenly Father has promised me children, but He has not promised to give them to me tomorrow. I will be patient in faith, and I will stay the course.

If your blessing doesn't come when you expect it to, hang on – it doesn't mean it's not going to happen. It means to trust HIM with all your heart and to not rely on your own understanding.

Struggling with infertility isn't something I foresaw for myself, nor would I wish it on anyone, but I know absolute faith and trust in the Lord will help us endure and overcome our struggles.

Thank you for the 2x4 moments that show us you unending ways! Your blessings both large and small are not forgotten.

Grace Days

This section is for the days you just need to take a deep breath, a break or a vacation! Life is busy. Our days are hectic. Infertility is stressful. And sometimes, we just need to slow down, rest and give ourselves a little (or a lot) of grace. Maybe you need to give yourself an extra helping of grace, or perhaps you simply need a reminder that God can rejuvenate you.

Let the words in this section help you unwind, relax and find a renewed sense of peace. Spending time in the Word can do that. Open your Bible, and ask God to take a load off your shoulders in the middle of the chaos. He's listening. He hears you. Let Him in.

Truly my soul finds rest in God. –Psalm 62:1 NIV

Grace Day One >>> Lisa Parvey

For in this hope we were saved. Now hope that is seen is not hope. For who hopes for what he sees? But if we hope for what we do not see, we wait for it with patience. — Romans 8: 24-25 ESV

Rejoice in hope, be patient in tribulation, be constant in prayer. —Romans 12:12 ESV

We were called back by the ultrasound technician at my OB/GYN's office. My heart pounded as we walked to the ultrasound room, where she gave me instructions and said she would be back shortly. I sat on the table, my husband resting in the chair next to me. He could see I was nervous and said, "It is going to be okay; I just know it." The technician came back in, darkened the lights and started with the ultrasound procedure. I remember grabbing my husband's hand and squeezing it as tightly as I could, my heart pounding through my chest as the tech told us what she was looking at. We were extra nervous for this appointment due to a previous miscarriage.

As I looked at the screen, I thought I saw a little flicker. I thought to myself, *Is this really happening? Is God answering our prayers of a healthy pregnancy?* I immediately asked the tech if it was the heartbeat, and she confirmed it was. My husband and I were ecstatic and so joyful. Over the next week, we continued to faithfully pray, as we were due for a follow-up ultrasound in a week.

Unfortunately, the next ultrasound did not go as we had hoped. We were not able to see a heartbeat and learned I was, in fact, miscarrying. I am not sure why God allowed us to see the heartbeat that day and not a week later. Romans 12:12 reminds me of that day and the hope it gave us that our prayers were being answered.

We had waited so patiently for this time to come, especially when we were so nervous from the previous miscarriage. We also were joyful in that moment and faithfully prayed for things to go right this time. I have asked myself, what's next? When will God make us parents? What if we never become parents? Romans 8:24-25 reminds me to have hope that someday we will have children and to patiently wait for what we do not yet have. Rest in the waiting, and know there is a plan.

Lord, I will wait. I will wait with a joyful heart and a patient mind. Amen.

On a Sabbath Jesus was teaching in one of the synagogues, and a woman was there who had been crippled by a spirit for eighteen years. She was bent over and could not straighten up at all. When Jesus saw her, he called her forward and said to her, "Woman, you are set free from your infirmity." Then he put his hands on her, and immediately she straightened up and praised God. Indignant because Jesus had healed on the Sabbath, the synagogue leader said to the people, "There are six days for work. So come and be healed on those days, not on the Sabbath." The Lord answered him, "You hypocrites! Doesn't each of you on the Sabbath untie your ox or donkey from the stall and lead it out to give it water? –Luke 13:10-15 NIV

Jesus said to the man with the shriveled hand, "Stand up in front of everyone." Then Jesus asked them, "Which is lawful on the Sabbath: to do good or to do evil, to save life or to kill?" But they remained silent. He looked around at them in anger and, deeply distressed at their stubborn hearts, said to the man, "Stretch out your hand." He stretched it out, and his hand was completely restored. –Mark 3:3-5 NIV

Rest. It's a word I don't like. I am the type of person who can't sit still for long. I don't go to movie theaters, and I can't even watch a 30-minute sitcom before I'm up folding laundry, checking Facebook or organizing a dresser drawer. Resting is just not in my nature. So, imagine my thoughts when after my third failed treatment cycle and recent news that I miscarried after IVF, God asked me to *rest* in His healing and cease all further fertility treatments.

It's been three years since that conversation with God, in which I agreed to *"rest."* Every time I start to feel anxious and think nothing will ever change unless I *labor* or *strive*, I begin to remember the healing of the paralyzed man at the pool of Bethesda. For 38 years, the man had been flat on his back, unable to do anything for himself or others, no matter how hard he struggled. I also think about the miraculous restoration of the woman oppressed with the spirit of infirmity. She had been bowed over for 18 years and saw very little of life's beauty – only the dusty ground, dirty sandals and bruised feet day in and day out. I even think about the man with the withered hand who must have felt useless with a very poor sense of self-worth.

I think about the stories in today's verses often because I can relate to each of them. I sometimes feel powerless to change my situation, or as though without children in my life, I am missing out on the beauty of being a mother. I, too, have moments where I have a poor sense of self-worth due to health conditions I have been diagnosed with. I can also relate because I believe all three of them, much like me, struggled for so long to get back on their feet, to try to lift themselves up, to attempt to do something about their situations, only to be disappointed each time they failed.

Yet, I mostly think about these specific stories because they offer me hope. Each one of them received the miracle they so desperately desired to receive on their own when Jesus came offering healing. *No struggling and no striving – just resting and receiving.*

I, too, want the kind of miracle they received, which is why I refuse to fall into the temptation of struggling and striving in my own efforts, but rather, through faith, embrace the offer of healing Jesus has extended to us all. I know, just like each of their situations changed in an instant, mine will, too. ***What is today, might not be tomorrow.***

Maybe you have struggled to lift yourself out of a problem that has weighed you down. Maybe you have attempted to do whatever you could, hoping it would amount to something, only to be frustrated to be let down time and again. If so, I encourage you to meditate on these stories because I find it no coincidence that all three received their miracles on the Sabbath, the day of *rest*. I believe God wants us to cease from all struggling and accept the offer He extends to turn our situations around. Jesus has already done the work on the cross for you to receive your miracle. Sometimes all you have to do is rest.

Father, thank you for extending your grace to me. Knowing I can rest in Your grace is a blessing. You are good, always. Amen.

Grace Day Three >>> Ali Forrest

For still the vision awaits its appointed time it hastens to the end—it will not lie. If it seems slow, wait for it; it will surely come; it will not delay. –Habakkuk 2:3 ESV

Picture this. You are at a stoplight. It's green, but as you approach, the light flashes to yellow. What do you do? Do you press your foot hard on that accelerator and zip right through, rushing to the next meeting, coffee date or appointment? Or, do you choose to hit the brakes and slow down?

Let's be honest here. If I can help it, I'm choosing to dodge the red light.

If God were driving my car, I think He would choose to slow down and hit the brakes at the yellow light. He tends to go at His own leisurely pace, don't you think?

Well, Elizabeth's story is a perfect example of a time God hit the gas when He was good and ready. Her story falls in the book of Luke and can be broken down into three episodes as a trilogy of sorts.

In episode one (Luke 1:5-25), we learn Elizabeth was past menopause. Her husband, Zechariah, was elderly. Their baby making days were over, and their hope had dwindled, as well. Factually and statistically, the science behind procreation was not on their side. But it happened. She became pregnant! Go, Elizabeth! Go!

She defied the odds.

I'm going to hit pause on her story for just a second and reflect. My husband and I have turned to treatments and medical advancements to help us conceive, and I have to admit that sometimes it makes me question the intersection of faith and science. With in vitro fertilization, how does God play a role? Science is doing all the work. Or, is it?

One day, my husband and I were talking about this very topic, and he said something that changed my viewpoint forever. He said, "If it were purely science, it would work every time."

Our God can move mountains. He can do the impossible, and His way will always prevail, whether we agree with it or not. Elizabeth learned this important lesson during her time at the red light.

Okay, so back to the story. In episode two (Luke 1: 57-66), Mary (you know, the mother of Jesus) visits Elizabeth while pregnant with John the Baptist. It's at this meeting that both women recognize their children, their baby boys, will be an extraordinary part of God's plan. Finally, in episode three (Luke 1: 67-80), Elizabeth gives birth to John, the child she had always hoped for. Elizabeth didn't, or rather couldn't, rush her pregnancy. Neither can we. Rushing to or through something is never as satisfying as taking it nice and slow.

Maybe the biggest takeaway here is we cannot rush our God. We cannot fully understand His ways, and so let's not be so busy trying to understand Him that we choose not to participate in our faith or lives. Let's use this time of waiting to come to understand He is good solely because *He is good.*

We can't put a rush order on our stork delivery, so let's slow down and soak in all the other blessings we do have, right now.

Lord, help me to trust in Your unfailing love. You are always good to me. Help me to recognize this. Amen.

Grace Day Four >>> Ali Forrest

They rose early in the morning and worshiped before the LORD; then they went back to their house at Ramah. And Elkanah knew Hannah his wife, and the LORD remembered her. And in due time Hannah conceived and bore a son, and she called his name Samuel, for she said, "I have asked for him from the LORD. –1: Samuel 1:19-20 ESV

Gosh, Hannah has a great story, doesn't she? The short version is that Hannah cries in anguish and prays, asking God for a son. The Lord remembers her, and she conceives and births a child.

How many times have you been like Hannah, praying unwaveringly for that child, speaking to God so intently from your heart? I mean, she is praying so hard her husband thinks she is drunk!

I know I have. Every single day, I pray that this be the day, month or year I will finally get my heart's desire: a child. I sometimes picture God sitting down to a multiple-choice test based on my life. The question: Will she get her baby this month? The answer choices: "Yes," "no," "needs to wait" or "I have other plans."

Hannah got a "yes."

And every time I read that last line, *So it came to pass in the process of time that Hannah conceived and bore a son, and she called him Samuel, saying, "Because I have asked for him from the Lord."* (1 Samuel 1: 1-20), I just want to jump in a time machine, backpedal a few years and give Hannah a high five. Knowing the struggle of wanting to be a mom, but experiencing a barren womb month after month, I can't help but rejoice when a friend finally, *finally*, sees two lines on a pee stick. It's a story of hope. A wonderful, glorious story of hope.

The more important message to remember here is that at the end of the day, the Lord remembered Hannah. So, although He may be saying "no" to your prayer request to be a mom today, He has certainly not forgotten you. Oh no, friend. We are on God's radar. Always.

I will be with you always, even until the end of the world. –Matthew 28:20

God didn't bring you this far to leave you. –Philippians 1:6

Do not be afraid I am with you. –Isaiah 43:5

The above verses are just a sampling of truths reminding us He is always there. Let that soak in. God is always there. More importantly, God is always there for *you*. He might check the box that says "no," "needs to wait," or "I have other plans," but that does not mean you are forgotten. It just means not today. Hannah waited and waited, but she got her "yes." Your story is still being written, and the ending is going to be good. I just know it.

Heavenly Father, waiting is hard! Sometimes I feel forgotten. Sometimes I feel abandoned. Sometimes I feel weak. While I wait, help me to see Your love and grace. I need it today and every day! Amen.

Grace Day Five >>> *Cassie Rief*

There's one thing I struggle with more than infertility. I'm sure many of you can relate. I'm incredibly hard on myself. And, I'll tell you something. The stress of it is guaranteed to break you down (and break you out!)

Especially if you, like me, have hormonal issues in spades. Thanks, Polycystic Ovarian Syndrome!

As hopeful as I am when it comes to infertility, I'll still do everything within my power to find a cure – some magic superfood, pill or tea. I've done the research. In fact, I'm quite embarrassed by what Google search knows about me. I've joined Paleo dieters. I frequent online support groups. I've bought the supplements, and the yoga pants.

But, when all is said and done, months of negative pregnancy tests and a chemical pregnancy as a 30th birthday gift are enough to make you feel it's all for naught. Toxic thoughts begin to linger with a vengeance. *Your body is literally unable to do the one thing it was designed to: create life.*

I'm soon sprinting full-on toward self-defeat and self-loathing:

- I ate two pieces of bread today – my Paleo diet is ruined. I guess I'll just eat that donut, too, because I'm not getting pregnant now!
- I didn't want to get intimate with my husband tonight, and it was my peak day. This could have been *the time*, and I missed it.
- I cried today after getting my progesterone shot. I should be used to this by now.
- This acne would be gone if I could just balance my hormones. Why can't I?!
- It's my fault my husband doesn't have a baby yet. I'm a burden to this marriage.

Ouch, right? I put *so much* unnecessary pressure on myself.

Our experiences with infertility teach us to be compassionate of others' trials. But, what about compassion for ourselves? We're going through *a lot* right now. And guess what? It's *OK.*

In times of sorrow, I search for God's beauty in the world and slowly begin to treat myself with the same kindness I bestow upon others. I show appreciation for my life by laughing robustly as our dog runs full-speed, tush-down around the house after bath time with such obvious pleasure to be free. I marvel over my garden teeming with veggies. I let go and let God by going out and letting loose. I live in the moment because it's filled with blessings the Lord has given me.

My mom tells me over and over again to be gentle with myself, my heart, and my hopes and dreams. After all, we are already beautiful and perfectly made in God's eyes. How dare I bash this very capable body He made with His own hands?

In times of self-doubt and when it feels like everything rests on my shoulders, I must look to God and remember Matthew 11: 29-30. God isn't asking me to take on everything by myself. He's asking me to give my worries and shortfalls to Him so I may rest. He is good all the time, and His graces extend beyond our comprehension.

Lord, my shoulders are heavy with my burdens and shortcomings. Please make me strong when I am weak. I give it all to You, who will make me whole in Your time. Take my imperfections and worries. Make my burdens light and my yoke easy.

While You are Waiting

There are two things I loathe equally: waiting and surprises. No thanks on either! Unfortunately, waiting is out of my control. While it's not my favorite thing to do (and probably not yours, either), we can choose to wait with strikingly impressive patience ... or try to at least!

The women in this section tell their stories about waiting, and more importantly, how waiting in the Word keeps them rooted in what matters most. As many clichés tell us, good things come to those whose wait. While we wait, let's do it together, and let's do it with great faith.

Father, while I would love to accelerate my wait time, I am trying my best to wait with patience and trust. Today, I ask You to fill the hearts of all those in waiting with an extra dose of Your great and ardent love.

Waiting Day One >>> Kathryn Shirey

Therefore you do not lack any spiritual gift as you eagerly wait for our Lord Jesus Christ to be revealed. –1 Corinthians 1:7 NIV

"Why do you think God gave you this specific timeline? Why 2 years?" The question made me pause as we talked about the work God is doing in my life. I took another sip of my coffee, then picked at the half-eaten bagel in front of me, stalling while I considered the question. Why this waiting period? I'm ready for a change, so why isn't He getting me there now? Is there a purpose in the wait?

How often have your found yourself waiting? Waiting for that special someone to enter your life, for the wedding you've always dreamed of, for a life together you so long for? Waiting for a baby when all your other friends are starting their families, but now you are caught up in the uncertain world of infertility? Waiting for that promotion, that next step in your career? Waiting for healing, for the long nights of grief to finally end, for the pain to subside and life to return to normal? Waiting to fulfill a calling God has placed on your heart, yet it seems impossible from your current circumstance? And the list continues…

I find it hard to wait, especially in our culture of immediate gratification. Restaurants that serve food within minutes of ordering, 2 day delivery on Amazon purchases (sometimes even same day!), instant internet access on the ever-present iPhone, all-electronic toll lanes on the highway so we never have to slow down. We are not a people who like to wait for anything!

Yet, the Bible is full of stories of waiting. Time and again, God takes a long-term vision to His promises, often involving long waiting periods for those to whom He has made promises. So, why this waiting? What is God's purpose in making us wait? When God asks you to wait, trust that He has a purpose!

These seasons of waiting do have purpose. To draw us nearer to God. To learn to rely on God's power instead of our own. To believe in His promises for our lives. To prepare ourselves or to allow time for God to prepare others for our next step.

I knew the answer to the question why I have to wait two years. I'm not completely ready for the next step. I need this time for God to continue preparing my heart, to build the skills and confidence I need for what's next and for God to align the pieces that will bring me to the next step. These two years are a gift of grace from God, an opportunity to stay in familiar turf for a little while longer while preparing for whatever is next.

The waiting period hasn't always been so clear, though. Other seasons of waiting have felt more indefinite, less clear on the reasons for the wait. Such as waiting through years of infertility to start a family. Wondering why I had to endure that wait when it came so quickly for others. Yet, that waiting period became a pivotal moment in my faith journey.

So, what will I learn from this latest period of waiting? I don't know yet, but as anxious as I am to get through the waiting and arrive at the next destination, I know the journey is important. The journey is where I'm learning and growing. The journey is developing me into who I need to be for the next destination.

There is purpose in God's wait. That wait is where we grow, where we build character, where we draw closer to God, where we test our determination and faithfulness, where we become who God wants us to be.

What are you waiting on today? Can you see the purpose in your wait? Look closer. Trust there is purpose in the waiting and lean on that promise for more hope and patience as you journey on.

Christ, help me to remember that waiting is a blessing. It's in the waiting that we can deepen our relationship with You, which is always a good thing. I am trusting You and Your purpose! Amen.

Waiting Day Two >>> Heather Step

But other people are like the seeds sown in good soil. They hear the message, accept it, and bear fruit: some thirty, some sixty, and some a hundred. –Mark 4:20 NKJV

The parable of the sower is about seed that is sown which lands in different places. Seeds may fall on a path, the rocky ground or in thorn bushes. The story is about God's Word, but it can also be a metaphor for infertility.

Perhaps Satan has you in a well of doubts and is stealing your joy in life (path). Perhaps you are in a place where you feel it is all too hard, and you want to give up (rocky ground). Perhaps you are so focused on comparing yourself to others with their cute, completed families that you can't bear fruit in your own life (thorns). Perhaps you're in a great place of trusting that God has the perfect idea of what your family is going to look like (fertile ground).

Wherever your location in your journey, know God is with you and understands exactly where you are. Don't judge yourself for where you are at the moment. The important thing is how you're going to move on from here. That being said, I'm the first to acknowledge it can be difficult for a woman to stay on fertile ground during infertility's hardships.

There is so much involved in terms of diet, lifestyle and daily choices we are faced with. There is the emotional weight of each cycle and the disappointment of a negative pregnancy test. The compounded stress of a treatment cycle: expenses, as well as multiple injections and drugs, the invasion of your body and pressure to make it all work.

Sometimes it just becomes too much, and it's easier to cast aside your better judgment and eat your emotions. So, you grab that chocolate cake even though you know sugar is going to deplete your vitamins and wreak havoc on your glucose levels, which you are already attempting to medicate with more pills.

Self-control is hard for those facing infertility because you never know when your endpoint is. If you knew you only had to diet one month to get pregnant, it would be a lot easier. In some cases, years can pass without a drop of real coffee. And you're left wondering, why am I doing this?

It helps to know God is in control and has the best plan for your family. It is something far beyond our human comprehension. God has the bigger picture, and we have such limited vision. In the meantime, it's up to us to make sure we find fertile ground. Grow your faith. Persevere. Focus on the good things in your life right now that bring you joy.

Lord, help me to be that fertile ground. Help me to seek Jesus again. Help me to control my emotions by focusing on Your best plan for my life, my family and all the positive things happening to me right now.

Waiting Day Three >>> Melanie Bryant

Let all that I am wait quietly before God, for my hope is in Him. – Psalm 62:5 NLT

Do you ever get tired of waiting? Or hoping? I sure do! I finally got pregnant one January with our miracle baby. A month later, I started spotting. I was told everything looked good and to remain hopeful. I did, and I prayed everything would be okay. Sadly, it ended with a miscarriage that March. I was back to waiting.

Only this time, all hope had flown out the window. I'll be honest; it didn't come back quickly, either. And, finally, it started creeping back when I began visiting my fertility doctor again. Well, that, and with many hours and days spent praying to God for peace and comfort. The song "While I'm Waiting" by John Waller reminds me God really does have perfect timing, although sometimes we have to wait more than we want to.

This song has deeply impacted me throughout this journey. It hits all the emotions that come with fertility treatments: *We should still serve God while we are waiting. We should still worship while we are waiting.*

We are all waiting on something, and it's not easy. However, we must be obedient to God. He knows the bigger picture, and we are strengthened because of our struggles. For me, one struggle will be Sept. 15. This is the due date of the baby we lost. If you have days you dread facing, just know I get you. You are never alone for the tough stuff. And, when Sept. 15 comes, my husband and I are going to honor the baby we lost, while keeping steadfast hope we will soon conceive again.

No, it won't be easy, but I am hopeful God will continue to use our lives to impact others. We understand how it feels to go through a miscarriage. To continuously wait for results, doctor visits or a positive pregnancy test. We understand how it feels to lose hope, only to find it again. We also understand there will be days in which you want to give up, while other days are filled with hope.

We continue to pray God will bless us with a child, and for all others on this journey. *Let all that I am wait quietly before God, for my hope is in Him.* – Psalm 62:5

My desire as you read this is that you find hope in your waiting, because God is hope! Thank you, Lord, for being our hope. Amen.

Waiting Day Four >>> Brianne Shoop

Do not be afraid. Stand firm and you will see the deliverance the Lord will bring you today. The Lord will fight for you; you need only to be still. —Exodus 14:13-14 NIV

Most days, I am go, go, go. When is our next doctor appointment? When can we afford in vitro fertilization treatments? When can we afford adoption? When will we ever get pregnant? When will it be our turn? When, when, when?

My husband and I found out we have a one percent chance of getting pregnant on our own without fertility treatments. Our world was rocked by this news. I already felt like we had waited long enough. We were patient enough. Ready enough. But our God has other plans.

Every time we are about to get what we hope is good news, it typically never is. My mind instantly goes back to thinking, *But, God, we have waited long enough! We've been patient long enough! Can't you see how badly we want this?*

This is when we need to remind ourselves to be still. We need to love where we are right now in our lives. This is the time we need to set our eyes on Jesus, spend time in prayer and really develop a relationship with our heavenly Father. We need to make Him our priority and not allow our wants to win out. Heck, we need to enjoy those uninterrupted naps and the ability to buy ourselves a new handbag. And, while we're at it, why don't we just get back to the basics and start dating our husbands again?! Let's simply enjoy these current moments we have been completely blessed with.

I often get caught up in the dreams of what it would be like to decorate a nursery. I imagine how our parents' faces will look when we finally tell them we are pregnant. Maybe you do, too. It is so easy to dream about that time in our lives, but I ask you to please focus on the now. Turn your doubts and frustrations to God.

Delight yourself in the LORD, and he will give you the desires of your heart. — Psalm 37:4 He knows our heart's desire, and I know He will provide. God has a bigger and better plan for us. All we must do is focus our hearts and minds on Him.

The Lord is fighting for us, ladies. He's fighting for us even when we have lost our hope, focus and strength. He knows our feelings of defeat. God is fighting for our husbands and our marriages. He is even fighting for those on the opposite side who may not know what to say to their struggling friend or family member. He is fighting for **US,** and He needs us to be still so we may focus on **HIM.** Faith makes the impossible, possible. *For nothing is impossible with God.* —Luke 1:37

Ladies, I ask that when you feel overwhelmed and you're tempted to take everything into your own hands, don't. I ask that you pray, talk to God, and listen to what He's telling you. *Cast all your anxiety on him because he cares for you.* –1 Peter 5:7

This battle is not yours. This battle is the Lord's. *The Lord WILL fight for you, you need only to be still.* –Exodus 14:14 Fight the good fight. Be bold in your faith. It will all be worth it.

God, thank you for fighting our battles. You know the desires of my heart and I can pour my troubles out to You. You are good. Amen.

Waiting Day Five >>> *Wynne Elder*

See, I have engraved you on the palms of my hands; your walls are ever before me. —Isaiah 49:16

You reminded me, Lord. Amidst a sanctuary full of women in my dusty, west Texas town, You told me. You reminded me, and now, Lord, now I know **You really do see me.** You love me, and You know me. You spoke to me through an obedient friend and sister tonight, and You reminded me You are doing work in me **during my waiting.**

Waiting seems to be something I *should* be really good at from the past five years of infertility plus adoption, but it's been easy recently to just sort of push it to the side. I haven't been waiting well. Instead, I've just reminded myself (and others) pretty consistently that "we are taking a break" from fertility stuff. Meaning, I don't want to think about it, talk about it, pay for it or pray about it.

It's amazing how the stages of grief come in waves. Once again, I felt this surge of anger and deep, deep sadness that God still hasn't answered my prayer to heal me of my sickness and give me a biological baby. Why, Lord? Why me? Why haven't You answered me? Why have You forgotten about me?

There have been years of people praying over me. God speaking to me through others and His Word, prophesy and encouragement that one day He will heal, restore and put life inside me. I feel like He has asked me to believe He is ABLE to do those things. And, in the process, He's also asked me to trust and believe in Him, EVEN IF HE DOESN'T heal or give life.

There have been so many paths He's taken me down the past five years; I've learned about His character and love for me in ways I might not have without this struggle. I've also felt alone, hurt, sad and forgotten. And today, I want to encourage myself and all of you who have also felt that way – that **no matter how we feel, God has NOT forgotten us!!!** Did you hear that? *God has NOT forgotten you.*

He has a perfect plan and purpose for your life! He knit you together in your mother's womb, and He loves you. He delights over you, the Bible says.

I know, in the middle of the storm, it's so hard to remember that. That's why I literally have notes saved in my phone when friends have spoken those words to me from the Lord.

I want to be the one to tell YOU today, sweet sister, that **God has NOT forgotten you.** I want you to believe with fresh eyes and fresh faith today that He loves you. He's called you His, and He has a wonderful plan. Hold on. It's so hard to believe a lot of days that He hasn't forgotten you, but believe it today. **Here's to believing again!**

God, you have not forgotten me or anyone in our time of waiting! My prayer for today is that I remember how You are doing good work today and right now. No matter what, You are good. Amen.

Worry Less; God's Got Your Back

I like Thomas Edison's gumption. In creating the light bulb, he found tons of ways that didn't work along the road to success. Sometimes, I feel that very same way about infertility. At this point, my husband and I are on, like, Plan E!

The thing is, in life, there will always be choices, forks in the road and something to worry about. Thank goodness God is already a step ahead of us, and we can cast every last worry right on Him. Whatever you are stressing about, release it all to the One who is in control.

Worry Day One >>> Holley Gerth

But you, O LORD, are a shield about me, my glory, and the lifter of my head. –Psalm 3:3 ESV

You are the light of the world. A city set on a hill cannot be hidden. Nor do people light a lamp and put it under a basket, but on a stand, and it gives light to all in the house. In the same way, let your light shine before others, so that they may see your good works and give glory to your Father who is in heaven. –Matthew 5: 14-16 ESV

I have been crucified with Christ and I no longer live, but Christ lives in me. The life I now live in the body, I live by faith in the Son of God, who loved me and gave himself for me. –Galatians 2:20 ESV

Dear you,

I see the way you sometimes duck your head, the quiet questions that fill your eyes, the subtle step you take back from the crowd. You're thinking, *I'm not enough to be here.* So, let me chase your heart for a moment to that corner where you're hiding and tell you the truth, instead.

"Oh, yes, you are enough … You are even more than enough. You might shake your head at me in a soft protest. "You don't understand," you might say. "You don't know my faults and failures. You don't know my past or the problems that chase me."

I'd nod, agreeing, and say, "You're right. I don't. But I know something even more important — I know who you belong to, and that changes everything." The reality is, none of us are enough on our own. We're all weak and fallen, broken and helpless, sinners in need of a savior. But our story doesn't stop there. We do have a savior. *And, He trades our nothing for His everything, our brokenness for His wholeness, our inadequacy for His identity.*

Are you perfect? No, ma'am. Neither am I. Nor is anyone else. But are you enough? Yes, ma'am. I am, too. So is everyone who belongs to Him. *We are enough because Jesus is enough in us.* You are made in the image of God. Isn't that miraculous?

So, when you want to go to the corner, dare to step into the center of His will, instead. When you want to shrink back in fear, go forward in faith. When the whispers and lies get loud, listen to the voice within your heart that can silence them all.

You are not meant for hiding. You are meant for highlighting the One who created you, calls you by name and invites you out of the shadows and into the light of His love.

Lord, shine light on the woman reading this today. Let her see that she is enough, more than enough. Let us not strive for perfection, but rather grace. Amen

Worry Day Two >>> Ali Forrest

One who is full loathes honey, but to one who is hungry everything bitter is sweet.
–Proverbs 27:7 NIV

In the middle of the night, I was suddenly awakened by a blaring alarm, which screeched, *"Fire! Get out!"* My bed was empty aside from two dogs (yes, my dogs sleep in the bed). My husband must have fallen asleep watching television upstairs. I grabbed my dogs' collars, not wanting them to dart away from me, and quickly opened the door to find Chandler. He was already walking down the stairs, thank goodness.

We didn't smell any smoke, so we walked around the house to see if there was a fire or something else going on. It turned out to be a false alarm (thank goodness again).

The thing is, if there really was a fire that night, we would have dealt with it. My first thought when I woke up to an alarm wasn't, *Oh, no; this is scary, anxiety-inducing or worrisome.* It was a calm, *Okay, what do I need to do* **right now**?

I am going to skip the small talk and jump straight to the point. When the fire alarm goes off, look for the honey. When you slam into somebody's car and it's too late to backup, look for the honey. When you get yet another negative pee stick, look for the honey.

Find the sweetest, best possible thing among the smoke, bent metal, or one pink line... and hold on to it. Thank Jesus for it. When you are in a season of summer and everything is sweet, thank Jesus for it.

It's because of the bitter that the sweet is so good.

One who is full loathes honey, but to one who is hungry everything bitter is sweet. –Proverbs 27:7

We need the crappy stuff (whatever that is to you) to appreciate the really good stuff. You know that. You've heard it before. We can't stop anything – good or bad – from coming. It simply will. This applies to everyone, not just those of us with finicky reproductive systems. But we're talking about infertility here (obviously).

We can take solace in the fact God's got it under control, and that *His* way *will* prevail. We will deal with the cards we are handed as they are dealt. So, maybe your IUI won't be successful this cycle. Maybe Clomid isn't your best friend this month. Maybe your IVF cycle didn't go as planned. Maybe you didn't see the spike or dip in your body basal temperature chart you hoped for. Maybe you are tired of doing nothing, but that's exactly what you feel God is telling you to do... nothing.

Find that honey.

It's going to take some work, y'all. It takes elbow grease and attitude adjustments to see the sweet among the bitter, but it is there. Seek it. More than anything, having Jesus on our side is enough to make every bitter thing sweet. Friend, God has it all mapped out.

In the bitter and in the sweet, I will look to You with gratitude. Hosanna! Hosanna! Hallelujah!

Worry Day Three >>> Megan Carlson

Do not be anxious about anything but, in every situation, by prayer and petition, with thanksgiving, present your requests to God. And the peace of God, which transcends all understanding, will guard your hearts and your minds in Christ Jesus. —Philippians 4: 6-7 NIV

My hubby, Kyle, and I have been trying to conceive for nine years. Nine LOOONNNGGGG years! I've done acupuncture, tried herbs, changed my diet and undergone plenty of procedures, tests and surgeries.

After doing almost everything under the sun, it seems in vitro fertilization or adoption are basically our final options. We have what doctors call "unexplained infertility," but what I call a terrible diagnosis. Our countless questions remain unanswered.

Last night, I had dinner with my mom. I was updating her on all of our life happenings as of late and telling her how I have an extraordinary amount of anxiety right now. I told her it's at an all-time high these days and that I feel like I'm on the verge of a panic attack whenever I'm in the car.

I had to be honest. I also told her I've been mad at God for a long time, pushing Him away instead of drawing closer to Him. I've prayed for so, SO long to have a baby, but it hasn't happened yet. Even worse is we don't know why, and all we want is to be parents. As a result of this anxiety, I haven't felt like investing in my relationship with Jesus because He's not answering my prayers.

After listening quietly, she told me that just yesterday when she was praying for me, God revealed to her a message. He said she must help me get through this anger and anxiety because she, herself, had spent so many years angry at God after her and my dad's divorce. She didn't want that to be my fate, as well.

So, here we stand. I don't know how this is all going to play out. I don't know how my mom is going to help me. I don't think she knows, either, besides lending an ear and words of encouragement when I'm feeling down. I guess time will tell.

But, as we sat in that Thai restaurant, with tears in her eyes, my mom showed me Bible verses I've heard a million times, but hadn't paid much attention to. *Do not be anxious about anything but, in every situation, by prayer and petition, with thanksgiving, present your requests to God.* The hardships of infertility are very real.

Finding purpose in the pain is even more difficult, especially as my prayers seemingly go unanswered. I'm working through the anger, and with not knowing the purpose of our infertility and what Jesus wants of me. In the meantime, I plan to spend more time with Jesus as my mom recommended, praying for Him to reveal His plans in His timing.

As such, what I've come to realize is I must give Him the opportunity to lead the way. That, and moms really do know best!

Lord, help me find purpose in the pain, even when it its difficult. Let our weary hearts turn towards you when we need them the most. Not only that, but let our hearts be full of gratitude and joy all the days of our lives. Amen.

Worry Day Four >>> Ali Forrest

Many are the plans in the mind of a man, but it is the purpose of the LORD that will stand. —Proverbs 19:21 ESV

A joyful heart is good medicine, but a crushed spirit dries up the bones. —Proverbs 17:22 ESV

Between a struggling adoption case and low success rates for treatment options, I can't help but be shaken with worry, fear and anxiety. Sweet friend, I have a feeling you get exactly where I'm coming from.

And, here is the thing about you and me. We are not in control. God is. God is in control of our lives. It's terrifying and beautiful all at once. *Many are the plans in the mind of a man, but it is the purpose of the Lord that will stand. —Proverbs 19:21*

To me, this means we can make plans all day long and jot down schedules in pretty calendars, but God's plans for us will always, always prevail. With that in mind, I openly confess I question how His plan intersects with my own. My plan is kids, and I don't care how they get here. Boat, plane or stork; it doesn't matter. I cling to this desire. Yet, I picture God laughing as He watches over me! *Those are your plans? Well, wait until you see what I have in store for you...*

But, what happens if I don't like God's plan for my life? What happens if you don't like God's plan for your own life? In this event, we choose joy. We simply choose joy anyway. *A joyful heart is good medicine, but a crushed spirit dries up the bones. —Proverbs 17:22*

Joy trumps all. Amidst the bitter circumstances, we choose joy. Amidst the magnificent circumstances, we choose joy. In all things, choose joy.

Christ, break the chains on my heart and mind so I can surround every cell of my body with joy. Let my life be filled with exultation, praise and adoration for You. Amen.

Worry Day Five >>> Rachael Gentry

"For I know the plans I have for you," says the Lord. They are plans for good and not for disaster, to give you a future and a hope. –Jeremiah 29:11 NLT

Our journey began when we decided to stop all birth control methods. After one year of trying naturally, we asked our OB/GYN what we needed to do next. I answered a ton of questions, and he diagnosed me with Polycystic Ovarian Syndrome. I began taking Metformin to stabilize my glucose levels, but after three months, we were still childless. He then added the fertility drug, Clomid, which – by the way – is now considered a curse word in our household. Three months later, still no baby.

Our OB/GYN referred us next to a reproductive endocrinologist (RE), who explained I have diminished ovarian reserve and an Anti-Mullerian hormone level of 0.167. Basically, that means I don't have many eggs left and the ones that remain are poor quality.

Test after test was completed, and negative pregnancy test after negative pregnancy test was the end result. Eventually, my doctor made it clear I would never have a biological child and suggested we look into adoption. Talk about heartbroken! I walked out of the office sobbing uncontrollably. My husband tried to comfort me, but I was inconsolable.

After the negative vibes we received from the doctor that day, we decided to see a different RE. I believe God puts signs, large and small, in your life to show you where He needs you to be for His will to be done. That being said, the day we had our first appointment with this new doctor, he did an ultrasound just to see if I was ovulating naturally that cycle.

The ultrasound showed a follicle 23 millimeters large – a very good sign! They gave me a trigger shot that day, and we had our first intrauterine insemination the next day. Although the pregnancy test came back negative, I took it as God telling us we were where we were supposed to be.

We have actively been trying now for two-and-a-half years, and each month, I have only produced one follicle. I know things are lining up the way they are supposed to, but it's hard not to question God. It's also so difficult to see everyone around me having their second and third babies while we are still trying for our first.

I know one thing for certain: when our angel makes it to this earth, he or she is going to be a blessing God purposely placed in our lives in His perfect time! If this struggle has taught me anything, it is to be patient. I have learned I can do everything in my power to make life work the way I want it to, but if something isn't God's will, then it won't happen.

While we wait, I will keep my head high and rest easy knowing His will is being done.

Sometimes, God, it can be hard to trust Your will when it doesn't match up with what I want. Today, I ask that my heart be aligned with Your way. I want to serve and live my life according to Your plan. Amen.

Created for Purpose

Birthed out of barrenness. I use those four words several times in this section, but I just love it. Sometimes, I think we have to create our own opportunities, even within infertility. I have no idea why we struggle with infertility, but I do know we can use our experiences for a purpose.

Maybe that purpose is helping another woman cope. Maybe it's simply having the time to follow the other desires of your heart. Be bold, and see what you can birth out of your barrenness. Waiting doesn't just have to be *waiting*. It can be a time to accomplish feats you've only dreamed possible.

The readings in this section are all about seeing infertility in a way that creates purpose, whether it's participating in something bigger than you or simply empathizing better with others. Jump in!

Purpose Day One >>> Ali Forrest

Twenty years. That is how long Rebekah waited for her twin sons, Jacob and Esau. — Genesis 25:24 ESV

Rebekah, wife of Isaac, waited 20 long years to conceive. *Twenty years,* you guys! Isaac prayed. *And Isaac prayed to the LORD for his wife, because she was barren. And the LORD granted his prayer, and Rebekah his wife conceived. —*Genesis 25:21 ESV

Rebekah prayed, too. Clearly, God's timing was vastly different from theirs. But then one day, boom! Twins! So, I have to ask. What is your timeline? My plan was always two kids by 30, but maybe, just maybe, it's time to throw out the timeline, and stomp on the clock.

Let's say your wait is six months. Let's say it's a year or two. Let's say you follow in Rebekah's footsteps and wait 20 years. During that wait, you are not a childless woman. You are a woman. You are not a childless couple. You are a couple. Get rid of qualifiers that limit your joy.

For too long, the infertility label robbed me of that joy, or rather, I let it. I had it in my mind that without motherhood, I had no purpose. Without children, life was just another series of days. Oh, sweet friend, how wrong I was! Infertility was my excuse for not really living, and then I broke the proverbial chains that were holding me back. I started becoming the person I want to be. I task you to find a purpose that sets your heart on fire.

Be open to saying "yes," "yes" to dreams you never thought you could accomplish. Decide. What kind of soul-satisfying, heart-on-fire mission is He whispering for you to do? Do it. Do not let your years without children pass you by. Make your mark. Leave this world a legend. Friend, the time is now.

Push yourself, and be bold. Live your story, love your story, and let God's mercy light the path before you. His timing is and always will be perfect. Those baby boys Rebekah gave birth to? Jacob and Esau? They grew up to play a critical role in the story God crafted. Both were fathers of nations. Jacob goes on to become the father of the 12 tribes of Israel. Esau teaches us about the ungodliness that happens when we put humanly desires over our spiritual blessings. You see, sometimes it isn't our timeline that matters. It's about something much, much bigger. You just never know what God has up His sleeve. Until your desires coincide with His, continue (or start) living a life with your heart set afire with love for our Lord.

Father, set our hearts on fire and help us to live a life of passion! While I am waiting on a baby (or anything else), let me use the time I am given for purpose, good, and love. Help me to use my talents! Amen.

Purpose Day Two >>> Ali Forrest

For if you keep silent at this time, relief and deliverance will rise for the Jews from another place, but you and your father's house will perish. And who knows whether you have not come to the kingdom for such a time as this? —Esther 4:14 ESV

Read the last line of Esther 4:14 again. *And who knows whether you have not come to the kingdom for such a time as this?* Translation: Perhaps you were born for such a moment.

Esther has an impressive story. When Mordecai (Esther's supposed cousin and guardian) refused to bow and respect Haman (one of the king's officials), Haman plotted to destroy all Jews in the kingdom. It was a pride thing.

Thankfully, Mordecai learns of the plot and relays the details to Esther. Cue her life-saving plan. She outsmarts Haman by getting the king to sign a petition, which protects the Babylonian Jews, thus thwarting Haman's devious plan.

Esther saves the day! She was courageous, bold and quick-minded. She took a chance, accepted a dare. And, ultimately, she became queen and saved her people. I love the message written in her story. Perhaps you were born for such a moment. Maybe God is using infertility for a greater purpose in our lives.

So, today, I ask you, how can you make your mark, take a chance or accept a challenge for the goodwill of others? Actively seek out ways to demonstrate God's love is everywhere, all the time, in all circumstances. It's a magnificent way to find the purpose you may be searching for.

It's true, your moment might not be saving an entire population from being hung in the gallows, but Esther's story is a fantastic example of how she was able to make her mark on the world. You aren't Esther. You are you, and you can do brave things. Find a way to make your mark. In your home. Your community. This world.

Dear God, help me to be courageous. Help me to stand up and embrace opportunities when they arise. Use my pain of infertility as motivation. Let the pain of this experience be worth it, and let it help me to serve others, even if it's just one person. Amen.

Purpose Day Three >>> Lauren Hartley

Trust in the Lord with all your heart, and do not lean on your own understanding. In all your ways acknowledge him, and he will make straight your paths. –Proverbs 3:5-6 ESV

Infertility is a disease that is not only a physical battle, but also a mental and spiritual one. I have struggled with accepting God's will and plan for my life. However, I know He is working to mold my life for His good.

One February, at 11 weeks pregnant, I went into my OB/GYN's office for my first ultrasound. It was confirmed my baby was no longer alive and had died at around eight weeks. I leaned heavily upon God, family and friends to get me through the rough next months.

July of the same year, I found out a close family friend was pregnant. Because my husband and I had been trying to conceive again to no avail, I thought life was miserable, cruel and unfair. Ironically, a few weeks later, after pain and mid-cycle bleeding, I took a pregnancy test upon decisively feeling pregnant. It was positive! But, I couldn't help feeling confused as I wondered what was going on with my body.

An appointment with my doctor soon confirmed another miscarriage. Why was this happening to me? I remember crying the whole afternoon.

I went back in a few days later to ensure my hCG levels were dropping appropriately, only to find they had about doubled! Something was definitely wrong. As soon as I made the 30-minute drive home, I received a call from the doctor urging me to come back to the office for an immediate ultrasound, which confirmed what I had dreaded all along. It was, indeed, an ectopic pregnancy.

After injections of methotrexate, horrible pain for several days, an ER visit, time off work and hCG monitoring for about a month, I was finally free and clear. But all the questions still haunted me. Why me? Why not someone else?

In the midst of all this, my friend who had gotten pregnant lost her baby, too. Our shared pain drew us closer together in a bond many reading this know way too much about. I wish I could write a happy ending of pregnancy, but there isn't one to tell yet. We currently have been trying for almost two years after the ectopic, with no success.

It has been a difficult journey! The emotions are often more than a person can stand. Many tears have been shed and many prayers prayed. It is hard when it seems everyone is pregnant or just had babies. We were trying when my sister had her first baby, and she has two kids now! I'm depending on God to bring me through this storm! No matter how difficult and unfair it seems, I know He is in control. He cares about me!

I also know He has a plan for my life, and He sees the future and the unknown. I must trust Him. Maybe I will never have kids. I don't know. But I know the One who does, and He sees me and holds me in His hands. As for now, I will believe and have faith that one day, I will hold our child in my arms. Through my pain, I have been able to help others and give encouragement when they experience loss. In this way, my own disappointments are turned into joy.

God, you can bring me through any trial! When everything seems unfair and difficult, help me to be a light and source of encouragement to others. Amen.

Purpose Day Four >>> Ali Forrest

But I will hope continually and will praise you yet more and more. —Psalm 71:14 ESV

The Bible is laden with words and stories about people waiting on *something*. We are not alone in our waits. Oh no, sister friend, even when it feels like we are the last little blip to ever exist on God's radar, He has a plan and a purpose for us.

With all of our fellow waiters within the Bible, the thing is, usually something good (something really, really good) was to come. Take Abraham for example? He waited 25 years for his promise of a son. Then there was Moses. He waited 40 years in the wilderness! Forty *years*.

Abraham and Moses can be our biblical role models during our wait. We're in good company. I take so, *so* much solace in the fact God did not forget them. Maybe it means He hasn't forgotten me, either. Maybe He really does have a plan for me. It's just not being revealed today. Consider this. Today is the day He has something else for *you* planned. How great is that? Let me repeat: He has something planned for you right now in this very moment on this exact day.

Take away what you want, of course, from today's readings, but I see a major common thread between our Bible friends: Their story of waiting impacted so many people. It was not just about them. Their stories impacted those around them. Heck, they impacted people hundreds of years later! And the cool thing is, so can your story. There are two big points I want to make here.

First, apply the waiting stories of Moses and Abraham to your life. How can your waiting season impact those around you? It probably isn't a question you can answer at the snap of a finger, but think about it, mull it over and then more importantly, act on it. Second, God is writing a story for us, friend. I can't say it enough. We do not know what is ahead, but it is likely to be something more beautiful than we ever could imagine on our own. Infertility is hard stuff. God, you didn't promise an easy life. So, through our baby waits and wants for all future things to come, let us inscribe Psalm 71:14 in our hearts: *Hope continually and praise always.*

Lord, take my infertility and let it change me, shape me, and empower me. Amen.

Purpose Day Five >>> Ali Forrest

But the fruit of the Spirit is love, joy, peace, patience, kindness, goodness, faithfulness, gentleness, self-control; against such things there is no law. —Galatians 5:22-23

My husband and I attended a church in North Carolina where the pastor ended each service with the Halverson Benediction: *You go nowhere by accident. Wherever you go, God is sending you. Wherever you are, God has put you there. He has purpose in putting you there. Christ who indwells you has something He wants to do through you, wherever you are. Believe this, and go in His grace and love and power.*

My encouragement for you today is that you trust this. So many obstacles are part of my infertility story (and probably yours too). I want to use a few examples from my experience to help build my case:

- When it seemed like we would never get our dossier approved, I met with yet another fertility specialist. At our second appointment, he told me he was leaving the practice and we would need to start with a new practice. That night, we found out our dossier had been approved.
- After two failed international adoption matches, I was adoption exhausted. This was followed by a miscarriage through intrauterine insemination. While painful, these events were simply part of my journey.
- We met with our clinic about in vitro fertilization. It didn't feel right to either of us, so we didn't do it. A month later, we received our adoption referral.
- I had a feeling there was a little girl out there for us. Five minutes later, we got "the" call saying come get your baby girl. 48 hours later, I was holding her.

I don't write these things to gloat. I don't write these things to say you should adopt. I don't write these things to say which treatments you should or should not do. I write these things because each obstacle put me one step closer to where I needed to be.

So, believe it. Wherever you go, God is sending you. He puts you and me in the exact right place at the exact right time. One day, we'll understand. One day, we'll see the pieces of our God-ordained life puzzle come together. In this season of waiting, let us find our purpose. While standing in the hallway waiting for the door of motherhood to open, let us praise Him!

Let us go wherever He puts us with grace, love and power. Let us put into practice the very things He calls us to do with the fruits of the Holy Spirit listed in Galatians 5:22-23. We can start exactly where we are, because that is exactly where He has put us. Amazing, right?

Even in the moments where you just want to give up and throw in the towel on God or your faith, remind yourself in the best and worst of circumstances that God has put you exactly where you need to be. It took me a long time to really believe this, but I do, now, more than ever.

Today I ask that you allow yourself to be open to His purpose everywhere in your life! You never know what will be birthed out of your barrenness. Waiting does not mean purposeless. It's an opportunity. Seize it.

Community: Lean on Your People

Infertility is an unexpected place to find community. You find community with your spouse, your family who hurts with you and friends who want what you want. Of course, there are steps you walk alone, but don't be afraid to let others in.

Over and over, women who have carried the cross of infertility say their experience made them empathetic, that they take heart in breathing fresh light into others' aching hearts. Reach out and connect!

God, sometimes it can be hard to reach out and be vulnerable. Grant me the courage to be bold and reach out, create community and love my people well. Help me to be a blessing to those around me. I ask that You surround me with a network of friends and family who can lift me up, encourage me and celebrate life with me. Amen.

Community Day One >>> Amanda Morrison

And now these three remain: faith, hope and love. But the greatest of these is love.
–1 Corinthians 13:13

On the day of my last in vitro fertilization embryo transfer, my husband unexpectedly had to be out of town for work, so my dad took me. On the drive home, he looked at me and said, in regard to fertility treatments, that perhaps I shouldn't be messing with something out of my control.

As a woman raging on hormones, my temper immediately became enraged, and my heart began beating faster. I was ready to attack! But, the words that came out of my mouth shocked me. It certainly wasn't what I was thinking!

I said to my dad, "I have to have faith. I believe the doctor wouldn't be able to perform the miracles he does if not blessed by God, so I am hopeful God has His hand in this." It was purely a God moment because I wanted to say so many other things.

Despite their best intentions, family, friends and even strangers can be hurtful. They can be wonderful and caring, too. They express their emotions to you depending on where you are at that moment in time. Yet, so often when you're trying to conceive or build a family, there are many days, nights and hours you feel so alone. At the end of the day, know you're not alone! My dad was just trying to help in the car that day. He wants for me what my husband and I want. My whole family wants to see me with a child because it's our dream. Without them all, I would be lost.

Sadly, a few weeks later, we found out IVF had failed yet again, but I never forgot the conversation between dad and me that day. That God moment helped me see without a shadow of doubt that God has been with me every step of the way. Even when I could not see or walk in my overwhelming sadness and anger, it was He who carried me. It was He who tamed my words.

So, next time you get into fight mode when someone offers you unsolicited advice about your infertility, remember it's a show of solidarity, and they are trying to help. They may not always understand, but they're trying. Extend them gratitude, and praise God for community.

Father, thank You for the people in my life! Guide me to always show love to the people I cherish, for they are a true blessing.

Community Day Two >>> Wynne Elder

There is no fear in love. But perfect love drives out fear, because fear has to do with punishment. The one who fears is not made perfect in love. —1: John 4:18 NIV

I left a three-hour, triple baby shower dinner before the tears started to flow. It's such a weird thing, when you've been walking with a group of girls for three to five years, and they know you, your heart and your desires. They know your struggles and your heartache. They want what you want almost as much as you do. *They want to change the hard stuff; they want to make it better.* **They love me so fiercely.**

They don't know what to say sometimes, so sometimes they don't say anything. And, sometimes they step out on a limb and send me a message just to see how I am. I'm sure they feel nervous doing so. I would feel nervous, too, if it wasn't something I was familiar with. But when they do, I am so grateful. I can feel the hurt in their hearts for me. I can feel them empathizing with me. It's nice to know I'm seen.

It's hard having been trying to conceive for five years. There are always seasons when everyone and their dog are pregnant, and this is one of them. I have way too many stories of crying in the bathroom at parties and dinners, just trying to hide and be alone. Then, I have stories of friends finding me in that bathroom, praying with me and letting me hide out until the tears dry. *Five years* of this. I've witnessed the first round of kids, then the second, and now, lots of my friends are onto round three.

It's weird. It's weird because **I don't want people to feel sorry for me.** But, at times, **I feel sorry for myself.** I'm learning a lot about dealing with grief and loss over what could have been. I'm learning it's OK to cry out to God to tell Him I'm mad and don't think it's fair. He can handle it.

I don't want people to feel sorry for me. In fact, I think because I feel sorry for myself, I perceive everyone else as emphasizing, too. But they *are* right there with me. They are confused, sad and hurt, and they want it to be different, too! They want what I want!

I sometimes find myself asking, "Why not me?" I question God, telling Him it's not fair. I know in my heart the truth – that His timing is perfect, and there is purpose in my pain. But, that doesn't mean it still isn't hard. Not every day. But some days, it's hard.

I'm grateful for this journey; *I really am.* I'm grateful I can now, for the rest of my life, *empathize* with other women going through this same struggle. I'm thankful my pain can be my platform. I'm thankful my heart can be broken, hurt and sad alongside other women, and at the same time, I can encourage and relate to them in a new way. I'm grateful this journey has brought me to a greater dependence on HIM. I know full well we are NOT in control; He is. **He is in control of it all, and He alone is the author and giver of life.**

Sometimes, though, I just want to get in my car after dinner and drive around town before going home, stopping at random parks to cry. ***Ugly cry.*** I know the truth. I know I am loved, that my friends and family are for me and with me. But, there are times in this journey that must be walked alone. And, so I walk forward confidently, with my head high and heart open.

Oh Lord, we never walk alone! You are always at my side. Turn my sorrow to gratitude and my pain into empathy. Amen.

Community Day Three >>> Stephanie Cline

I give you thanks, O LORD, with my whole heart; before the gods I sing your praise.
—Psalm 138:1 ESV

"You are the light of the world. A city set on a hill cannot be hidden. Nor do people light a lamp and put it under a basket, but on a stand, and it gives light to all in the house. In the same way, let your light shine before others, so that they may see your good works and give glory to your Father who is in heaven. —Matthew 5:14-16 ESV

My story. I have a story? Me, the one who chose not to put God first many years ago, which, in turn, led me down a path of immeasurable pain, disappointment and heartbreak? The one who had to face a double dose of shattered dreams and heartbreak that infertility and divorce each bring? The one who continues to struggle holding onto hope that the Lord will bring me a godly husband and then bless me with children? How could these be things that are used for anyone's benefit, let alone to glorify Him?

Despite our brokenness, we each have a story to share. A story of God's faithfulness, grace and forgiveness. A story that is so unique, no one else can tell it. A story that will glorify God through our brokenness to those hurting around us. When our circumstances seem bleak, it is easy to lose perspective and to feel hopeless, invisible and like an unworthy wife and an incomplete woman. It is easy to feel as though the Lord has become callous to our heartbreak and abandoned us in our brokenness. It is easy to feel as though our stories aren't worth the paper they're written on, or that we have no story at all since we don't hear the pitter-patter of our children's feet in the quietness of the morning.

We must realize that we have a story to share, not because we have it all together, but because we *don't* have life figured out. We *don't* have all the answers. We must become vulnerable and allow the Lord to comfort us, bind up our brokenness and shine His light through our imperfections, even when we don't understand.

We must then learn to become vulnerable enough to allow Him to use our experiences to reach out to other hurting people. *You are the light of the world. A city set on a hill cannot be hidden. Nor do people light a lamp and put it under a basket, but on a stand, and it gives light to all in the house.* —Matthew 5:14

In the same way, let your light shine before others so they may see your good works and give glory to your Father in heaven. I encourage you to read all of Psalm 138. Psalm 138:8 states, *The Lord will fulfill his purpose for me; your steadfast love, O Lord, endures forever. Do not forsake the work of your hands.*

What are the pieces of your story? Take time to write down small ways you can look back to see the Lord working for your good through your circumstances. What have you learned through these examples of the Lord's faithfulness in your own life? How can you reach out to other hurting people and bring His light into their darkness, despite your own brokenness? Pray about how you can become vulnerable and transparent enough to let the Lord shine through you into a hurting world.

Let our stories be a light for others. Father, my prayer today is that through my brokenness, I can encourage my community, my loved ones, my friends, and all of Your people. Help me to be a blessing always. Amen.

Community Day Four >>> Suzy Idley

From the end of the earth I will cry to You, When my heart is overwhelmed; Lead me to the rock that is higher than I. –Psalm 61:2 NKJV

I would have lost heart, unless I had believed that I would see the goodness of the LORD in the land of the living. –Psalm 27:13 NKJV

You know your struggle with infertility has lasted a long time when your husband starts to become emotional about it, as well. When we got married, my plan was to wait about three years to start a family. He definitely was not ready at that mark. However, had we known we would be 10 years into marriage and still without children, we probably wouldn't have balked at the baby gifts his mother insisted on buying from almost the time we tied the knot.

Just this week, as we left yet another gathering of younger friends who now all have children, my husband became unexpectedly emotional. He didn't cry, but he expressed his opinion that he didn't know how much longer he could sit on the sidelines of fatherhood and watch.

I can't count how many tears I've cried over my struggle with childlessness. Feelings of loss flood me at the oddest times, and I become overwhelmed. It's been said infertility is like grieving a death every month. I don't know of a better way to express my feelings than to borrow that thought.

Those with a mother's heart and empty hands like mine are the only ones who could possibly know what that kind of grief feels like. Or, are they? God gets it, too, and I serve He will truly take my overwhelmed heart, and, in the words of David, "*lead me to the rock that is higher than I.*" –Psalm 61:2

Sweet sisters, I don't know where your journey toward motherhood will lead, whether to a house full of babies or to a lifetime of barrenness, but I do know God is in control of it all, and His plan is better than ours.

If I could give you one promise from His Word to hold onto, it would be this one from Psalm 27:13: *I would have lost heart, unless I had believed that I would see the goodness of the LORD in the land of the living.* You will see His good promise, my sister, and you will see it here on earth, not just in heaven. Your husband will see it, too. Let's not lose heart while we wait. Instead, let's surround ourselves with community and witness God's love together.

Lord, I know You are my rock and I am so thankful! Help me be a rock for others in need. I am here and ready to surround those around me with Your love. Amen.

Community Day Five >>> Ali Forrest

This is my commandment, that you love one another as I have loved you. Greater love has no one than this that someone lay down his life for his friends. —John 15:12-13 ESV

Today's verse is about *community*. Love others, and let others love you. *This.* This is something we can do. We can let people in, and we can be there for others.

You don't have to pour out your story to a stranger in the grocery store line or the waiter taking your order at a restaurant. But, lean on your people, and do not feel like you have to walk this journey alone. You are not alone. Let those words sink in, sweet friend: You are *not alone.* Even when you don't know a single person going through this season, you have a silent sisterhood rooting for you, praying for you and understanding exactly what you are experiencing.

Think about it, and when you are ready, break the chains of your fears – whatever they might be – and seek camaraderie within your own arsenal of close friends and family. Sharing your story with them can result in a monumental change within your life. What if that friend you think has the perfect life instead has her own silent suffering and needs a friend to help her get through it? Maybe she feels just as trapped as you.

Let's open up about our shame, fear and embarrassment. At the very least, surrender all your vulnerabilities to God. Just don't feel like you have to be silenced in your story.

This is my commandment, that you love one another as I have loved you. Greater love has no one than this that someone lay down his life for his friends. —John 15:13

Find encouragement in these words to open up and rally your own troops as you go through infertility. Support others in their battles. Do it with abundant love, just as our great God loves us.

Opening our imaginary gates is scary and hard. Hiding behind them is easy. But opening the gates? It lets you live authentically. We don't have to be alone in our fight. Let's let each other in.

Father, help us to build a thriving community that allows us to celebrate one another, our unique stories and our faith in You.

Rooted In Joy

Rejoice in the Lord always. I will say it again: Rejoice! –Philippians 4:4 NIV

Writing about joy in relation to infertility was the hardest part of putting this book together. Yet, somehow, I felt like it was one of the most important topics.

The thing is, whatever the situation, I'm encouraging you to find a place of abundant joy! We praise a God who created the earth and can make mountains move. Believe that He WANTS to see you happy, just as an earthly father wants to see his daughter happy. You, my friend, are a royal daughter of Christ. That is a huge reason to be joyful every day!

Though you have not seen him, you love him; and even though you do not see him now, you believe in him and are filled with an inexpressible and glorious joy, for you are receiving the end result of your faith, the salvation of your souls. –1 Peter 1:8-9 NIV

Joy Day One >>> Chelsea Ritchie

Dear brothers and sisters, when troubles of any kind come your way, consider it an opportunity for great joy. –James 1:2 NLT

This verse fills me with conviction every single day. James said "when" – not "if" – which means we should expect there to be times and seasons in our lives for trials to hit. Maybe you are reading this book today because you feel isolated as you deal with infertility. Maybe you're craving to add to your family. Perhaps you've faced another miscarriage or failed cycle. Whatever it is, it's easy to tuck those emotions away and feel abandoned by God. Be encouraged to know that while troubles *do* come, it's not *just you* dealing with them.

Now the good stuff – *consider your troubles an opportunity for great joy.* "Consider" means to think about something carefully. This means we have to pause and intentionally reflect on our troubles; you know, the ones we hate and want to push away forever. Yes; those ones. We are supposed to think about them as an *opportunity* for great joy. Hang on; rewind.

Opportunity? Um, if you are anything like me, infertility doesn't feel like an opportunity. Worrying about paying the medical bills, dealing with a bad test result, facing another big fat negative … no, those aren't opportunities, are they? Yet, the very definition of opportunity says we are given a set of circumstances – in our case, infertility troubles – that make it possible to do something. That something? It's to have great joy.

Whoa, James. Calm down here. We are on *verse 2 of the first chapter*, and you are telling us that the suckiest, hardest and most taxing seasons of our life are ones we are supposed to reflect on and use as a chance for joy? And not just joy, but GREAT joy?

God's trying to tell us something here.

If we continue reading James, we learn so much about *where* we get this joy from and *how* it helps us grow. We develop endurance, which leads to us becoming more complete. We grow into a person who knows to ask for wisdom and understands He will provide it to us with love. We grow, and it's that cycle that makes great joy a real possibility. I have learned trials can either make us bitter and angry or they can help us blossom into women with character that comes only from God.

I would much rather live a life that uses my hardships as opportunities to fill me with GREAT joy. For me, great joy has to be intentional. It doesn't just happen. We have to work at it by spending time with God and asking Him to show us virtues about His own character that He wants to develop in us. We have to pray and talk with Him so we can build a relationship of trust. It's then I see how He is working and trust Him despite the hard "opportunities" that come my way. We have to consider our attitudes and responses when faced with a challenge – would they look like great joy or would they look like a toddler tantrum?

These seasons of development, despite how truly painful and heartbreaking they are, really can be beautiful.

So friends, where in your life do you need a shift in perspective? Are you considering your troubles as opportunities? Are you developing great joy? Are you opening up to someone about the season of infertility you are in? I know God doesn't want our pain to be in vain. Let's use it for His glory and be filled with great joy.

Christ, write the words of James 1:2 on my heart so I never forget them. All opportunities are a chance for great joy! How amazing, how awesome! Amen.

Joy Day Two >>> Brittany Trentham

So to keep me from becoming conceited because of the surpassing greatness of the revelations, a thorn was given to me in the flesh, a messenger of Satan to harass me, to keep me from becoming conceited. Three times I pleaded with the Lord about this, that it should leave me. But he said to me, "My grace is sufficient for you, for my power is made perfect in weakness." Therefore I will boast all the more gladly of my weakness, so that the power of Christ may rest upon me. For the sake of Christ, then, I am content with weaknesses, insults, hardships, persecutions, and calamities. For when I am weak, then I am strong. –2 Corinthians 12:7-10

National Infertility Awareness Week is in April. Five years ago, I would have never known that. Infertility isn't something that is talked about; however, more people are beginning to share their stories. Those of us who suffer from infertility typically sit in silence and shoulder the pain, but through it all, I am thankful for infertility. So, you must be thinking, *This girl has gone off her rocker. Why in the world would she be thankful for infertility?!*

Don't get me wrong here … it hurts. It still hurts – everyday. Without my journey, I wouldn't have connected to some really great women who are also going through infertility. I wouldn't be able to relate or to empathize with their struggles. Infertility is much more common now than many realize. There is no reason for couples to suffer in silence anymore! More than anything, infertility brought me my son.

Without experiencing infertility, we probably wouldn't have pursued adoption so soon. We always wanted to adopt, but I thought it would happen after our biological children. God had different plans, and I'm so thankful He did! Our baby boy is exactly the child we were meant to have. My husband and I have also been brought closer together through infertility.

We have had to deal with emotional, physical, spiritual and financial situations that many couples our age aren't burdened with. Through this, we have learned to lean on one another, and we have grown closer though the process. Would I wish infertility on anyone? Heavens, no. Do I enjoy infertility? Not at all. Am I thankful for the journey God has me on and the sweet blessings He brings? Absolutely!

My infertility reminds me of when Paul talks about the thorn in his flesh in 2 Corinthians. We have no idea what this thorn is, but Paul asks God to remove it several times, yet He never does. We don't know why, but we know it kept Paul humble.

I don't know why God has allowed me to suffer from infertility. I pray He will take this burden from me. If He doesn't, I will praise Him. If He does, I will praise Him! Sometimes things happen that we don't like, but we must always remember God has a plan. I know it is hard to be happy and thankful in the midst of infertility! However, God does have a perfect plan for each of us.

Father, thank you for my infertility! The blessings and lessons this trial has brought straightened me, my faith, and my compassion. Let my story shine hope on the girls in need of positive stories today.

Joy Day Three >>> Amanda Morrison

Delight yourself in the Lord, and he will give you the desires of your heart. —
Psalm 37:4 ESV

Today's verse from Psalm 37:4 is full of hope. *Delight yourself in the Lord, and he will give you the desires of your heart.* The desire of my heart is for a family. We probably have that in common, don't we? Until that time comes, I will continue to have faith, hope and joy, which life is abundant in. I'll give you three reasons why.

First, my husband and I recently started a new journey. We are joyfully awaiting our first (and hopefully!) permanent placement of a foster-to-adopt child.

Second, I will never forget the journey I've been on and the alternate routes I've been given. It wasn't my plan, but it has been God's plan all along. I still struggle and wonder how my husband and I will make foster-to-adopt work. How will I ever fully accept this is the plan for my life? Yet, with faith, I now know I can do all things through Christ who gives me strength!

Third, I hope my story and how it has unfolded will help another struggling woman find her voice along the path of infertility! On our latest adventure, I have met some amazing women already in my shoes. Without their stories, I'm sure the decisions that come with pursuing this path would have been much more difficult!

Sure, I am hopeful every day that God sends us a biological child or children, but I also pray we are sent the children He wants us to have. That is my daily prayer. Well, that and to have more faith. We could all use more of that, couldn't we?

The truth is, I would relive my infertility journey all over again, because while I wait for the desires of my heart to be fulfilled, I have gained so much along the way.

I have learned to love myself and to trust. I have learned to have a little more faith. All I can do is hope for the best and appreciate the petite joys and tiny blessings along the way, like the quiet evening trail rides on our beloved horses with my husband and the notes of encouragement from our family and friends.

Love what God has currently given you, while joyfully waiting to see what He has in store for you. More importantly, never lose hope. He hears what your heart wants. Believe it.

Father, as I wait for my heart's desires to be fulfilled, I will praise You and put my hope in Your faithfulness! Amen.

Joy Day Four >>> Ali Forrest

Sing and make music from your heart to the Lord. –Ephesians 5:19 NIV

I'll tell you; what a great verse! *Sing and make music from your heart to the Lord.* Even if you don't feel like praising God, do it anyway. How is that for tough love? Hear me out. You know those days when you binge-watch Netflix and the more you couch potato it up, the more sluggish you feel? Praising God has a similar, yet exceedingly more positive effect. Joyful thoughts lead to joyful attitudes.

Remind yourself right now that each waking day is an opportunity to praise and serve our God in ALL we do. It can't just be wishful thinking; it requires effort. And, while we're focusing on every opportunity in each moment, let's sing and make music from our hearts to the Lord, just as this Ephesians verse suggests. Let's adorn Him with praise and thanks. Yes!

When I was finally in a place without so much bitterness and hurt, I opened my heart, my eyes and my ears to a life with joy. It is at the intersection of gratitude and choice where my infertility story changed. Sure, I wasn't a mom yet, but I was finally able to start seeing life in Technicolor.

Of course, there are still rough days and moments when I am caught off-guard with a wave of grief, but I have come to appreciate my infertility journey and the lessons I have learned.

I can truly say I am a stronger woman. Infertility didn't kill me. It made me an empathetic person. It made me the type of woman who chooses to build others up. It made me have faith-filled stories of infertility, adoption, foster care and loss. It shaped who I am, and I like who I have become.

Joy comes in many forms, big and small. Celebrate them all, and cloak yourself in happiness. Maybe I needed infertility to get me where I am today, but I am joyful. Friend, wherever you are today, seek joy. Infertility impacts your life forever; let the impact have a joyous effect. It might just change your whole world.

Today is a fresh start, Lord, and I want to make it a day filled with joy! Open my eyes to the blessings that surround my life and the world around me. Amen.

Joy Day Five >>> Rachel Hayden

Now I want you to know, brothers, that what has happened to me has really served to advance the gospel. As a result, it has become clear throughout the whole palace guard and to everyone else that I am in chains for Christ. Because of my chains, most of the brothers in the Lord have been encouraged to speak the word of God more courageously and fearlessly. –Philippians 1:12-14 ESV

I had been meeting with a group of fellow women for more than a year. Together, we read the Bible and shared prayers. However, I kept my infertility a secret because I had it all planned out. I would tell them about my struggles once I had finished this chapter of my life.

The picture was clear in my head. On that future day, I wouldn't have that little, aching twinge when my friends walked in carrying diaper bags on their way to drop off their littlest ones in the nursery. Why? Because it would be *the* day!

My testimony would bring everyone tears of joy as I recounted my story of how I waited and prayed for more than five, long years for this pregnancy. I would praise God and speak with wisdom as one does when they can look back on a long struggle with perspective.

Something shifted before I got to *the* day. What I came to realize is for this struggle to have purpose, for God to be glorified at all times, I needed to invite others into my pain. I began by sharing my current struggle with those in my Bible study. My friends' prayers helped me see how these chains of infertility could serve as a platform, a platform to speak love and joy into others' lives that I would never have if I wasn't deeply entrenched, myself.

That realization allowed God to open my eyes to others having similar struggles, and I have felt blessed to be able to pray with them, to discuss doctor appointments, to just listen. My introverted personality has made this new platform a scary one to walk on, but seeing God's hand at work gives me such confidence. This strength of God was most clearly displayed when He gave me the idea to bring roses with me to the office of my fertility doctor as a little way to bring joy to others.

On the day of my appointment, I prayed as I waited for the doctor, the bag of roses with notes of encouragement and Scripture tied to their stems beside me. I had no way of knowing if I had brought enough roses. As I finished up with the doctor and opened the door to the waiting room, I saw women sitting there in silence, looking at the ground or at magazines. I awkwardly walked to the middle of the room and feebly gained their attention, stammering something I can't recall.

As I walked around the perimeter of the room, passing out single roses, I soon had passed out all but one. As I turned to open the door to leave, I met one last woman entering the office and offered her the remaining rose and note. God had brought just the right amount of people to the clinic that day for me to be able to distribute hope, love and joy.

In the above verse from Philippians, Paul is writing from his jail cell as one who understands the purpose within his pain. Instead of becoming bitter toward the injustice of his chains as others walked free, he used this new platform to reach "the whole palace guard and to everyone else" with a gospel of hope. Think of how much more impact this made on those who listened to his message when they saw his chains.

May we see our struggles as a unique way to spread God's message of joy, hope and love to those on a similar journey.

Father, in You we find the best joy! Help me to seek You in both my trials and my triumphs. May I always look for opportunities to spread your holy, hopeful message. Amen.

Anger in the Heart

One of my favorite lines in this whole devotional book comes from Jayme's devotional in this section. *Where we see holes, God sees opportunity.* Whoa, girls! That is good stuff. Speaking from my own experience, I have seen many holes in my quest to motherhood. At times, I have never known such angry, raw emotion.

The last thing I want to do is turn to faith in those angry moments. After all, it's much easier to blame God for creating the circumstances surrounding the pain and the holes. Yet, that is where He sees opportunity. Let's turn our anger into opportunity, too, by becoming rooted once again in His Word. Always.

Father, we storm the heavens in prayer, asking You to shine light on those with angry hearts. Please bring peace and joy to all those in need so we can have softened hearts to serve You.

Anger Day One >>> Valentina Wysocki-Hall

In the beginning You laid the foundations of the earth, and the heavens are the work of Your hands. They will perish, but You remain; they will all wear out like a garment. Like clothing You will change them and they will be discarded. But You remain the same, and Your years will never end. —Psalm 102:25-27 NIV

The inexactitude of words, for me, is nowhere more apparent than in a conversation surrounding infertility. Cliché phrases both received and offered fall superficially on the growling, gnawing beast that is Polycystic Ovarian Syndrome and an empty womb. It feels like a script, honestly – your questions and my answers: "Yes, I would love to have children." "No, we hadn't heard about the latest diet." "That worked for your daughter? We can try that, too."

What I can't quite ever get across is that it is not sadness I contend with, but hollowness. Despite how fragile I feel, there is hope as thin and intricate as lace attaching itself to the walls of my empty spaces. Some days, this hope holds strong. Other days, it is nothing more than a whisper. I could tell you, oh, questioner of our family, about the hatred I have for pregnancy tests with single lines, false symptoms and those moments when I am doubled over without breath because I had forgotten and then remembered. I could tell you of the ache that radiates down my arms and into my stomach during those moments.

But all that might be too intimate for our little conversation, so instead, I will tell you it is hard and hope the silence explains the rest. It is easy for me to get lost in the ambiguity and to feel not only alone, but personally wronged by well-intentioned acquaintances, fertile sisters and God, Himself. A large rock of self-pity lands in front of me, and it becomes hard to see around. I become bitter, unkind and narrow-focused. The world drops away, devalued to nothing when weighed against my desperate need for someone or something to give my ovaries the jump-start they need.

And don't think You can escape from this measuring stick, Lord! Oh, no. In fact, Maker of All Things, You have some questions to answer. How is it You embellish the sky with billions of stars, yet I am still left without a child? How is it that the sparrow is forever within Your watch, but my heart's desire seems to go unnoticed? Don't You see me? Can't You hear me? Don't You love me?

Woven into those words of fear and pain is a lament echoing the psalms of the prophets. This lament draws me out of myself and pulls my eyes upward, where I see God's face for the first time in a long time. And there, I am reminded once again of the things in my life that do not fade. I see again the God who does not change.

To catch sight of our great God, who enduringly loves, effectively humbles me and unravels my sense of self-absorption. My pain becomes attached to the greater ache of the universe to be made like new in the work of Jesus, and my anger falls aside in the face of beauty that looks like promises given and kept. Even among the inexact words and aches, like a beating drum, I feel the words, "but You remain," echo among the hollowness.

But You remain. From this sprouts the simple prayer, "Abba, in my grief, I will turn away. Daddy, in Your grace, please don't let me go."

Lord, in anger and pain, I lift my prayers to You. I know You hear me and won't abandon me. Please let me feel Your presence on the days I need You most. Amen.

Anger Day Two >>> Jayme Wurtenberger

In this you rejoice, though now for a little while, if necessary, you have been grieved by various trials, so that the tested genuineness of your faith—more precious than gold that perishes though it is tested by fire—may be found to result in praise and glory and honor at the revelation of Jesus Christ. –1 Peter 1:6-8 ESV

My story is not over. For all I know, it could just be beginning. Regardless if this is chapter one or chapter 29, I'm thankful to have found light in this darkness. When I noticed I was beginning to feel unhealthy bitterness toward birth announcements and other babies, I knew I would lose the battle with myself if I began to crumble rather than find joy in other people's happiness.

As soon as I acknowledged those ugly feelings, I began to teach myself how to deal with them. The energy you put out is the energy you receive, and my stubborn self knew I was not going to accept negativity heading in my direction. I learned to recognize that pain and tell myself the same thing every time I felt the initial *woe is me* feeling:

It's okay to be sad during infertility. But it is not okay to feel defeated by others' blessings. This is not about you; it is nothing personal. It's about timing and trust. Trust in His timing. Be thankful for their blessing, as you will want them to celebrate with you when your blessing comes.

And just like that, I began to feel their happiness before my pain. Of course, I still want to throw my phone across the room sometimes when I'm perusing Facebook and feel caught off-guard, but that's normal (I think). And yes, sometimes I still roll my eyes when I find myself on the receiving end of a brag session about someone's kid.

I suppose a large part of this epiphany is God's grace and knowing the weaker I am, the stronger He is. I smile when I think about how weak I must have been at the beginning of this journey. Where I saw holes, God saw nothing but opportunity. Learning how to control my feelings and knowing it is mind over matter has become a light that has found its way through the darkness. It is one more way I know God's timing is perfect.

Father, I want to be the strongest woman possible for that child of mine who will look up to me someday. Today, I draw strength from You, my rock. Amen.

Anger Day Three >>> Meredith Erickson

Has the Lord rejected me forever? Will he never be kind to me? Is his unfailing love gone forever? Have his promises permanently failed? Has God forgotten to be gracious? Has he slammed the door on his compassion? –Psalm 77:7-9 NLT

When I first started opening up to people about my infertility, my "I-can't-seem-to-get-pregnant-but-God-is-faithful-and-good" confession would oftentimes be met with, "That must be so hard. It's okay to be angry with God. You don't have to always 'be okay' about it. Be mad!" I struggled with this. A lot.

I lamented this excerpt from Psalm 77 to the Lord in frustration and anger, but was this really what He wanted from me? Is anger a Godly response to the pain and frustration of infertility? There are two types of anger in the Bible – righteous anger and unrighteous anger – and understanding the difference between the two is important. God's righteous anger in the Bible is His love of justice and hatred of evil, such as His anger toward the Israelites during their seasons of idol worship and rebellion. Jesus demonstrates righteous anger, as well, in Mark 11:15-17 when He throws the money-changers out of the temple for using it as a place to buy and sell animals for sacrifices instead of prayer. So today, we might feel righteous anger when we are reminded of the many injustices in the world.

You might say, "My infertility is obviously an injustice!" but first, let's make sure we understand unrighteous anger. Unrighteous anger is selfish. Its concern is to protect or promote *oneself*, which is the direct opposite intention of its righteous counterpart. In fact, unrighteous anger in the Bible is almost always accompanied by jealousy. Proverbs 14:29-30 says, *"People with understanding control their anger; a hot temper shows great foolishness. A peaceful heart leads to a healthy body; jealousy is like cancer in the bones."*

If jealousy is the root of our anger, then I think we will be hard-pressed to identify it as righteous and justified in the eyes of God. So, what do we do? How do we work through the unrighteous anger we feel?

If our anger is triggered by jealousy, then we must first work through our covetous attitudes toward the pregnant women and mothers in our lives. If we confess these feelings of jealousy to the Lord and ask for His forgiveness (over and over again), if we relish in His love for us, and if we read His Word and are reminded of the countless ways He showed His faithfulness to His children – *then*, we will experience a peace that surpasses all understanding. The anger will dissipate, our hearts will be still, and *that* is exactly where the Lord wants us to be.

Heavenly Father, I confess I sometimes lose sight of the story You have written for me and instead covet the story You have written for others. Thank You for Your forgiving heart and for gently reminding me Your way is best. Help me seek the comfort of Your Word and Your love for me in this trying season of my life. In Your righteous and holy name, Amen.

Anger Day Four >>> Melissa Forster

You intended to harm me, but God intended it for good to accomplish what is now being done, the saving of many lives. –Genesis 50:20 NIV

We tried for three years before finding out I was pregnant. If I am being honest, I had waited my entire life for that positive test and couldn't stop smiling. The smile was short-lived, however, as my world was rocked by two little words: ectopic pregnancy. I don't think I will ever forget the look on my husband's face when the doctors said I couldn't leave the hospital. I had to have surgery that afternoon to save my life. I hope to never see fear like that on his face again.

For the next several months after surgery, I felt confused and angry. Why did we have to wait three years to get pregnant only to lose the baby? Why did we have to walk this road? Why did we have to experience such heartbreak? I felt broken and lost.

I wonder if that's how Joseph felt as he sat in jail in Genesis. Because his brothers were jealous of his strong relationship with his father, they sold Joseph into slavery. He was later thrown in jail, again from others' jealousy. How could that be part of God's plan? Was his purpose really to waste away in jail? Where was God? Had He forsaken him? I am sure Joseph spent at least several days feeling confused, broken, angry and lost.

However, through a series of events, Joseph eventually won the respect of the king, and his brothers ultimately begged for his forgiveness. In Genesis 50:20, Joseph said something that continues to rock my world. He said, *"You intended to harm me, but God intended it for good to accomplish what is now being done, the saving of many lives."* Joseph forgave his brothers and praised God for putting him in a place to change history.

An ectopic pregnancy almost destroyed me. It could have taken my life or stole my faith, but God taught me so many lessons through that loss. Not once did God turn His back on me.

The day after we found out I was pregnant, we called our families to tell them we were expecting. My mother-in-law started praying for "baby Trudy" right away. We laughed when she told us that name, but I am forever grateful for that "silly" name. I carried baby Trudy for exactly six weeks.

The week we lost her, my in-laws celebrated their 40th wedding anniversary. They had been trying to plan a vacation for months, but nothing seemed to come together. My first memory after waking up from surgery is my mother-in-law holding my hand, stating, "God knew we needed to be here."

God never turned His back on us. He provided a support system during the darkest days and guided the doctor's hands so surgery and recovery went well.

It has been two years since we lost baby Trudy. I have learned God is still good in the bad parts of life and that the sun shines after the storm. I have learned God is faithful, and His grace is enough for each day. I have learned what it means for God to be our refuge in times of trouble. My perspective has changed, and I am more thankful for the little blessings in life. The loss brought my husband and me closer together, and I've been able to bring hope into other people's lives because I understand the heartbreak loss brings.

Baby Trudy made me a mommy, but most of all, she changed my life and the lives of many.

I may not always understand the why behind what happens in my life, but Father, let me turn my anger into joy and let my pain be used for good. Amen.

Anger Day Five >>> Melanie Dafler

For I am sure that neither death nor life, nor angels nor rulers, nor things present nor things to come, nor powers, nor height nor depth, nor anything else in all creation, will be able to separate us from the love of God in Christ Jesus our Lord. –Romans 8:38-39 ESV

Did you catch that? NOTHING in all of creation can separate you from the love of God. Not even infertility. But for me, it came close. I'll never forget the day we found out my husband had azoospermia, or wasn't producing sperm. For days immediately following our diagnosis, I remember as though a thick, dreary fog had fallen over my entire life, but one memory in particular stands out.

It was a phone call I made to my good friend and spiritual mentor, Lynn — I called her my "mom away from mom." After telling her the bad news, she made me promise that no matter what, my husband and I wouldn't turn away from God, that we wouldn't stop praying, worshipping, reading God's Word or loving Jesus. It wasn't what I wanted to hear. I still get emotional every time I recall our conversation because I had known back then she was right, but I had already felt my heart hardening against God because of our diagnosis.

The next weeks and months, I reluctantly continued heeding her advice, but my heart ached so much that it was impossible to get through a church service without bawling my eyes out. I tried to tell God how much this hurt, but it felt like He wasn't listening. I needed someone to direct my anger toward, and He made the perfect target.

Slowly, I began to pray not only for a child, but for God to heal my heart. I prayed for wisdom, clarity and for Him to help us see opportunities before us. Eventually, my grief subsided. At times, I "relapsed," but the fog did eventually clear and healing began to occur, both spiritually and physically.

I don't know where you are in this infertility journey, but I do know this – God does not desire for you to be apart from Him for any reason. Praise God that He is true. No matter how much we want to disassociate our hearts with His in times of anger, the love He has for us through His Son is infinitely stronger than our fickle love for Him.

Abide in the hope God always opens His arms to us, and nothing – not even infertility – can separate us from His love.

Lessons from Pain

We live in a world where pain, injustice and failure run rampant. Have heart, dear friends, knowing these feelings are fruits of the enemy. There is power in Jesus' name, and His Word paints a story of hope and love even amidst the pain and trials. Turn toward Him, not away from Him, in your time of suffering.

The women writing this section get you. They've been there. They *are* there. My prayer for you today is that their words breathe fresh life, purpose and perspective into your mind, heart and soul.

Father, take away the pain of all women struggling to conceive and become mothers, whatever their methods. Give them light enough to know the next step to take, and be with us, always. For even during our turbulence, we thank You for Your many blessings and enduring love. Amen.

Pain Day One >>> Caroline Harries

...and if children, then heirs—heirs of God and fellow heirs with Christ, provided we suffer with him in order that we may also be glorified with him. For I consider that the sufferings of this present time are not worth comparing with the glory that is to be revealed to us. —Romans 8: 17-18 ESV

Lately, I can't stop reading Romans 8. I highly recommend reading it if you haven't. I could probably share every verse in the whole chapter, but today, let's revisit verses 17-18.

It is inevitable we will face trials in our lives. We will suffer. But Paul, who experienced way more suffering than any of us have ever seen, points out in verse 18 that the **suffering we will face doesn't even compare to the glory and joy that is coming.** Nothing we face here on earth compares to the price Jesus paid to save us and the joy that comes when we enter heaven. But even before that day, a life surrendered to Him results in His power, presence and gifts that help us and provide victories in our present struggles and trials.

When we face a trial, we must weigh what we are going through against our glory in knowing Jesus more completely because of our suffering, as well as against our glory in heaven. During my recent (triathlon) race, I wanted to quit. I didn't think I could make it, but the feeling I got crossing the finish line totally outweighed the pain and discouragement from the race. Our hardships here on earth are the same. Even though we can't see it now, we can trust **the glory revealed will be worth it.**

Whatever you are facing, know the pain is never too great and the trial never too big. Jesus made the ultimate sacrifice for us to live, and even though there will still be trials, **the suffering we go through for Christ while here on earth isn't for naught.** Until your day of triumph, seek His face in every struggle you encounter. His glory will be present in your life through His victorious and overcoming power.

Lord, nothing is impossible for You! I know You don't promise a life without pain, trials or tribulations, but thank You for Your unwavering love as I walk through my valleys. Amen.

Pain Day Two >>> Diana Montes

And when he was entered into a ship, his disciples followed him. And, behold, there arose a great tempest in the sea, insomuch that the ship was covered with the waves: but he was asleep. And his disciples came to him, and awoke him, saying, Lord, save us: we perish. And he saith unto them, Why are ye fearful, O ye of little faith? Then he arose, and rebuked the winds and the sea; and there was a great calm. But the men marveled, saying, What manner of man is this, that even the winds and the sea obey him! –
Matthew 8:23-27 KJV

A few months ago, I found myself sitting in my car, crying. I felt alone and hopeless because I was afraid becoming a mother was an unreachable goal. Anger began to set in, and I found myself thinking, *What's the point of holding onto the promise of a child who may never come?* The fear of those thoughts becoming reality was overwhelming.

It was as if I was in the middle of a raging sea while waves crashed all around me, engulfing me with doubt and fear. The storm was too strong. I was losing hold of my faith and the promises made to me. My strength was gone, and my heart was broken. As I sat there, God in His mercy began to speak to me through a song on Christian radio. The words confirmed He knew my pain and would be there to get me through.

In that moment, God's overwhelming presence and love began to pour over me, and my pain turned into joy. Once again, God had kept His promise to never leave nor forsake me. The doubt and fear began to fade away. God had come to my rescue, calming the storm inside, speaking words of faith and reassuring me: "My child; I am with you. Your Father is here! You will be ok."

As I remember that moment, I think of Matthew 8:23-27. These men had walked with Jesus daily and witnessed many miracles of healing and deliverance; yet when the storm came, they let fear blind their trust in Jesus. Was Jesus going to let them drown in that storm? Of course not! Jesus had been in control the entire time! When you feel unable to continue, remember that the Jesus who saved the disciples is the same Jesus who carries us through our own storms.

We might think He sleeps at times and may even feel forgotten, but have faith God is in control of every situation. His timing is always perfect! God knows the pain and disappointment we feel every time we see a negative pregnancy test or when the life growing inside our womb ends abruptly. He knows when an infertility treatment fails yet again. When our marriage suffers. When we see the pain in our husband's eyes. When our arms feel empty and our hearts ache.

God knows the pain we feel, and He's always ready to rebuke the wind and crashing waves and bring peace and reassurance. He is faithful, and His promises are true. When Jesus left this earth, He gave us His Holy Spirit to comfort and be with us always. Take time today to write a list of promises God has made you, and proclaim them every day!

Father, today we surrender all of our fears and doubts. We ask that You take control of the storm we are facing. Strengthen our faith, and let us hold tight to Your promises. In Jesus' name. Amen.

Pain Day Three >>> *Valerie Rohde*

...as your days, so shall your strength be. –Deuteronomy 33:25 ESV

I don't remember when I came across this scripture, but it continues to speak to me as a reminder of who God is when it comes to infertility, pregnancy loss, and now, my successful pregnancies and births.

Despite any and all earthly circumstances, I am called to follow Him and put Him first. As Proverbs 4:23 says: *"Above all else, guard my heart, for everything you do flows from it."* This means not getting so wrapped up in the "trying to conceive stuff" that has the potential to overwhelm your mind and, some days, consume almost every thought. It means clinging to His Word and *abiding* in Him – the One who offers life, safety, peace, comfort, strength and faithfulness – no matter what happens in this world.

It takes me back to the story of David and Goliath from 1 Samuel 17 and reminds me we are called to be obedient to His authority in our lives. There is a difference between facing giants and finishing them. 1 Samuel 17:37 gives us an example of what we can do as we approach our own goliaths. In the story, David recounts ways the Lord delivered him in the past. Long before David ever put a rock in his sling to defeat Goliath, he put an entry in his journal declaring the work of God in his past.

God's activity in our past serves as a reminder of how closely He is walking with us and caring for us today. He has not forgotten us, and He cares about every hair on our heads. Look back, sweet friend, at what goliaths God has overcome in years past. He knew you and was working on your behalf before you even knew Him. When facing the "giants" of infertility, remember what God has done for you and all He can and will do for you yet.

When those giants are screaming all around you, taking over every thought in your head, put them to silence. Seek God in the still, quiet moments of your day, as well as in your frustrations. Remember, although giants scream, God is quiet because He is near you. He has life to give you in every moment you think you can barely go on. And, He doesn't want you to face your giants alone; He wants you to put them to rest, to finish them and to finish well.

Take time each day to physically write out what God has done for you in the past so you can remember Him today. Doing so will help you see the good work He is performing in and through you. When you realize God is all you have, you'll come to understand He is all you need. You are not alone. Others have walked in your footsteps, and God will provide the perfect amount of strength according to what your day demands.

Father, just as David fought his giant, help me to fight my own battles. Help me to remember that You are near and that I can persevere. I turn to you and ask for renewed strength and faith, for You are my everything. Amen.

Pain Day Four >>> Ferial Trammel

Therefore let those who suffer according to God's will entrust their souls to a faithful Creator while doing good. —1 Peter 4:19 ESV

Suffering. *Merriam-Webster Dictionary* defines suffering as pain that is caused by injury, illness, loss, etc. – physical, mental or emotional pain. It's such a deep word. Recently, I read through 1 Peter, in which the theme of Christian suffering is ongoing. Peter is writing to believers who are undergoing various trials, likely persecution due to their faith. He reminds these people of their identity in Christ and gives very practical encouragement for how to live the life of faith, even and especially through suffering.

Reading through this book made me wonder about suffering. I wanted to be able to take Peter's words to heart and apply them to my life, but first, I needed to determine if I have ever truly suffered. After meditating on these thoughts for a few weeks, I realized we all suffer. Our levels of suffering differ, of course, but we all have experienced and will experience pain. Although I have never felt the pain of, say, poverty and other societal injustices, I do currently feel the pain of infertility.

So, now the question is, what should we do with these pains? The short answer is we can accept Peter's exhortation. 1 Peter 4:19 offers practical and powerful insight into how to approach suffering as a Christian: *Therefore let those who suffer according to God's will entrust their souls to a faithful Creator while doing good.*

Peter is writing specifically to Christians who are suffering under persecution for their faith. However, I believe the exhortation remains true for those of us suffering as a result of the fallen state of human existence – it is calling us to accept and live by Peter's encouragement.

What he is saying is our suffering is not purposeless; it has been ordained by God for His Glory and our good. We need to stop scrabbling around for control. God made us, and He is faithful to us. Don't just wallow in your pain; use your time to do good. BOOM. There it is. Trust God. Do good. Who's with me?

Lord, in my pain, help me to surround the world around with Your good and faithful message. Your love outweighs the pain of infertility. For that, I am full of gratitude.

Pain Day Five >>> Elisha Kearns

Now to him who is able to do far more abundantly than all that we ask or think, according to the power at work within us. —Ephesians 3:20 ESV

But he was pierced for our transgressions; he was crushed for our iniquities; upon him was the chastisement that brought us peace, and with his wounds we are healed. —Isaiah 53:5 ESV

He heals the brokenhearted and binds up their wounds. —Psalm 147:3 ESV

You shall serve the LORD your God, and he will bless your bread and your water, and I will take sickness away from among you. None shall miscarry or be barren in your land; I will fulfill the number of your days. —Exodus 23:25-26 ESV

The rod shattered and jewels went flying across the room as she accidentally dropped her new Elsa wand on the floor. As I sat there in my chair, awaiting her reaction, I held my breath. I wasn't sure if she would cry, throw a fit or both. But, to my surprise, she did neither. Instead, she calmly picked up the pieces and, after examining them and realizing she couldn't fix it, confidently carried them to her "Daddy Dan," knowing he could.

As I silently watched this simple exchange between a father and child, I began to think about how often I cry and throw a fit over the broken pieces in *my* life without first taking them to my heavenly daddy and placing them in His hands so He can fix them. Or, how often I accept life's troubles just because there is nothing "I" can do to fix them. And shamefully, I decided I do this far too often.

But, friend, as I watched her confidently skip away knowing in her heart Daddy Dan would soon fix the wand, I wondered how much easier my life – or rather, our lives – would become if we went to Him with our pain. If we brought Him the shattered pieces of our lives. And, if we gave Him the problems that keep us up at night. What if? The Bible says when we come to Him in faith, He will mend our broken hearts. He will bind up our wounds. He will heal and restore our bodies.

He did it for Hannah in 1 Samuel. She cried out to the Lord in the temple, and after the priest finally ruled out her "ugly cry" wasn't a result of drunkenness, he told her God had heard her prayers. And, not only had He heard them, but He had answered them. So, she left, no longer feeling downcast. She went back to eating. Enjoying her life. Living it knowing she had given her problems to her Father, and He had fixed them. And in the end, He did this not only once with the birth of her first born, Samuel, but five more times. Because, friend, when God does something, He doesn't do it halfway. He goes above and beyond anything we could ever ask, dream or imagine.

So today, let's pick up our broken pieces – the ones we can't repair ourselves – and confidently take them to our heavenly Father. Let's place them in His loving hands and skip away knowing He is ready, willing and able to do what we can't: make our lives whole again.

Lord, I turn to You in my pain. When I am brokenhearted, pained, and hungry, You are the cup that fills me up. You are the one who can satiate, heal, and bless. Amen.

"P" is for Patience

I once saw a funny little saying that went something like this: "Bless me with patience." Not the opportunities to be patient, but actual patience. Can you relate? Infertility feels like a marathon in which endurance is a prerequisite. But, for whatever reason, it's our reality. While running toward our dreams, let us be patient in the wait as God would want us to be.

This section is all about it. I'd wait forever for God's glory, and I'd wait forever for a baby. However long it takes, I'll wait in good company with His Word and a sisterhood of women who get it.

Father, help us to use our season of waiting for Your good and the good of those around us.

Patience Day One >>> Lisa Culver

When Pharaoh finally let the people go, God did not lead them along the main road that runs through Philistine territory, even though that was the shortest route to the Promised Land. God said, 'If the people are faced with a battle, they might change their minds and return to Egypt.' So God led them in a roundabout way through the wilderness toward the Red Sea. —Exodus 13:17-18 NLT

About three years and two states ago, I was talking to God on my way home from work and trying to explain why now was the perfect time to start a family. We had a house with spare bedrooms, vehicles to get us from Point A to Point B, well-paying jobs, close proximity to our families and a wonderful church family. It seemed perfect. What else could we need?

I firmly believe God has a sense of humor, and I'm sure He got a kick out of the fact I thought I had figured something out that He had overlooked! Needless to say, He told me to be patient and that He had a plan. I knew that all along, but it didn't fall within my timeline, so of course I wanted to make sure He saw the logic to my idea; you know, just in case! Around a year later, I was participating in a Beth Moore bible study at my church when I came across this particular verse in Exodus and had one of those "aha" moments!

This scripture showed me that while we think we know the shortest route or easiest plan, God has the big picture in mind. Trust me. He knows what He is doing. The Israelites took the long way around to the Promised Land. While I know this passage isn't directed at my ability to have a family, it stands as a reminder that He is in control and is always looking out for our best interests.

Over the last three years, we've moved away from our home state of Georgia to Florida, and then to Tennessee. I was able to fulfill a lifelong dream of recording a song I wrote (which would have been much less likely to happen if we had already started our family). Lately, I've been praying for opportunities to share my experiences in some capacity. Again, this very book gave me the ability to share my story in a way that would not have been possible had I not still been going down this path.

My prayer for you today is that you remember God really does have a plan for us, even if we don't always know what He has in store along the way. As we continue to patiently wait, He will reveal His will to us, and we will find sweet moments as we travel this roundabout way. Ultimately, our lives are to bring glory to God. If the road we're on is the longer route, we might as well make it worth the wait and faithfully serve Him along the way.

Patience Day Two >>> Rosie Marlatt

Come to me, all you who are weary and burdened, and I will give you rest. –Matthew 11:28 NIV

Our journey started off like most couples. We started dating and quickly knew we wanted to spend the rest of our lives together. We talked about having children throughout our engagement and were so excited to start trying after we tied the knot. Once married, we enjoyed having the first few months to just ourselves before we began trying to start our family. For the next year, I thanked Jesus every day for our future baby. I probably sounded like a broken record. And, every time my cycle came around, I wept.

Needless to say, after a year of trying and lack of success, I decided to make an appointment with my doctor to look into reasons why. Fast forward to my first appointment with a reproductive specialist. The doctor told me I had stage 3 endometriosis, a cyst on my right ovary, a polyp and early signs of diabetes. Wow! I wasn't expecting any of that news! It was devastating, and after going through countless injections, appointments, a laparoscopy and four failed inseminations, we decided it was time to take for IVF. This journey of infertility so far has been long, disheartening and full of disappointment and tears.

But, through many prayers, I grew closer to the Lord. One Bible verse I draw strength from is Matthew 11:28. *Come to me, all you who are weary and burdened, and I will give you rest.* As I have deepened my relationship with Jesus, I have come to understand He is a resting place through all the obstacles this journey has presented me with. When I am weary and burdened, He is my constant respite amidst the chaos. Commit this great verse to your memory. Find peace in His Word.

Although our journey is not yet over, we are one day closer to our next step. We believe Jesus will find a way to bring the finances we need to begin IVF. He has already led so many people to give to our cause, and to give generously. It is a blessing amidst future unknowns. We are so ready to welcome Baby Marlatt into this world!

While we wait, we will do so with continued hope and faith. That is my prayer for you and me both!

Patience Day Three >>> Ashley Kimble

Be still before the Lord and wait patiently for him; fret not yourself over the one who prospers in his way, over the man who carries out evil devices. —Psalm 37:7 ESV

I've never been good at waiting. Patience does not come easily for me. In fact, I only really like waiting if I know what's going to happen next. Ironic, I know. Do you have a hard time with it, too? It seems as if all we do is wait when experiencing infertility. We wait to see if that ovulation stick turns positive. We wait two weeks after each procedure to see if it worked. We wait for test results. We wait for that stick to show two pink, beautiful lines. But we're not always waiting patiently, especially when it comes to infertility.

Be still before the Lord and wait patiently for him; fret not yourself over the one who prospers in his way, over the man who carries out evil devices.

As we travel together along this path of infertility, we must patiently wait for God to answer our prayers. This can be difficult, especially when we see others blessed with babies and big, full families as we sit casting yet another frustrated glance up to the heavens.

But when I take a step back and ask the Lord, "Why? Why not me?" I have to remember He has a plan. A plan for me. It's hard not knowing what it is, but fretting over those who are blessed with children will not bring this plan to fruition any quicker. Instead, He reminds me of how blessed I am.

Impatience can be a silent evil, can it not? I know if I let that silent evil creep further into my daily life, I'm not being a very powerful woman of God. And I know the power is in me. He has given me the strength to wait patiently. Even when it's most difficult, when I only see that one pink line or when I'm fretting about someone else's joy – I must trust in His plan.

Whatever path you're on, whether it relates to infertility or not, you may be fretting, too. But right here, right now, will you trust with me? Let's push aside that silent evil. Let's be still. Let's trust in Him today.

Lord, I trust You! On the days I have a hard time understanding Your plan, guide me back on the right path. Keep my heart and mind focused on what matters most: You. Amen.

Patience Day Four >>> Cassandra Griffo

For everything there is a season, and a time for every matter under heaven. He has made everything beautiful in its time. Also, he has put eternity into man's heart, yet so that he cannot find out what God has done from the beginning to the end. —Ecclesiastes 3:1; 11 ESV

This past spring, my husband and I started a vegetable garden. We went to the hardware store and spent a small fortune on all the things we would need to build a few, raised beds. We created our plan and began laying it out. It was so cool to see the garden come to life!

We knew we had a long wait to endure before we would be able to harvest the fruits of our labor; so, waiting is what we did. Days went by, as did months. Each day, I looked for new growth or progress, but it seemed like I was wasting my time as I watered to no avail.

Then, one day out of nowhere, new shoots – albeit, tiny shoots – started to appear. It was like magic! I knew then the effort we made in tending to the plants day after day would pay off. This whole planting experience made me reflect on my own growth in waiting on the Lord. Throughout all the infertility testing, blood draws, appointments, waiting for results and trying different treatments and medicines, I now know that one day, the Lord will bless us with the child our hearts so desperately ache for.

I always found courage in stories from the Bible. For example, Jesus could have healed Lazarus when he was still alive, yet, He waited to raise him from the dead. Jesus could have given Abraham and Sarah the child they prayed for, yet He waited until Abraham was 100 years old. There are countless examples of how our Father makes people wait. In the waiting, we don't see growth or the purpose for it. But, if we hold onto our faith and cling to the Father, we will begin to see new shoots in our lives start to appear out of nowhere.

My morning ritual with my plants, watering and caring for them, has become so ceremonial to me. It's almost like I'm spending time with the Father, too. With each new leaf or sprout, I give thanks to God for allowing a new season and new growth. Just in the past few weeks, we began harvesting the fruits of our labor. Basil, tomatoes, peppers and so many more tasty veggies are in abundance!

I give thanks to God that I didn't stop watering or nurturing those plants when I first saw nothing. In the same way, I'm thankful the Father doesn't stop working on me and my husband when moments of defeat overcome us or in moments when we want to just give up. I'm thankful today that there is great joy in waiting. And, not only waiting to see the reward, but also experiencing great happiness in forming a deeper bond with our Creator. He is the One who knows all things and does fantastic things for us beyond our imagination.

Psalm 27:4 gives me great joy in saying, "Wait for the LORD; be strong, take heart and WAIT for the LORD."

Father, thanks for the awesome words of Psalm 27:4. Today, I will make it my goal to live them out. I will be strong, take heart, and wait for You with great patience.

Patience Day Five >>> Pier Lefebvre

Let us hold fast the confession of our hope without wavering, for He who promised is faithful. –Hebrews 10:23 ESV

Right now, my husband and I have two girlfriends very close to us who are both expecting children right around the same time. We are thrilled for both of them! Several months ago, I wouldn't have been. I would have been wallowing in my own misery. Why not me? It's not fair!

Then, something happened. Christ broke the stronghold of infertility over our lives. No longer are we remorseful and full of self-pity. Rather, we are fully confident He is going to bless us – and at the very best time – His own.

And, do you know what blessings have been brought about by leaning on Him throughout this trial? By letting Him take the burden of infertility? We have been able to fully enjoy the blessing that is being "just us" – a young (almost not-so) newlywed couple with our furry little rascals along for the ride. We have walked through the grocery store – no longer avoiding the baby aisle like the bubonic plague, but instead, purposefully walking down it KNOWING we will HAVE TO soon enough.

We are planning, in our new home, a nursery for the child we know we will be blessed with. As we have looked at homes and considered places to live, the Holy Spirit put it on my heart that we are to build a nursery in our next home. Being that we are not with child, this is a plan that has taken root in the form of Noah building his ark. The flood (or blessing, in our case!) hasn't arrived yet, but we are PREPARING because we KNOW it WILL.

It is Satan who instills into us doubt, fear, sickness and worry. Allow the kingdom of God into your heart – where there <u>is no doubt, fear, sickness or worry</u>! *...nor will they say, "See here!" or "See there!" For indeed, the kingdom of God is within you.* –Luke 17:21 And here, we chill, waiting on His <u>perfect</u> timing and enjoying His many blessings along the way!

Lord, because of my faith in You, I have no need for worry or doubt!

Living with Loss

A loss is a loss is a loss. There is no one-upping when it comes to miscarriages, failed cycles, failed adoptions or any other loss you have experienced in infertility. They all suck. The brave women sharing their stories in this section have hearts wide open to help other women cope with loss. They shine light on how they saw God's love right smack dab in the middle of the dark days surrounding their loss.

I pray for the women who wrote these devotionals and their desires to help bring purpose in the pain. I pray for women all over the world who have experienced loss as they meander through their infertility journeys. Maybe that woman is you, reading the words on this page right now. As a community, we come together. We see you. We understand you. From a sisterhood of women who get it, know that tomorrow is a new day, and God's love surrounds you at this very moment.

Father, bless the empty wombs and hearts of the women most in need. Let them see Your goodness, and help them recover from their losses.

Loss Day One >>> Kim Gorman

This I recall to my mind, therefore have I hope. It is of the LORD's mercies that we are not consumed, because his compassions fail not. They are new every morning: great is thy faithfulness. The LORD is my portion, saith my soul; therefore will I hope in him. — Lamentations 3:21-24 KJV

Have you ever wondered throughout your journey with infertility if God really does love you and, if so, why He is allowing this painful time in your life to happen? Is this His form of punishment for something you did in your past? I admit I am guilty of thinking both these thoughts along with a myriad of others. My hope is that by the end of this devotional, you will be able to know God is always with you. No matter how many times life may knock you down, He will be there with His outstretched arms of love to pick you back up and fill you with a fresh dose of hope.

My journey with infertility began almost eight years ago when I was diagnosed with stage IV endometriosis. I remember sitting in my doctor's office and being completely clueless about this disease and the impact it would have on my ability to conceive. My husband and I were given a very dismal statistic that stated we would have less than a two percent chance of a natural conception. We were devastated.

Fast forward through multiple surgeries, fertility drugs, shots, too many failed intrauterine insemination attempts to count, and the heartbreaking loss of three precious babies, and this is where our journey finds us today. One of my favorite movie quotes of all time is from *The Notebook* and states, "Science can only go so far, and then comes God." We have found this to be such a very powerful truth. You see, we had done everything humanly possible to try and conceive a baby, outside of in vitro fertilization, without even one successful treatment cycle ... and then came God.

That's the only way I can explain how we have been blessed with our three angel babies, Hannah, Taylor and Grace. I was able to carry both Hannah and Taylor for eight weeks. Two years ago with our third daughter, Grace, I went into preterm labor. It was at only 17 weeks that she was born into the arms of Jesus. God gave us the opportunity to hold our precious baby girl, love on her and see His beautiful creation. Looking back, it still amazes me how God showed such love and beauty throughout the most horrific day of my life.

Although we never had an opportunity to raise our little ones here on this earth, what a wonderful truth to know we have three eternal children waiting for us in Heaven someday! But for now, we are happy resting in the hope we have in God and believing He has a divine plan for us that will be perfectly revealed in His time.

Life is definitely not always rainbows and butterflies. It is tough! It knows how to kick you while you're down and really make it hurt. Then comes God! He loves you. He cares for you. He wants to heal you. All you have to do is cry out to Him! He will take all your brokenness and exchange it with His joy (Psalm 126:5). So, what are you waiting for?

Your compassion does not fail. Bless those enduring loss with these words. It's difficult to remember Your faithful and good ways in the middle of dark times, but you are always near. Hallelujah!

Loss Day Two >>> Jessica Mernin

How long, O Lord? Will you forget me forever? How long will you hide your face from me? How long must I take counsel in my soul and have sorrow in my heart all the day? How long shall my enemy be exalted over me? –Psalm 13:1-2 ESV

These are the questions I find rolling around in my head lately. How long will this sad season last? How many more days before He makes beauty from ashes in my life? How much pain will I have to endure before I get to hold my child?

After seven months of trying and a first, devastating miscarriage and its resulting health complications, I found myself staring in disbelief at a second positive pregnancy test

The sweet, innocent excitement of my first pregnancy did not greet me in the second –I spent the weeks after my positive pregnancy test treading lightly, following all of the doctor's rules, pleading with God and asking that I would get to meet *this* baby. I prayed this baby's heart would beat for 36 more weeks and then 100 years after that. I told God how much I wanted this little one, how much I already loved her or him, and how I so desperately wanted to be a mom and end this waiting period. I explained to God that if I had to say goodbye to another sweet babe, I wouldn't be able to do it. The thought of it brought me to my knees in sadness.

But then, at our nine week appointment, silence. No heartbeat. It felt like my heart sank to the bottom of the ocean. My husband and I grieved, cried, prayed and had angry words for God. We got honest with how we felt and didn't sugarcoat anything. We were ticked, devastated and losing hope.

And that is where I still sit, existing in this in-between season after my second pregnancy loss, before the miracle and before God's restoration in my life. I am living in the valley, an uncomfortable place where I am waiting for answers. Can you relate?

But I'm not alone in the valley, I'm realizing. As I look around, I see so many others carrying their own heavy hearts. I feel more empathy for my single friend who would love to be dating or married. My heart hurts more deeply when I hear the news of a friend's mother in the hospital again. I feel my own dad's job loss. My dear friend's chronic health condition resonates in a new way. I see I'm not the only one struggling, and I'm not the only one needing God and the hope He gives.

The Book of Psalms does that same thing for me, reminding me I am not the only one who hurts and experiences loss. My feelings are validated because it's honorable to bring these emotions to God. He wants me to –

and that brings comfort and meaning to my pain, even though I'd prefer to bypass this season of my life.

Psalm 13 ends with these hopeful words: *But I trust in your unfailing love; my heart rejoices in your salvation. I will sing the Lord's praises, for He has been good to me.*

God is with me, and He is with you, too. He will be faithful. For I know a valley is only a valley; it will not last forever.

In the valleys, Oh Lord, You walk with me. I will remember to thank and praise you today. Today, I will make a list of three things you have done for me on this infertility journey so I can have a concrete reminder of how You are right beside me. Amen.

Loss Day Three >>> Lisa Pawey

The Lord is a stronghold for the oppressed, a stronghold in times of trouble. And those who know Your name put their trust in You, for You, O Lord, have not forsaken those who seek You. —Psalm 9:9-10 ESV

When I was younger, one of my favorite things to do on a Sunday morning was look at the newspaper ads. I always looked forward to the Target ad. At one point, I told my parents I wanted to work for a Target store. God had different plans; I never worked for Target.

To this day, I still enjoy shopping at Target. However, shopping there changed the moment I stood amid the aisles one September. I was expecting a phone call from my OB/GYN's office regarding my hCG level. We had been praying over the last couple days that it would double. Standing within rows of cards, my phone rang. It was the physician's assistant I had seen a few days earlier in the clinic. All I can remember next is being told, "I'm sorry, but the number did not double. It is not a viable pregnancy." I hung up the phone, and it felt like a fog washed over me. I quickly picked up a few things we needed and rushed to get out of the store as tears welled up in my eyes.

Reaching my car, I texted my husband and sobbed on the phone to my mom, who helped me calm down and take a few deep breaths so I could make it home safely. My husband left work early that day to meet me. When he got home, he immediately hugged me, and I cried many tears into his chest as he held me tightly.

In the days ahead, I remember asking myself, how can I continue to **trust** God? We are good people. How come this happened to us? Did God forget how much we prayed for this moment? I am reminded in Psalm 9:9-10 that God was there with us the entire time. He did not abandon us, even though it felt like it. God knew our prayers of wanting to grow our family. Looking back, we now see God was teaching us to put all our faith and trust in Him. My husband and I looked to God as our rock and our strength in the days ahead to get through the difficult moments and grieving and to move toward healing.

Lord, how comforting it is to know You will not forsake me! Today, I say a special prayer for those with a broken spirit. Amen.

Loss Day Four >>> Carrie Slaughter

For I know the plans I have for you," declares the Lord, "plans to prosper you and not to harm you, plans to give you hope and a future. —Jeremiah 29:11 NIV

This has become one of my favorite verses. Since I was a child, I had hope. I always felt things happened for a reason. As an adult, I lost hope for a little while. Somewhere in between battling infertility, divorce, lost friendships and life struggles, it all seemed too much. I never forgot the verse. I never gave up, but my armor sure got thin for a while.

When you're fighting infertility, you do one of two things. You buy stock in ovulation and pregnancy tests, then cry when either or both are negative month after month. Or, you refuse to test. I've done both. I cannot tell you the amount of money I've shelled out in the process. One day, I gave up. I was tired of it. Tired of the pills, tired of the injections, tired of the doctor visits. I just wanted a fish-bowl-sized margarita and Mexican food. However, something kept stopping me. My best friend, in particular, kept bugging me about testing. "Why?" I asked.

After all, it's either negative or will end unsuccessfully. I felt ignorance was bliss. However, one night after work, I thought, *OK; here goes.* Now, I'm aware you shouldn't test at night. hCG is not high then. It may not even show up early on. I peed on the stick, coming back several minutes later to throw it away. It was then I saw two pink lines. I was speechless. After all, according to doctors, odds of this happening were slim.

Well, someone upstairs had a bigger plan. I prayed over that baby for several weeks. As I went to my weekly ultrasounds, I knew it would be a complicated pregnancy. I just prayed for viability. I found hope. I wrote this verse everywhere and held it close to my heart. One night driving home from work, I started spotting. To say I went crazy is an understatement. I knew what this meant. I yelled, cried and called my doctor. I went to the ER and was put on bed rest. The spotting eased up.

A few nights later, it was like a dam broke. I knew what was going on and cried for hours. Given the option to go back to the cold, insensitive ER, or pass my baby at home and see my doctor in the morning, I chose the latter. It's a heartache not many understand. According to most, my baby wasn't even a baby yet. At this stage in my pregnancy, women could technically still choose to abort their babies.

As I sat in the bathroom, I was suddenly reminded of this verse and felt God's presence. This was not the end for me. This was not God's final plan. He did not want to harm me. He has given me hope and a gentle reminder that doctors and modern medicine aren't omniscient. God has the final say in things. As much as my nursing education has taught me, my fate can change in an instant if it is His will. He gives me hope for another day.

Lord, You give me hope for another day! Everyone has their own trials and I just ask that you can help make light of the pain in due time. Thank you for Your mercy and grace through it all. Amen.

Loss Day Five >>> Kassie Hart

He must become greater, I must become less. –John 3:30 NIV

With seven years of marriage under our belts, my husband and I have two sweet blessings who are four and almost two, and three angel babies. We struggled tremendously with infertility. Having visited St. Louis, Missouri weekly to see specialists year after year without any success, we got pregnant only to lose our first blessing a few weeks later.

We conceived our little four-year-old a few months later, but sorrowfully experienced a tubal pregnancy shortly after him. Deciding to try one last time to add another blessing into our lives, we lost our daughter's twin a few weeks after finding out we were pregnant.

Seven years of marriage, two blessings in our lives and three angel babies at just 30 years old. During our infertility struggle, I had a hard time trusting in God and His timing.

I didn't understand why this was happening and why our trials were numerous compared to others. But, now that we feel our family is complete, I understand more each day why these events occurred. Do I still have days I am sad and struggle? Of course! But, I am able to talk with other mothers who may have experienced something similar. Not everyone has the same story, but knowing there is someone to talk to who has also struggled is a huge help.

When we went through infertility, it felt like no one was around, no one was in the same boat as us, no one wanted to listen. We also found out no one talked about it. The more I opened up about our situation, the more I felt relief. I posted our story on social media and had an overwhelming response, including messages from friends who didn't know we struggled so much, or notes from those going through situations who needed to talk. God is using me to help others in a way I did not think was possible. *He must become greater in my life, and I must become less.*

Although I know the pain will never go away, using our losses to help others has given my husband and me a feeling of pride we know only comes from God. Watching our son and daughter play means more to us than anything now, knowing what an extremely huge blessing they are.

Father, turn my pain into a blessing! Let it be used to encourage others. Amen.

Trust Him Always

I am a gigantic fan of reliability. I like sure things, stability and the opposite of everything that starts with an "r" and ends in "isk." I like having my ducks in a row, and I like trustworthy people. During the obstacles of infertility, though, God can sometimes seem, um, untrustworthy.

Oh, but friends, He *is* trustworthy. He is more loyal to us than any human ever could be. Still, I get it. Trusting the process and the waiting is hard. The women in this section help encourage us and remind us that trusting Him is precious ... even when we think things aren't going our way.

Father, help me to fully trust You! Help me to understand what is holding me back so I can have greater confidence in my faith.

Trust Day One >>> Cassie Rief

And there appeared to him an angel from heaven, strengthening him. —Luke 22:43 ESV

On my journey toward motherhood, I've encountered paths that weren't just rocky, but blocked by boulders. Unable to go it alone, I found myself talking more and more to God and listening for His voice. My faith grew by leaps and bounds as a result.

Much of this had to do with the listening part. I came to realize I voiced my problems to God and prayed fervently that He fix them, but wouldn't listen for His response.

Sitting attentively in silence, I wondered if I would literally hear God speak. It was then I understood He chooses special methods of communication for each of us. I believe in my case it is through angels – God's messengers – who appear through others and with perfectly timed signs.

After this moment of clarity, remarkable things began happening. My hope in sharing my stories is you will hear God, too, and be strengthened to overcome your life's boulders.

Sign #1 occurred after visiting my doctor to verify my hCG levels were increasing in early pregnancy. As my spotting became heavier, I didn't need lab work to tell me what I already knew. Sobbing on the way home, a Jeremy Camp song entitled "He knows" came on the radio:

How hard your fight has been / How deep the pain within / Wounds that no one else has seen / He knows, He knows / Every hurt and every sting / He has walked the suffering / He knows, He knows / Let your burdens come undone / Lift your eyes up to the One who knows

Powerful stuff, right? In my pain, God was suffering alongside me. I was not forgotten or alone.

Sign #2 was a note on my car at work. Written on it was Proverbs 3:5-6 - *Trust in the Lord with all your heart, And do not lean on your own understanding. In all your ways acknowledge him, and he will make straight your paths.*

I still don't know who left it (I asked *everyone* and even reviewed security tapes, which malfunctioned at the time the note was left). What I do know is the message consoles and comforts me to this day.

This brings us to **sign #3**. Standing in my backyard, I found myself encircled by feathers. Some were large and striped. Others were pure white and fluffy – like angels' wings. The striped feathers pointed straight up, like someone had stuck them in the ground. The others rested gently nearby.

Two thoughts came to me: 1.) Either an ugly bird brawl went down in this very spot, or 2.) God's love is literally surrounding me. I chose to believe the latter. After all, the saying is, "feathers appear when angels are near."

That day, I was worrying about a diagnostic surgery coming up that would hopefully give us answers to our infertility. I was terrified this might be only the beginning of our struggle.

Those feathers were God's voice telling me it was going to be alright. Life was going to work out. In that moment, I felt peace. Instead of tears of sorrow and fear, tears of joy and love for God filled my eyes.

Later that evening on a run with my dog, I looked up to see another feather white as snow floating softly down toward me. I smiled knowing God's love for me.

When life becomes difficult, allow me to open myself to listening and patiently awaiting Your answers, Lord. They may appear spiritually within my heart or mind, or physically around me. Give me faith to recognize Your voice and strength to move the boulders in my life.

Trust Day Two >>>Cara Holdman

Relax, everything's going to be all right; rest, everything's coming together; open your hearts, love is on the way! –Jude 1:2 MSG

Every time I would visit my fertility clinic for a check-up, treatment or follow-up, I would breathe this verse in and allow myself to find hope in its loving, life-giving words. The thing is, I never imagined I would find myself infertile. "Infertile," when used to describe yourself, is like a punch in the stomach.

When you want nothing more than to give your husband a child, when you long to hold a sweet soul who blesses you with motherhood, and when you plan a future sketched around a big, full family, hearing the words, "It's going to be hard for you to get pregnant," casts a deep, dark shadow on all those dreams. Infertility is not what I wanted; however, I learned to embrace its season in my life, and I am truly thankful for the harvest it produced. I do believe that in our pain and suffering, we are aligned with some of the most important divine appointments in which we need to fulfill.

Many of these appointments can only be understood in our darkest times. I believe if you allow God to unfold His plan before you with an open perspective, you will gain a new depth of understanding of His love for you. We have been placed on this earth for a bigger purpose than we can ever fully imagine. We entered the world exactly when God needed us to be here to make our divine appointments, and He is preparing and providing in the same way not only for us, but also for our future children. I know your heart is heavy, sweet sister, but wipe your tears away.

Come to see the Lord wants His best for you. Trust He is bringing it at the exact moment when it will set a new, fresh season into motion for you. It will be a season you come fully equipped for because of what you have gained from infertility's hardships. Look around for those people in your life who were placed there purposefully by Him to help you cope, grow and move forward.

Don't miss out on this opportunity to allow the Holy Spirit to transform your mind and heart for the wonderful journey ahead. If I would have had a child when I wanted, I would have missed out on so much the Lord needed me to take in. Instead of becoming a casualty of despair and cynicism while carrying the weight of infertility, become a resilient warrior. Find your strength by "resting" in our Savior; find your perseverance by "relaxing" in His skillfully crafted plan for you.

Dear friend, don't lose hope; love is on the way! I offer up a special prayer today for those reading this right now. This journey is hard, but you are not alone. God is with you, and so are we, the women walking this journey alongside you.

Trust Day Three >>> Felicia Kruse

For I know the plans I have for you, declares the Lord, plans for welfare and not for evil, to give you a future and a hope. —Jeremiah 29:11 ESV

My husband and I were so ready to become parents. I got pregnant right away. Our first baby – oh, how exciting! I heard my baby's heartbeat, and it was music to my ears. We saw our baby on the ultrasound screen. All I could think was, this is our beautiful creation from God. When we lost her, we named her Dani.

Sadly, we would go on to lose our second baby, Arin, and our third baby, Jessi. We lost all three around six to eight weeks along after seeing them on ultrasound and hearing their heartbeats. Through my infertility, God began to show and teach us that when we are weak, He is strong. We discovered I had a condition in which I didn't have a hormone that matured my eggs.

A simple shot was the solution, and with it, God gave us hope. We learned to trust in His plans, and one June, we found out we were pregnant again. At first, the doctor thought I was pregnant with six babies. Praise God! Having a baby was what my husband and I wanted, so if God wanted us to have six babies, well, we were going to have six babies. We thought, *His will be done.* If He choose to take one, we would praise Him without fail. We were trusting in God's plan, even if it would cost me my life. We were very excited, but extremely nervous.

I was transferred to a high risk pregnancy specialist, who discovered we were pregnant with quintuplets. Yes, *five* babies. We knew God had a plan for each one and that their lives were important to Him. From 10 days to 19 weeks, we watched our babies grow. We learned there were two boys and three girls.

We gave them names. Our sons would be born first: Jeremiah William and Josiah Dean. They would be the big brothers who would protect their little sisters, Miriam Faith, Lilyann Marie and Phoebe Annette. We saw their heartbeats, and we watched them grow, wave, kick and do flips. Then, in September, at 19 weeks and one day, I went into premature labor and delivered all five of the babies.

We were told they would only live seconds or minutes, but God showed up and showed off. Although they were only able to live two hours outside of the womb, those two hours were the most blessed. During that time, we held them in our arms.

I watched them move their hands and feet, each with 10 perfect fingers and toes. Their little mouths opened. We could see their hearts beating. At only 19 weeks, they were God's masterpieces. One of the ultrasound techs who was with me when my first son was born came to see me later that evening. She said she saw God that day. God's plan may not have been for me to have five babies. Instead, His plan was for someone else to see Him through them. So, I hope you see that as short as their lives were, they was important, and each baby was created so beautifully.

God has our futures planned out from the beginning and can provide you strength to face each and every storm. Trust in His plans. I may know all about loss and heartache, but I also know all about Jesus' everlasting hope. He loves you. Believe it.

Lord, help those needing an extra dose of Your love to believe and trust. No, it's not easy, but it's worth it. You do miraculous things and You have a plan. I put my faith in You. Amen.

Trust Day Four >>> Ali Forrest

And God said to Abraham, "As for Sarai your wife, you shall not call her name Sarai, but Sarah shall be her name. I will bless her, and moreover, I will give you a son by her. I will bless her, and she shall become nations; kings of peoples shall come from her." Then Abraham fell on his face and laughed and said to himself, "Shall a child be born to a man who is a hundred years old? Shall Sarah, who is ninety years old, bear a child?" –Genesis 17:15-21 ESV

And the LORD said to Abraham, "Why did Sarah laugh, saying, 'Shall I surely bear a child, since I am old?' Is anything too hard for the LORD? At the appointed time I will return to you, according to the time of life, and Sarah shall have a son." –Genesis 18:13-14 ESV

I want to know if and how Sarah avoided being a fair-weathered friend to Jesus. We've all experienced a friend like that at some point in our lives – that person who supports you when it's easy and convenient, but gets going when the going gets tough. I try so hard not to be fair-weathered with my own faith, but I sometimes am, despite the best of intentions.

When things are going my way, it's so easy to exclaim, "High five, God! You're the man." It's simple to sing His praises. Faith is effortless. It's the honeymoon phase full of joy and thanksgiving. When my husband and I got our first positive pregnancy test, we were elated. God is so good! When we got our first adoption referral for two, three-year-olds (a boy and a girl), we were elated. Again, God is *good!*

When things *aren't* going my way, it's a different scene that looks more like I'm talking to a brick wall or a dead telephone line. "Hello? God, are You there? It's me, Ali. Hellooooo?"

That first (and only) positive pregnancy test turned out to be a chemical pregnancy. That first referral we received? We found out there was a paperwork error less than a day after getting the news and the two kids wouldn't become part of our family after all.

God had abandoned me. Or at least that's how I felt. It can be extremely hard to have faith when circumstances are unyielding. Multiply that by two when it comes to infertility.

If anyone can relate, I feel like it would be Sarah. At some point, she likely gave up on her dreams to be a mother, right? After all, she and Abraham both laughed when they found out she would bear a son. The mere thought was inconceivable (no pun intended)!

I mean, can you imagine the headlines today if a woman inching closer to her centenarian years was expecting? It would be crazy! Yet, nothing is too arduous for our God. Nothing is impossible. And, He proves it with Sarah's story.

There had to be times when Sarah questioned it all. She's human. I can't help but imagine she had her own moments of weakness when she felt God was being a fair-weathered friend. But He wasn't. He knew her story all along. And, it was a really, really good one.

God is not a fair-weathered friend. God is for us. He loves us completely, and His love can carry you, sustain you and rescue you. Let us do the same for Him. Let us love, trust, adore and thank Him. Let's not be a fair-weathered friend to Him.

Oh, Lord, shower me with resiliency in all circumstances, and help me to see Your abundant love and glory, even when I am empty, lost and straying. You are always good, and I will praise You all the days of my life.

Trust Day Five >>> Ali Forrest

And Michal the daughter of Saul had no child to the day of her death. —2 Samuel 6:23 ESV

So now there is no condemnation for those who belong to Christ Jesus. And because you belong to him, the power of the life-giving Spirit has freed you from the power of sin that leads to death. —Romans 8:1-2 ESV

Do you ever ask God, "What did I do to deserve this? Why can't I have children, yet the mom who killed her two kids and stuck them in the freezer can?" Although I try to catch myself, I sometimes get into this trap of thinking it's not fair they can have children, but I can't. After all, that sort of thinking goes against humility and creates a flawed notion I am better than X person. No bueno; not good at all.

This devotional, right here and now, is dedicated to all you women who ever thought, even for a single second, your barren womb is a punishment. It's not. Your infertility is not a punitive measure for past sins and indiscretions. It's not a curse bestowed on your reproductive organs. Yes, Michal was barren all of her days. No, it was not a punishment for anything she ever did. Why am I so sure? Romans.

Romans 8:1-2 says, *So now there is no condemnation for those who belong to Christ Jesus. And because you belong to him, the power of the life-giving Spirit has freed you from the power of sin that leads to death.*

Why, then, is infertility a chapter in our lives? I can't answer that more than I can answer the question of why cancer might take away a beautiful mom of two young children.

But what if the pain and suffering of our here and now has a big story? What if the good works of our God can be displayed in the pain we feel? It's bigger than us. Our story, our life, is grand in ways God planned from the very beginning.

That is where the whole trust thing comes in. We trust because we believe. Faith is not always logical, and it can be impossible to understand. My husband is an engineer. His brain is wired around the concrete, and so he struggles with faith and God. Things that happen are simply coincidental to him. Or are they? It's his biggest roadblock with faith.

The thing is, it is impossible to understand God. Let's stop trying to understand His purpose for us and the why behind His powerful ways. Simply surrender. Make the common phrase, "let go and let God," a mantra for you.

Get out of His way, and trust the plan He created for you. It's a risk worth taking.

Contributors

Logan Andreotta in a nutshell: Mama, book lover, hot tea drinker and Christ follower. She blogs about her journey and experience over at her website, withgreatexpectation.com.

Melanie Bryant lives in Decatur, Ala., and she is a third grade teacher. Her passion is to help her students be the best they can be. She has been married to her husband, Scott, for three years, and they have been trying to conceive for two of the three. Melanie battles endometriosis and PCOS. As a couple, they have been going to the fertility doctor for a year now and have had one pregnancy, which ended in a miscarriage. They will continue to seek God's will for their lives!

Megan Carlson has big dreams of mommyhood, and while she waits, she lives her life to the fullest. Fun facts about her: She met her husband in the fourth grade, and she has earned the name "Baby Whisperer" by friends and family. Learn more about Megan's journey by visiting her blog: www.infertilemyrtles.com.

Stephanie Cline is a lifelong resident of the Midwest. She was saved at 13 and walked with the Lord for about seven years. While in college, she began dating the man she would marry. She didn't see that he didn't know the Lord, and gradually, she also stopped walking with Him. About eight years later, they began experiencing unexplained infertility. Toward the end of this time, her husband confessed to multiple affairs and refused to reconcile. Following the ending of the marriage, Stephanie came back to the Lord. She is learning to share her experiences and the healing the Lord has brought with other hurting people. While single, she is hopeful the Lord will bless her with a husband and children. She enjoys motorsports, traveling, pets, fishing, baseball, hockey and anything outdoors.

Lisa Culver lives in middle Tennessee with her husband and their four wonderful pets: two dogs and two cats. She is an administrative assistant, and in her spare time, she is learning to play guitar and write songs.

Melanie Dafler and her husband (Wes) have been married since 2011 and began trying to have children very soon after. They were diagnosed with azoospermia, but with the help of lifestyle changes, IUIs and the grace of God, their first daughter was born in November 2014. Melanie is now a stay-at-home mom who also teaches voice and piano lessons. She is active in her home congregation and loves yoga, drinking tea, blogging, sewing and crocheting.

Nadine Easty lives in St. Paul, Minn. She has been married to the love of her life for 17 adventurous years. The Lord gave them their greatest blessing when he brought their son to them. Nadine lives each day to faithfully and happily serve God, her husband and her son. She gives God all the glory, for she feels blessed by Him beyond her dreams!

Wynne Elder is a Texan, wife and mom to two children adopted from Ethiopia. She loves people and finds joy sharing pieces of her life on her blog, Gloriously Ruined, at www.wynneelder.com.

Meredith Erickson is an accountant, wife and daughter of the King. She started the website, The Baby Wait, as a means to provide hope and encouragement to those struggling with infertility, miscarriages or adoption. The Baby Wait shares reminders of God's goodness through scripture, song and story. Meredith and her husband live in Chicago, Ill. They love to do house projects, get in a good workout, and most of all, have friends around their table. They are still waiting for God to reveal the rest of their story, and look forward to the day their home is filled with children.

Kelly and David Evans are proud parents to four dogs: Dakota, Coby, Annie and Molly. They bring this couple so much joy and tons of laughs every single day! Kelly and David are currently waiting for their human miracle from the Lord, and they have learned so very much (the good, bad and ugly) during the three years they have been trying to conceive. They invite you to visit their blog, 1 in 8: Our Journey While We Wait, at https://bella209.wordpress.com.

Melissa Forster lives in Missouri with her husband, Dan, and their two cats. She and Dan have been married for more than eight years and have always dreamed of having children. Melissa assumed after eight years of marriage, she would be done having children, but God had other plans. Although she would love to be a mommy to children in her home someday, she loves the journey God, infertility and the loss of one baby have taken her and her husband on. The couple is currently working on choosing faith over fear and trusting God with whatever their future holds.

Rachael Gentry is married to her husband, Jaime. She was blessed not only to become a wife that day, but to also become a step-mom to a handsome five-year-old boy! They live in a small city in Alabama with their six furry pets. Their journey to parenthood has been one of the most challenging things a newly-wedded couple could face. It has brought them closer to God and to each other.

Holley Gerth is an author, encourager and life coach. She blogs over at HolleyGerth.com, a place where you can sit back, relax and have a cup of coffee for your heart.

Kim Gorman was born and raised in Georgia, but now resides in North Carolina with her husband, Bradley. After the loss of their daughter, Grace, Kim's mission was to create a legacy in which her daughter's memory could live on. Kim and a friend decided to start a small business, Love, Faith, and Southern Grace, to do just that. Kim enjoys making metal-stamped jewelry and other crafts. She is a stay-at-home wife and hopes to add stay-at-home mom to her title someday soon. Kim enjoys sharing her story of love, faith and hope to encourage others to never give up!

Cassandra Griffo is originally from South Africa. After she graduated college with a business degree, she lived and taught English in Korea for two years. While there, she met her now husband, Chad. They dated long distance for a while before finally moving to the U.S. and getting married. They are a military family with the sweetest kitty, and they are currently stationed at Fort Bragg, N.C. Cassandra is an avid reader, food blogger and a lover of Christ. She loves sharing her faith with those around her.

Caroline Harries is first and foremost a daughter of Christ. She loves fitness, healthy living and traveling. Caroline lives in Texas with her husband, Colby, and blogs over at www.in-due-time.com, where she talks about all things faith and infertility related. Be sure to stop by and say "Hi!"

Lauren McCain Hartley, age 26, lives in Rock Hill, La. She got married on Jan. 1, 2010, to Kevin M. Hartley. She works as a registered nurse at a local hospital, and her husband is self-employed as a portable building mover. Both Kevin and Lauren perform volunteer children's ministry work at their home church, Tioga Wesleyan Methodist Church. They love God and want to fulfill His will for their lives. They have one Catahoula Cur/Lab mix named Rambo. Lauren enjoys traveling and shopping at thrift stores, and Kevin enjoys tinkering outside in his shop and working with his hands.

Rachel Hayden is a mom, wife, daughter and friend who also happens to be walking the secondary infertility journey since a miscarriage in 2010. She works as a part-time physical therapist and a full-time disciple of Jesus

Christ from her home base nestled between a frog pond and a corn field in southern Indiana.

Kassie Hart is from a small town in Illinois, about 45 minutes from St. Louis, Mo., but grew up close to Columbia, Mo. She has a bachelor and master's degree in accountancy. She married the most amazing and supportive man in 2008. They have two children, ages four and two. She has been growing closer to Christ more this past year than she ever could have imagined. What a wonderful feeling it is knowing He's there with you every step of the way!

Amber Holmes is a wife to her southern gentleman high school sweetheart, Joey. She is a radiation therapist at Central Alabama Radiation Oncology, and she has a background in radiologic technology. Amber and her husband call Valley Grande, Ala., home with their two furry pets, Remi and Oscar. Amber is a Jesus believer, "Roll Tide" screamer and boutique shopping junkie, as well as an IVF warrior and conqueror! She and her husband welcomed their first child, a girl, into the world this year on Halloween!

Cara Holdman is the wife of her husband, Daniel (a firefighter), and the mom to their miracle son, Jude (age two). Jude, after many obstacles, was conceived through IVF. Cara began a blog after a year of struggling to conceive. She had no idea how her story would turn out in the end, but knew she could trust God's goodness. The most important lesson she learned was to pray for peace about her situation. She knew if she had *peace that passes all understanding,* she could handle whatever outcome was given to them.

Marianne Jennings is a middle school reading teacher from Delaware who enjoys spending time with her husband, two boxers and cat. She loves traveling, baking, spending time with her closest friends and going for long rides in the car. She and her husband try to find joy in everything and travel as much as possible with their dogs.

Elisha Kearns is a wife, foster mom, cat owner, Jesus follower and Type A organizer. She writes all about her own infertility journey and offers words of hope and encouragement on her blog, Waiting For Baby Bird. Be sure to check it out at www.waitingforbabybird.com.

Ashley Kimble is a 29-year-old girl living in West Michigan with her husband, Jordan, and two crazy cats. Ashley is a writer and graphic designer who loves wine, curling up with a good book, and is way too proud to be a

Gold Card member at Starbucks. She and her husband are in the midst of their infertility journey, but taking it one day at a time with the support of God, their friends and family. You can follow her journey at futurebabykimble.wordpress.com.

Felicia Kruse became a Christian at the age of 16, a week before her 17th birthday. She trusts God's plan for her life. She has been married seven years to her best friend, Justin. They are proud parents of eight saints in heaven: Dani, Arin and Jessi, as well as their quintuplets: Jeremiah, Josiah, Miriam, Lilyann and Phoebe. They hold tight to the promise of reuniting with their children in heaven. Felicia and Justin have a very energetic dog, Bebe. They became foster parents three years ago, and God has brought some special blessings into their lives. They are so grateful to be part of this wonderful mission work of God.

Pier Lefebvre is a young woman on fire for the Lord and striving to serve Him in every facet of her life alongside her husband, Craig, who is a commercial airline pilot. After a whirlwind year serving in Maine as a youth minister and speaker, Pier returned to her native Georgia town, where she is an active member of her church and worship team and a Christian blogger at The Newlywed Lefebvres. She survives infertility one day at a time. Pier continues to speak to women and church groups about God's work in her life through her website, I Am A Daughter Of The Risen King. The couple lives in Dallas, Ga., with their precious fur-babies, Miss Daisy, Lucy and Caroline.

Suzy Lolley is a longtime Georgia girl, pastor's wife and mama to three sweet, but crazy dogs. She is having a good time blogging about all her issues at thebeaminmyeye.com and looks forward to the day when she will get to put all her bossiness to good use as a mother.

Rosie Marlatt's journey started off like most married couples. She and her husband talked about having children right away. They were married in May of 2012 and starting trying in July of 2012. Three years later, they are still waiting for their miracle. Their journey has been an emotional rollercoaster filled with lots of tears, many nights of crying out to God, four failed IUIs and a lot of doctor's appointments, as well as unpleasant fertility medications. They have already invested thousands of dollars in fertility treatments in hopes they would work. To date, their journey has led them to IVF. Since May, they have raised more than half the money for the procedure. They are giving all the glory to God. In November, they will do their first round of IVF and are looking forward to welcoming Baby Marlatt next year!!

Jessica Mernin has been married to her husband, Zac, for almost four years. She is 28, and they have been trying to conceive for 16 months. She knows so many women have experienced longer and more treacherous journeys before overcoming infertility and understands she could still be at just the beginning of her journey. However, it has been such a deeply difficult process on her heart, and she needs the comfort and love of God more than ever. Part of her story is marked by two pregnancies that ended in miscarriages. The losses have been heartbreaking. She prays for God to use her for His good if she must remain in this difficult season of waiting and trusting.

Brandy Miller lives in Delaware with her outdoor-loving husband and 100-pound doggie. She loves sharing day-to-day stories about Jesus, marriage, hope, infertility and the newest addition to her womb(!!) on her blog, A Sweet Aroma. Though she loves standing atop mountains, she's found that deeper fellowship (with God and others) is found in valleys, laced with transparency.

Diana Montes and her husband have been married for almost 10 years and battling infertility for the past five years. They are part of the youth ministry at their local church as volunteer youth counselors. She has been part of the youth ministry and church worship team for 15 years. Working with the youth group and cooking for her family are two things she is passionate about. Her hobbies include reading books, writing in her journal and listening to worship music. The couple resides in Midland, TX.

Amanda R. Morrison is from small town, USA. She grew up in a town called Salt Rock, W.Va., but now lives in Milton, W.Va. She married her childhood sweetheart, John, and they celebrated their 16th wedding anniversary Aug. 28, 2015. She is a registered nurse at a local hospital. Amanda and John have three Tennessee Walking Horses and two spotted Saddle Horses, whom they dearly love. They are all show and trail horses. They also have one bloodhound, two labs and two cats, and they hope to add children to their nest soon.

Joanna Nissley is wife to her farmer honey, Kirby. She enjoys the solitude of helping on their farm and being a homemaker. She is a lover of Jesus Christ, spending quality time with family and friends, working in her flowerbeds, traveling, hanging out with their two dogs and three friendly cattle, relaxing at the beach, reading, appreciating beauty and indulging in dark chocolate.

Lisa Parvey lives in Wisconsin with her husband, Dan, and their two dogs. She and her husband enjoy spending time with family and their dogs, going for motorcycle rides, riding snowmobiles and traveling. Lisa and Dan have been married for five years and have always dreamed of having children. Lisa knew conceiving children might be difficult due to a history of fibroid tumors. In fact, prior to meeting her husband, she had her first surgery to remove a tumor. Their journey of trying for a family started after Lisa was finished with nursing school and had her first nursing job. Lisa and Dan continue to faithfully pray and trust in God's plan for their future with the hope it includes children – that is, if it is God's will.

Chelsea Ritchie is a Midwestern girl who loves connecting with fellow women and bloggers about the topic of infertility and living authentically. She's been married to Josh for almost 10 years, and their current family is rounded out with the perfect little fur-baby ever, a Morkie named Cali. Chelsea loves a good Americano and cozy bookshop and is a sucker for paper and pens. She values engaging her faith in this trial and embracing the season with joy.

Cassie Rief lives in eastern Nebraska with her husband of two years, Clayton; their cat, Chloe (Chlo-meister); dog, Macie Doodle (The Doodler); and five chickens come spring! Throughout her season of infertility, which includes PCOS, a chemical pregnancy and endometriosis, she has found immense faith in God and NaProTECHNOLOGY, as well as fellowship with other faith-filled women battling similar circumstances. Cassie enjoys hiking, traveling, fishing, writing and working out. She makes a mean pesto sauce and firmly believes you can never have enough boots. She and her husband met playing softball, and they can't wait for their "home run" baby! *She also edited this book. Cassie, you're amazing! Thanks for everything.*

Valerie Rohde lives in metro Atlanta with her husband, Douglas, and her two boys, Ryne and Benjamin. She experienced pregnancy loss and subsequent infertility, which fostered her passion to serve as a birth doula, lactation consultant and educator to families on their own journey to parenthood. She truly believes in God's sovereignty over her journey to where she and her family are today. Valerie also loves exploring on hikes with her little ones, baby wearing, cloth diapering, and is beginning to learn more about homeschooling. You can learn more about Rohde family adventures through her blog at www.valerierohde.com.

Kathryn Shirey is a writer, author of Pray Deep prayer journals, and a mom. She is learning to say yes to God day by day. Learn more about Kathryn by visiting her blog, kathrynshirey.com.

Brianne Shoop has been married to her best friend, David, for two-and-a-half years. They just bought their first house and are working on making the house a home. She is completely in love with their three-year-old Boston Terrier named Basil. She is an avid iced coffee drinker and essential oil user and loves photography and writing. Brianne grew up in a Christian home and has been a follower of Christ since elementary school. She really feels that through the struggle of infertility, she has been more drawn to Christ and feels there can be triumph over any tragedy. Brianne was born and raised in York, Pa.

Carrie Slaughter is a nurse who has battled infertility for 10-plus years. She is married and has three fur-babies, a pug named Davidson, a lab mix named Cheyenne, and a cat named Zoey. She also has some angels looking down on her. Writing became her therapy after a divorce and was her way of being able to say things she couldn't speak aloud. She enjoys exploring with her husband, relaxing on the beach and anything artistic. Her goal is to let women battling infertility know they are not alone in it.

Heather Step is a stay-at-home mom to Nicholas, born June 2012. After enduring five years of infertility, he was totally worth the wait! When she isn't following him around, she likes writing and blogging at http://onestepatatime.co.za. She also founded a network for South African mom bloggers at http://samomblogs.co.za. Heather used to be a first grade teacher and has an interest in children and psychology. She has a BA (Hons) degree in psychology. Heather lives in Johannesburg, South Africa, with her husband, little Nicky and their two dogs.

Brittany Trentham is a wife, new mom, Christ follower, and food and fitness junkie! She blogs over at www.DelightsandDelectables.com. Be sure to stop by and say "Hi!" She is a great resource for both adoption and pregnancy discussions.

Ferial Trammell is a northern California girl who loves Jesus, her husband, her cat-kids, coconut milk iced coffee and pursuing the best community this side of eternity has to offer. Ferial was diagnosed with PCOS in 2012 and has been journeying through the rocky paths of infertility ever since. You can find more on her journey at http://www.ferialshmerial.com/.

Jayme Wurtenberger is a girl who comes from a large family and loves traveling, her dog, praying before dinner, golfing, cooking and the

Kentucky Wildcats. She puts her faith in His plans and can't wait until her home is filled with little ones.

Valentina Wysocki-Hall resides in Columbus, OH with her awesome, bearded husband. Having grown up in the middle spot of three girls born within three years of one another, Valentina learned early the value of having a voice and using it loudly (as well as late night chats/laughing fests). A graduate of both Ashland University and Ashland Theological Seminary, she studied political science, history and philosophy and earned her Master of Divinity. She currently works in finance, thus proving God's plans can often surprise us. When not working, she spends her time crafting, writing, reading, attempting to learn Spanish and living a messy-transparent life in community.

Scripture Index

2 Chronicles 20:15, p. 25
2 Chronicles 20:17, p. 25

Colossians 3:15, p. 143
1 Corinthians 1:7, p. 42
1 Corinthians 13:13, p. 71
2 Corinthians 5:7, p. 13
2 Corinthians 12:7-10, p. 81
2 Corinthians 12:9-10, p. 16

Deuteronomy 33:25, p. 100

Ecclesiastes 3:1, p. 109
Ecclesiastes 3:11, p. 109

Ephesians 3:20, p. 103
Ephesians 5:19, p. 84

Esther 4:14, p. 64

Exodus 13:17-18, p. 106
Exodus 14:13-14, p. 47
Exodus 23:25-26, p. 103

Galatians 2:20, p.52
Galatians 5:22-23, p. 68

Genesis 6:13-14, p. 13
Genesis 8:14, p. 13
Genesis 17:15-21, p. 128
Genesis 18:13-14, p. 128
Genesis 25, 21, p. 63
Genesis 25:24, p. 62
Genesis 30:22-23, p. 27
Genesis 50:20, p. 93

Habakkuk 2:3, p. 35

Hebrews 6:19, p. 14, 20
Hebrews 10:23, p. 111
Hebrews 11:1, p. 7

Isaiah 43:2, p. 11
Isaiah 43:5, p. 37
Isaiah 49:16, p. 49
Isaiah 53:5, p. 9, 10, 103
Isaiah 66:9, p. 27

James 1:2, p. 80

Jeremiah 7:17, p. 18
Jeremiah 29:1, p. 21, 59, 118, 126

John 4:18, p. 72
John 15:12-13, p. 77
John 20:24-25, p. 13
John 20:29, p. 13
John 3:30, p. 120

Jude 1:2, p. 124

Lamentations 3:21-24, p. 113
Lamentations 3:25, p. 21

Luke 1:37, p. 47
Luke 13:10-15, p. 33
Luke 17:21, p. 111
Luke 22:43, p.122

Mark 3:3-5, p. 33
Mark 4:20, p. 44

Matthew 5:14-16, p. 52, 74
Matthew 8:23-27, p. 98
Matthew 9:18-19, 15
Matthew 11:28, p. 107
Matthew 11: 29-30, p. 40
Matthew 28:20, p. 37

1 Peter 1:6-8, p. 94
1 Peter 1:8-9, p. 78
1 Peter 4:19, p. 102
1 Peter 5:7, p. 48

Philippians 1:6, p. 37
Philippians 1:12-14, 85
Philippians 4:4, p. 78
Philippians 4:6-7, p. 53
Philippians 4:13, p. 8

Proverbs 3:5, p. 29
Proverbs 3:5-6, p. 65, 122
Proverbs 4:23, p. 100
Proverbs 14:29-30, p. 91
Proverbs 17:22, p. 58
Proverbs 19:21, p. 58
Proverbs 27:7, p. 54
Proverbs 31:25-26, p. 28

Psalm 3:3, p. 52
Psalm 9:9-10, p. 117
Psalm 13:1-2, p. 115
Psalm 23:4, p. 27
Psalm 27:4, p. 110
Psalm 27:13, p. 76
Psalm 28:7, p. 22
Psalm 37:4, p. 47, 83
Psalm 37:7, p. 108
Psalm 46:1, p. 11
Psalm 61:2, p. 76
Psalm 62:1, p. 31
Psalm 62:5, p. 20, 46
Psalm 71:14, p. 67
Psalm 77:7-9, p. 91
Psalm 102:25-27, p. 88
Psalm 126:5, p. 20
Psalm 138:1, p. 74
Psalm 147:3, p. 103

Romans 8:1-2, p. 130
Romans 8:17-18, p. 97
Romans 8:24-25, p. 32
Romans 12:12, p. 12, 32
Romans 8:38-39, p. 95

1 Samuel 17:37, p. 100

1 Samuel 17:38-39, p. 23
1 Samuel 1:19-20, p. 3

Dear Reader,

The day I declared this book finished, I was sad! I loved working on *Anchored in Hope*! I love being so connected to His Word and an amazing community of women, some of whom I now call friends. I call it an honor that God laid this project on my heart.

If you read the introduction of this book, you'll remember I said I was the girl who had it all planned out. I am beyond thankful God came along and wrecked my plans. His redemption was worth the wait.

I could not be more thankful – thankful for Jesus, thankful for the opportunity to put this book together, and thankful for the unexpected opportunities life presents when I allow myself to stand still.

I pray daily for all women going through infertility in some way, shape or form, as I know this path is not easy. My hope is that this book brought you some joy, sense of community, and deeper hope, faith and encouragement. In short, I hope it brought you something positive!

Friends, stay anchored in hope. Always.

xoxo,

Let the peace of Christ rule in your hearts, since as members of one body you were called to peace. And be thankful.
–Colossians 3:15 NIV

ABOUT THE AUTHOR

Ali Forrest has a heart for girls in the trenches of infertility. She gets it. She's been there. She wants women to remain grounded in God's word during this chapter. While she may not have pregnancy stories to share, she is collecting an arsenal of tales from fertility doctor visits and international adoption adventures. She lives in the suburbs of Nashville, Tennessee with her husband, the daughter they adopted from Nicaragua, and two unruly rescue dogs. Whatever your story, she wants to listen. Connect with her at www.aliforrest.com.

39686831R00082

Made in the USA
Middletown, DE
23 January 2017